AFFAIR*y*TALE

No more Searching...
No more wandering....
He was the one.

Cover Design: MSPIRE

www.mspire.com

Cover Photo: Shawn Rode

www.shawnrodephotog.com

Digital Productions: Lewis Grant

Editor and Interior Designer: Hannah Kiges-Hutton

www.writeawaypublishing.com

In order to maintain anonymity, in some instances, places, the names of individuals, identifying characteristics, and other recognizable factors have been changed. The details and events in this memoir are based on my unique recollection and perception with no harm intended to anyone. I recognize that individuals involved in these events might have memories that are not the same as my own. Much of the content has been taken from original journal entries and other written correspondence. The text messages are the originals. So that the reader is not confused, spelling and grammatical errors within text and journal entries have been corrected in some instances.

www.affairytalebook.com

Paperback ISBN: 978-0-9863042-0-0

E-Book ISBN: 978-0-9863042-1-7

MY LOVE,

YOU WERE SO WORTH THE WAIT.

"IF A MAN COMMITS ADULTERY

WITH THE WIFE OF THY NEIGHBOR,

BOTH THE ADULTERER AND THE ADULTERESS

SHALL SURELY BE PUT TO DEATH."

—LEVITICUS 20:10, 538

Prologue

I didn't mind flying, but not like this. I hadn't prepared for this. I wasn't supposed to be taking this long trip alone. Nausea rolled through me in waves.

"Now boarding all passengers on flight twenty-two fifty-six to Kahului. Please have your passes ready at the gate."

I stood up, stretched my legs and got in line at the gate. I was dreading the grueling flight.

The gate attendant scanned my pass. "Thank you, Ms. Summers," she said.

I walked through the narrow jetway, tugging my carry-on stuffed full with bikinis.

It would be the first time I put on a bikini since the surgery. The scars across my stomach and back were still numb and jagged. They still looked fresh. I would stare at someone who had scars like mine. Scars that ran along a spine like a two lane highway, scars that were out of place on a youthful body.

Nightmares about my joints shattering into a million pieces still kept me awake at night. I would crumble brick by brick until I was nothing but a pile of broken rubble.

Normally I wouldn't be scared to travel alone, but on this trip, I feared I would collapse again and not be able to get back up. I would have to crawl on my hands and knees down the narrow aisle, pushing my suitcase in front of me just to get off the plane.

I tried to get comfortable, but my back hurt, my ears rang, and tears wet my eyelashes. I stuffed a pillow between my seat and the window, closed the shade, and squeezed in purple earplugs. I gagged down a Dramamine, but it got stuck, adding to the large lump lodged in my throat already. Loneliness tucked me in with a thin red blanket and offered me its cold shoulder in the place where his should have been.

Emotionally exhausted and on the brink of a meltdown, I was a felony disaster.

A few months ago, he'd asked me if I was up for an adventure, and I always was. I loved our adventures, like the time we'd shimmied across that rickety footbridge over the raging Temperance River, or when we had thrown human body–sized logs into a rushing gorge just to see how we might die. The adventures I loved the most were the ones at sunset, like the time we'd laid concealed among the tall grasses looking up at the sky. We watched in awe as one, two, then three bald eagles soared overhead. I adored the many nights we'd slept outside under a millions stars, and made love.

We'd made extraordinary love.

We'd hidden when we had to. Those had been the sultriest nights. Locked in his candlelit bedroom where he'd taught me the tango and the rumba, and played his guitar as I lay naked under his cool sateen sheets. I'd been longing to lie between those sheets for nearly a decade.

Now, after all that, the empty seat next to me wasn't my idea of an adventure. It was a heartbreaking reminder of how desperately I needed him in my life, a flashback of how painful it was to live without him. We'd come so far, overcome the impossible, now the grand finale was me, alone.

Maybe I was finally getting what I deserved for what I had done.

The loud speaker crackled, "Ladies and gentlemen, from the flight deck, this is your captain speaking. Our flight time today is seven hours and fifty-one minutes. Looks like clear skies all the way to Maui."

***

U are my wish:)

Chapter 1

Twelve Years Earlier

The pink neon sign glowed *"Psychic"* in the midnight darkness.

I had been driving home after a long shift of serving bar food and beer when I saw it blinking in the window, like a beacon calling for lost souls. Souls like mine, discontent souls looking for answers and comfort within a life of uncertainty and dis-ease. Something urged me to turn around.

The psychic's face was youthful, and her hair bounced with voluminous curls as she walked toward me.

"I don't know why I'm here," I said.

Without another word she led me to a small rectangular table where I sat down, pulled my tip money out of my pocket and laid out twenty crumpled up one dollar bills on the table, her fee for half an hour.

The psychic talked with her hands. "Something is wrong with your car," she said.

I shrugged and shook my head, "I don't think so."

"Yes," she insisted. "Something wrong with your car and you need to get it fixed."

I rolled my eyes. *This is already a waste of my time and twenty bucks.*

I didn't care about my car. I wanted to know about what every nineteen-year-old girl wanted to know about—my love life. "My boyfriend. Is he the one?" I asked.

Without hesitation and with a sense of absolute certainty, she said, "This man you are with is a fine man, and if you want to make it work with this man, you can." She leaned over the table toward me, her eyes commanding my full attention. She continued, "but if you stay with this man, it will be difficult, very difficult." She paused, and then what she revealed next made my heart beat in wild thumps, "the man you are destined to be with is still out there."

It was enchanting—the idea that there might really be one true somebody for everybody. That maybe my somebody was still out there, waiting for me, and that just maybe, she was going to lead me to him.

She reached over the table, wrapped her warm, soft hands around mine, and held them as if she were extracting information from my skin.

"You haven't met him yet, but you will. He has dark skin like yours and dark hair. He is very handsome."

I tried not to show how enthralled I was with her prediction. I didn't want to give any obvious signs that I was buying what she was selling, but involuntarily, an enormous smile grew on my face at the thought of *him.*

She closed her eyes as if to admire him and collect further information from the ether.

With a look of surprise and delight, she continued, "You will know it's him because of his eyes. They are the color of ice. It would be a great love, a rare love, with this man."

Then, as if my body knew something my mind did not, a shiver came over me, and my heart pounded even harder against my chest as she divulged more thrilling information.

"If you choose this rare love," she went on, "it will be the greatest love you have ever known. You are one of the lucky ones."

Every hair on my forearms stood up like I'd been zapped with electricity.

She spoke faster now, information quickly coming to her, "You will have three children with two different men, but this path can change. It has not been decided yet."

Great. Several children with different men? I can't wait to tell my mom.

"If you decide to make it work with the man you are with, it will be hard. Your love will grow cold, and you will become bitter. You will never be truly happy."

Blood pooled in the soft pith of my throat, the way it does when my heart flutters out of rhythm. I didn't want to make the wrong decision. I couldn't dump my new boyfriend because of the prediction of some psychic lady.

What if she's is wrong? What if Levi is the one?

I wanted Levi to be the one. I needed him to be the one. I didn't want to wait anymore. I hated being alone. I liked being loved, and Levi did love me. If he proposed, I would say yes. I would make it work. Like she said, it might be hard, but if anyone could make it work, I could.

Crazy gypsy. What does she know?

The bells on the door jingled as I walked past the neon sign and outside into the night. My mind raced with thoughts of my future, of my here and now, of my car.

My car was parked under a tall, dim streetlight. As I walked up, I took a quick look at all four tires to make sure they weren't flat.

Nope.

I slid into the driver's seat and quickly locked the doors. I fastened my seat belt and wiggled the key into the ignition. After half-expecting it not to start, I was relieved when the engine fired up without a hitch.

Huh. See?

I punched the gas and fled the shady, run-down neighborhood. It was the kind of neighborhood that was eerily silent and dark at night, the kind of neighborhood that allowed an old, white house to become a psychic's studio.

I was heading for the safety of the streetlights when I saw it.

Is that a crack?

It was a crack, one that hadn't been there before, and now, there it was, a lightning bolt that zigged and zagged horizontally across the center of my windshield.

I'll never know if the crack in my windshield was what she had been referring to, but if it were, she was right about that, and a few other things, too.

Although I didn't know it was *him* when it happened, the man with dark hair and eyes like ice showed up in my life only a few months later.

However, I wasn't single, and he was far from being available. In fact, I walked right into his wedding.

***

It was late summer when my older brother Dylan married his high school sweetheart. Lacey was an intelligent blonde beauty, and he was an aspiring bodybuilder with a gigantic laugh that matched his mountainous muscles.

A wildflower garden of yellow sunflowers and lavender hollyhocks stood tall around the well-manicured lawn. Rows of white chairs lined each side of a weathered boardwalk that weaved its way to the altar. Everything that could be was adorned in satin bows and burgundy lilies.

As Dylan kissed his new wife, wedding guests holding small plastic bottles wrapped in silver tulle blew thousands of multicolored bubbles into the air. The shimmering bubbles floated down, landed on our posh attire, and then exploded into a soapy mist. The wedding party, myself included, trotted down the boardwalk and disappeared behind the tinted glass of a polished white limousine.

An entourage of stretch limousines took the wedding party from bar to bar and dance floor to dance floor, with champagne flutes and shots of Grey Goose in between. My limousine shuttled me immediately to the reception for fizzing, tangy punch until some distant relative was kind enough to by an underage girl a drink to celebrate her brother's wedding.

When the bride and groom arrived at the reception they walked through the doors of the Crystal Ballroom where hundreds of well-dressed guests greeted the regal couple with roaring applause. Lacey was stunning in a timeless princess gown entwined on the arm of my brawny brother as she floated effortlessly through the ballroom. They looked and seemed like a perfect match in every way possible.

I wanted that. I wanted to find someone who belonged with me like the stars belonged with the sky. Someone I could get lost in, who would make me forget about reality for a while, who would adore me second to none.

I wanted the fairytale. Perhaps I could have that with Levi. I didn't know. It was still too new to even invite him to my brother's wedding.

A thin partition split the chandelier lit ballroom down the center, and I could hear music coming from the other side. With my burgundy bridesmaids dress bunched up in both hands at my sides I wandered over to check it out. From the hallway the door pulsed with music. It was another wedding, another bride getting her fairytale.

I had to peek inside and see how beautiful and beaming she was on the happiest day of her life. I wanted to see how enamored her groom was by her. I wanted to see the magical way a man looked at his new wife on their wedding day, like she was the only woman on earth.

Just before I was about to intrude something caught my eye. Handwritten in elegant calligraphy and centered inside an ornate baroque frame were two words:

ENGLISH WEDDING

I gripped the oversized door handles, slipped inside, and was greeted by the warm glow of hanging glass. This room was also ultra-posh and filled with its own luxurious amenities, like glittering champagne flowing from two tiered fountains, elegant ice sculptures, and chocolate rivers. The tone was set for an unforgettable night of celebration. The crowd was jubilant and tipsy, and people seemed to move as one organism across the polished wooden floor. Bliss lingered heavy in the air.

It only took a moment for me to spot the bride and groom. He was a dashing gentleman with his arm around the waist of his new wife. They smiled and laughed as they moved through the crowd, exchanging pleasantries and receiving congratulations.

Jealous of their jovial fate and feeling the intrusiveness of my presence on their most beloved day, I slipped out and closed the doors.

Eventually, I would learn that on that inauspicious summer night, nothing was as it'd seemed.

**

We're still on for
2morrow night, right?
Mwah!

Chapter 2

Three Years Later

At the top of the stairs of our tiny twin home, an argument of gargantuan proportions ensued. Every muscle in my body wanted to push Levi down the stairs.

We'd met on ladies' night. I had been underage, using a fake ID, and he had been the guy swinging hand over hand from the rafters above the dance floor. Levi was spontaneous and daring. I didn't have to try to have fun with him, he had enough fun for the both of us. He was the perfect escape from loneliness. He showed up with a carefree spirit and lived in the moment, but his recklessness was contagious. Being with Levi had become destructive and addictive.

Looking back, it had been volatile from the beginning. Although it was that very volatility that had made us want to kill each other that had also kept us together. Our personalities clashed, but the clash gave us variety and excitement.

I'd once read couples fight about three things—money, sex, and parenting. In the three years after Dylan had gotten married, Levi and I had become engaged, and we regularly battled over the latter two.

Our first two years together had been great, filled with sex, parties, and enough quality time to meet double my emotional needs. It wasn't until year three when I'd found out I was pregnant that things became complicated.

I was twenty-one when I had Danielle, and I'd quickly realized that our party lifestyle wasn't how I wanted to raise a child. I'd vowed to become the best mom I could, finish college, and do something productive with my life. So that was exactly what I had done. My priorities had changed, so I had changed.

Through college I excelled, checking off one degree then starting another, always sprinting toward another life challenge. I had quickly established a booming career working for myself consulting with private clients and corporations on health and wellness, as well as teaching part time at a local University. I was well spoken, on my way to receiving a master's degree, and employable with a plethora of credentials in health and nutrition. Despite the success, I was hopelessly discontent.

Through the lens of Levi's hazel eyes, all he wanted was for me to be content, for me to slow down, stop bouncing my knees and for once, be happy with what I had in front of me. He was the guy who could stay in a job for two decades with a yearly three percent raise and be satisfied.

I wished I could be that way, I just couldn't. I was a chronically discontent, obsessive compulsive overachiever.

Levi and I were very different. We had conflicting opinions on just about everything that was important to us. We struggled to find balance between our family and our relationship. It didn't seem so uncommon to have a difficult relationship like ours. In fact, it seemed to be fairly normal, like most of the other relationships I'd seen.

We rarely agreed on anything and regularly engaged each other in petty arguments over problems like inequitable household chores or opposing libidos. These arguments became a frequent and toxic cloak over our relationship and smothered our future.

Every sentence began with, "You always," or, "You never," and since no argument was ever fully laid to rest or resolved, snippets of previous arguments were continually reconstituted and poured back into the pot, making a more concentrated poison each time we fought. It was a poison laced with resentment over everything that had ever been said or done that hadn't been resolved. This resentment ate at me from the inside, callousing my heart and turning me into someone I was not.

Resentment killed my spirit in a record quick time. I became a hardened, empty partner lying dead on a cold metal table with a toe tag that read, *"Don't fucking touch me,"* and, *"Don't even dare try to have sex with me."*

We circled each other like bloodthirsty hyenas in a perpetual power struggle. Hating each other over everything that had ever happened, yet nothing was really worth fighting for. The bottom line was that not only were Levi and I not compatible, at some deep biological level we were also lethal to each other.

Violent words spewed off my tongue.

"I hate you."

"I wish you were dead."

"I wish I could fucking kill you."

My mouth was stuck wide open, covering years of ground in just minutes as I unleashed a hellfire of words until words weren't enough. Then, like a feral animal, physical anger forced its way out from inside of me to get its share of the kill. I wailed and kicked and screamed and pushed him down the hallway, lining him up with the stairs. I wanted to hurt him more than I had ever wanted to hurt anyone before. I wondered if I actually could kill him. Was I capable of that? Was that the mental derangement lawyers called temporary insanity? Had I slipped into the state of mind where a woman wanted to lop off her husband's penis?

He stumbled as I tried to launch him down the stairs, but not even a shot of angry adrenaline could give my five foot four inches and one hundred twenty pounds the power to push him more than a few wobbly inches. He easily restrained me. I flailed my arms and legs, trying to jolt free, but my efforts were futile. Levi was thick, not huge like my brother Dylan, but he was lean and muscular. He'd been an athlete in high school and he was still agile and strong.

When he finally let go, the evil inside of me rose up again but it was another failed attempt to overpower him. I conceded. I ran in to our bedroom and locked myself in but not because I was scared of him or what he might do. He would never hurt me. I was frightened by my own psychotic break and the ease at which I could abuse.

I had become the alpha abuser. I was the horrible partner who verbally and physically abused, and I hated myself for it. I hated the person I'd become in our relationship.

That night I cried then slept, then cried. He never knocked on the door to see if I was alright, and I never apologized. I didn't even know what we had been fighting about. Pointless arguments had become a familiar pattern and created a hatred that lingered between us.

After each freak-out, I always regretted my uncouth behavior, but inevitably I would be pushed to my breaking point again and throw more berserk tantrums later. Each one made me a little less whole and a little more crazy.

***

God, it just sucks that
we can't do what we want.
2 stay together tonight.

Chapter 3

"HIS PRESENCE IN A ROOM WAS MORE CHEERING THAN THE BRIGHTEST FIRE."

—CHARLOTTE BRONTË, *JANE EYRE*

Dani and I were sitting cross-legged on our lakeside patio, coloring with sidewalk chalk, when I heard Dylan yelling from the end of the dock.

"Come here, quick!" He was looking up at an endless ocean of blue sky.

Dani stumbled as I tugged her plump little hand alongside me. Nanook trotted behind us, tongue flopping and white froth dripping from his black gums. Summertime in Minnesota was brutal for my Siberian husky but a glorious warm vacation for me.

Just as we reached the end of the dock, a red-and-white plane swooped down unusually low, buzzing what seemed like inches from our heads.

I instinctively ducked. "What the—who is that?" I asked Dylan.

He squinted with his hand over his eyes, following the plane through the sky. "Grant," he said.

***

The cabin was nestled into a hillside surrounded by lush Minnesota forest. Our backyard sprawled out into a secluded wetland that morphed ubiquitously into a hundred miles of rolling hills in the Land of Ten Thousand Lakes.

The cabin itself was a time capsule that hadn't changed since 1979, the year I was born. There was carpet in the bathroom, no shower, and curtains hung where doors should have been. The well water tasted like pocket change, and the electricity went out with every summer thunderstorm. Although Mom made sure we had the fanciest cabin on the lake with a lit palm tree, pink plastic flamingos, and a handwritten sign by the toilet that read: "Here in the land of sun and fun, we never flush for #1."

Dylan and I were natural-born lake kids who never missed a weekend. We didn't care that we had to bathe in sixty-degree lake water and sleep in bunk beds that smelled of mold. The cabin was our warm summer reprieve from the icy cold Minnesota winters. Now that we were grown, the cabin was the only place Dylan and I could reunite with our parents before they flew back to their Arizona home each winter.

That night, pale pink and tangerine smudged the Western sky. The sunsets over the cabin were enchanting, each one a unique fingerprint yet each one the same. The wetlands surrounding our evening bonfire seemed to come alive at night. Toads and tree frogs croaked, fireflies blinked across the expanse of the damp marsh, and the resident pack of coyotes bellowed their lonesome howls into the darkness.

Dylan and I were sitting on tree stumps, listening to the crackle and smack of the fire and sipping our sweating Coronas when he asked:

"Where's Levi this weekend?"

I was always ashamed to answer, and my answer was always the same.

"Working," I'd say.

Or I'd make up some other lame excuse about how Levi needed to mow the lawn or repaint the kitchen for the sixteenth time.

"What?" Dylan replied, "Tell him to get down here, he's missing out. Work can wait, the summer is way too short to miss a weekend."

The truth was, Levi just wasn't a cabin type of guy. Missing a weekend was his vacation.

"It's too boring there," Levi would say. "What am I supposed to do all weekend? I don't like sitting around all day on the deck or in the boat."

I did. Doing nothing at the lake on the dock, or deck, or in the boat with an apricot brandy slushy were the best parts of lake living, and I wasn't about to cut my time short. It was my escape to solitude. It was the place where, if only for an hour, I could get lost in the woods without anyone caring.

My mom and dad were happy to see their granddaughter and occupy her for hours and hours. Every weekend, Dani and I would pack up our beach stuff and leave Levi behind on the hot pavement of our city home to head for the lake.

As a car approached our cabin its blinding headlights drowned out the color of the flames.

"Who's that?" I asked as a car door slammed shut.

Dylan didn't answer. He never answered—not to me, not to anyone. If he didn't like the question or didn't want to talk, he just simply didn't answer. For no other reason than it was just his way.

When we were kids he was the kind of brother who shot me with a rubber-band gun while I was sleeping and clipped his toenails in my bed. He made me walk ten feet behind him to school and showed me how to stuff my winter coat behind the bushes because "walking to school in a coat is so not cool."

A car door slammed shut and the slap of flip-flops coming toward us grew louder. Dylan stood up to greet the stranger.

"Hey, bud! Glad you could make it."

"Hey, Dylan. Thanks for inviting me."

I was instantly flustered by this man's good looks. He had an All-American smile that was intimidating and distracting.

"This is my sister," Dylan said.

They both looked at me.

I mustered out a clumsy, "hi."

"C.J., this is Grant," Dylan said. "He's the one with the plane from this morning."

"Very impressive," I nodded in Grants' direction.

He was humble and gave a polite, "thanks, nice to meet you."

I went back to doing nothing on my tree stump as they engaged in casual conversation. Except I *was* doing something; I was secretly analyzing this handsome stranger like an undercover agent would analyze her newest assignment. I listened intently as he and Dylan spoke. It seemed like they knew each other but hadn't spoken in long time.

Grant was well spoken, kind mannered and unusually intelligent. Though he also seemed a little distant, perhaps a little lost.

I twirled my engagement ring, alternating it between my middle and pinkie fingers, as I reminded myself: *Ignore him. Stop looking at him. What are you doing? You already committed to Levi, you're taken.*

After thirty minutes I'd gathered that Dylan and Grant had already become good friends, they'd talked on the phone regularly and even planned his stop by our fire tonight.

"Come on, bud. Join us for a few more drinks." Dylan said as Grant finished his beer. "We're going to hit the lake bars after this one. It'll be fun. Come with us."

"No thanks Dylan, I can't tonight but I will sometime soon," He said.

I was secretly excited and terrified to hear that he'd be back and that he was already a close friend of Dylan. *How could I have not known about his super-hot friend before?*

I knew the answer, Dylan was secretive, not a gossip, he'd only tell you what you needed to know in real time. He hadn't been hiding his hot friend, he just never thought to tell me about him.

Then Grant looked at me and nodded. "C.J., nice to meet you. I'm sure I'll see you again soon."

It was in that moment I first saw his eyes. They were nearly transparent, a shade of blue I'd never seen before. They were mesmerizing.

As soon as Grant's headlights disappeared into the dense blackness of the rural road, Dylan leaned forward like he was about to tell a ghost story at summer camp. He set his meaty forearms down on his thick thighs and inched to the edge of his stump.

"It's so terrible," Dylan said, his face twisted in disgust. "Grant's wife cheated on him three months after they were married."

"What? That's terrible. What happened?"

"I don't really know all the details. I haven't seen him in years. All I know is that they were high school sweethearts, and he was with her since he was seventeen."

Who in the hell would cheat on that? I thought.

"I ran in to him a few weeks ago," Dylan said. "I feel so terrible for him. C.J., Grant is the nicest guy. I always knew he had a cabin but I never knew it was on our lake! Can you believe that? He's been on the lake all this time and we never even knew it. It's so great to have another person we can hang out with now."

Our lake wasn't big, not more than a mile across, so it was weird that we never knew he was there, but not impossible. We stayed on our side of the lake, knew our close neighbors but that was all. Knowing someone across the lake was like knowing someone who lives six blocks down.

Dylan reached his thick hand into the cooler and pulled out two more longnecks. "Guess what?" He said, "You're never going to believe this. Grant was the guy who got married on the same day I did. Remember there was a wedding party next door to us in the Crystal Ballroom?"

"Yes, I remember." I said, "I looked in there. That was *him*?"

"Yes. He plays in a band, too. Country music, like us." Dylan was thrilled as he told me about his new friend who we seemed to have so much in common with.

In fact, I'd never seen Dylan like someone so much. He wrenched off the beer tops and handed me a dripping bottle. I flung the ice-cold water back on him but got no response.

"We talked about buying a wakeboarding boat together," Dylan said.

"Really?" I gulped and coughed, immediately feeling panicked that this handsome man was going to be around a lot more. "When? You mean, like, this summer?"

"No. The season is almost over. Now is the best time to buy a boat for next year. C.J., it'll be so fun. We'll be able to do all the things we've never been able to do behind Mom and Dad's boat."

I'd known Grant for thirty minutes, and already I felt like getting married to Levi was the wrong thing to do. Forget about the arguments, everybody argues, if I could be so smitten with another man almost immediately then maybe I was with the wrong person.

It didn't matter how I felt. I'd said yes. We had a child, I could never back out now. Besides, he treated me fine, he wasn't abusive, and he took care of Dani and I. What more did I need?

I soon found out what I needed was someone who I was so enthralled with that the thought of anyone else didn't even exist, which is exactly what happened during the remaining summer. However, it wasn't my soon-to-be-husband who stole my attention.

Surprise appearances from our new friend were becoming more frequent, and my high school crush on my brother's new best friend intensified. I tried to curb my appetite for him. I tried to reason with my mind, but he just kept coming around. Every. Single. Weekend. My fever never had enough time to cool down. Over the course of only a few months, he became like a festering ulcer of guilt and desire.

It wasn't only me who lusted over him. Everyone he met seemed to immediately fall in love with our new single and talented friend.

Dylan had a group of regular friends who frequented our place on the lake, as well as a revolving door of new friends he'd meet and invite over. There were always neighbors around, and my parents had friends and family stop by sporadically too. There was never a shortage of bikini clad bodies lying on the dock or hanging out on the lawn paying bocce ball or throwing a Frisbee.

It didn't take long for Grant to become a part of our regular group. He'd stop by with his new, shiny silver Jet Ski and offer take anyone waterskiing or just take them for a ride. He helped Dani fill up water balloons and instigate a war. We played ladder ball and tossed bean bags and did all the things lake-people do. Just like that, Grant had become a regular fixture with us. No one could believe he'd been right under our noses all those years.

"Who's the new hot guy? Why is he still single?" Our friends and neighbors would ask.

Even my parents doted over him. After Grant brought over his guitar and played music with them, they were instantly enamored with his charm. When he wasn't around they'd ask where he was and why they hadn't met him before and ogle over what a talented musician he was. They sold him vitamins and exchanged phone numbers.

They were right to swoon. He had an enticing charisma that drew you in. After saying not more than a few polite words, he held you captive. Men and women alike seemed to adore him.

Why would a smart, handsome entrepreneur with mysterious eyes and dark hair be single? I often wondered and wasn't the only one.

He was frequently assumed to be either gay, or too damaged from his first marriage to ever settle down again. No one, especially me could believe he wasn't taken.

"He's picky," Dylan would say when someone asked. "He'll never settle."

Grant was irresistible to everyone, except for Levi. They'd met less than a handful of times since Levi was seldom at the lake, but Levi would hear how people talked about Grant. How Grant was a pilot and a musician, a business owner and taught ballroom dance. He actually sounded like a fictitious character when people would list his attributes. I could see how it drove Levi nuts.

When the summer ended, I was surprised at how quickly my schoolgirl crush went with it. Everyone went back to their winter homes and regular lives. During the winter months, we rarely saw each other. Nine months passed without a single glimpse of him. In that time Grant faded in my mind, existing as only an apparition in the long gray winter.

***

Summertime arrived again, and overflowing ponds and streams became home to the returning waterfowl. My chapped winter skin rejoiced in the sun. With the first dose of vitamin D I'd had in nine months, my seasonal winter gloom lifted.

It was a new summer, a new beginning, and just as soon as I settled into my weekend routine, it began: Grant and I were slowly becoming friends, it was as if we'd both missed each other. My spark for him had ignited again. He looked at me, and truly saw me. When his crystalline eyes met mine, everyone else in the world seemed to fall away. My infatuation was back with vengeance.

Our friends and neighbors gathered around the fire to sing and dance in the sand and enjoy the summer libations. There were harmonicas, washboards with plastic spoons, drumsticks on logs, twelve-string guitars, and everyone sang along.

Grant was a jukebox that didn't need a quarter. You could just put in your request and get a personal serenade.

"Grant, play Bon Jovi."

"Grant, play 'Hotel California.'"

"Grant, play Keith Urban."

His brain was a catalog of music he'd collected over years of singing and touring. Playing all genres and every weekend around the bonfire, he wooed us with his encyclopedia of songs. Grant was a modern prodigy, a musical muse. He lured me in with his tenor and then held me captive with his timbre.

The weathered picnic table of my childhood creaked as he shifted his weight, situating his guitar on one knee. I watched him from behind the flames. He was plain and gorgeous—gorgeously plain, in worn-out jeans and an unkempt tousle. His face was bronzed, his voice smooth, and his transparent eyes drew me in closer. I could almost smell his breath and feel the vibration of his words on my skin. He closed his eyes as he sang my request—a love song, of course. Every syllable sent me deeper into a lucid dream, a dream in which I imagined what a life with him might be like.

I floated on the melody, exposing the curves of my neck, secretly inviting him in. When he opened his eyes, they met mine. He looked away, looked back, and then continued my request as if he were singing to my heart alone.

Is he singing to me or just in my general direction?

I analyzed further, examining his body language, where he looked, whom he looked at, and what it all might mean.

Is it possible? Could he be feeling the way I'm feeling? Why does he keep looking at me? Is it a nervous tic or something?

When the fire fizzled out and only the weekend warriors remained we would make our way down to the water and take a midnight ride in the new boat.

Grant and Dylan bought that wakeboarding boat they'd talked about, and stored it right outside my bedroom window.

That summer I found myself in a conundrum worse than any before. I was engaged, tied to Levi with a mooring rope, but I couldn't stop thinking about someone else. All week, I would look forward to the weekend, hoping to get a glimpse of him—the man who just happened to be Dylan's best friend, the man who I'd never seen with a girlfriend because he was so picky, the man who had been cheated on, the man I would never be able to have.

So why not leave Levi? I asked myself dozens of times and the answer was always the same.

I loved Levi. Levi loved me. Things weren't great but they weren't terrible. We had our dark moments, but everyone does. Why would I call off our engagement for a crush? For a man who is way out of my league? No, I would stay with Levi. *This thing that I feel for another man is completely normal*, I convinced myself, *a biological desire for the opposite sex, an inborn chemical attraction that would eventually dissipate.*

It didn't, and it seemed that nothing could uproot the seed that had been planted in my subconscious. I had a wanton desire for Grant that kept growing even under the most inhospitable conditions. For reasons I didn't yet understand, I became inextricably bound to him.

***

I will always take care of u
always... sucks that I can't completely
be my loving, caring self around others.

Chapter 4

"HE STEPPED DOWN, TRYING NOT TO LOOK AT HER,

AS IF SHE WERE THE SUN, YET HE SAW HER,

LIKE THE SUN, EVEN WITHOUT LOOKING."

—LEO TOLSTOY, *ANNA KARENINA*

It was no surprise when Levi turned a shade of jealous green the night I walked away with Grant. Had Levi gone missing with an alluring, charming, multi-talented female—if *they* had wandered out of sight and couldn't be reached—I would have dumped his ass. That's what he should have done to me. Even if Grant had been just a friend, which technically that's all he was—having a male friendship, especially one complicated by my secret emotional affair, was unacceptable and I knew it. I just couldn't help myself.

Several years had passed since that inauspicious wedding night and Dylan and Grant now shared the same fate. Dylan too was divorced. He'd since moved on to Lexi, a platinum blonde cosmetologist and model who was the sweetest girl I'd ever met, and who also made me want to hold her hand when she crossed the street.

Every year in August a drunken horde of country music fans flocked to our otherwise peaceful lakeside town for a week of Country music, Jiffy Johns, and beer bongs. WE Fest was a rowdy adventure rain or shine with thirty thousand half-naked bodies wafting around their four-day-old stink.

We had tickets. Grant had tickets too, VIP tickets, and he'd offered to share them with us. Dylan, Lexi, Levi, and I stood at our designated meeting spot by the French fry stand and waited for Grant.

I dressed subtly sexy that night, wanting Grant to desire me. At the same time, I clung to Levi's arm, wanting Grant to know I was taken, untouchable. I peeked out from under a tattered cowboy hat and scanned the crowd looking for him. When he emerged, his stellar blue shirt illuminated his eyes. They were a color so completely opposite from my own blackish-brown eyes that it was hard not to stare.

I was an instant cosmonaut.

I knew he would look hot, but really?

A pair of VIP passes hung from around his neck as he walked through the crowd with an air of confidence. I looked away uninterested, trying to hide my star-struck expression and curb the growing smile that threatened to give away my sinful attraction. If I let on even in the slightest amount that I found Grant to be funny, charming, or in any small way superior to Levi I would be forbidden to go to the cabin forevermore.

Grant looked our way, but he looked past me, not making eye contact. He never made eye contact when Levi was around. He barely even looked in my direction. Although when we were alone his behavior was quite different. He was his normal polite, charming, engaging self.

"Hi, everybody. I have two passes," Grant said as he slipped one off and held it toward us. "I can take one of you back at a time, who wants to go first?"

My heart arrested.

ME! ME! ME!

Inside I squirmed, jumping up and down with my hand raised high.

But why could he only take one of us? Why couldn't he just give up the two passes and let each couple go?

My hopeful mind instantly made the leap: *the reason only one of us could go at a time was because he wanted to be alone with me—right?*

I noticed a brood of girls walking by that were staring at Grant— their radar picking up that he was the only single person in our group. He ignored them, he didn't even look in their direction, but I stared them down with an evil sneer only women understand. Mine or not, I was claiming him.

Grant took Lexi first. They were gone for half an hour before they emerged from a crowd of bare torsos scribbled with Sharpies. Dylan and Levi had forfeit their turns, so I was up next. My mouth was dry and the muscles in my thighs twinged with anxiety.

"Ready to go?" Grant asked.

I waved and smiled at Levi as we walked away, "I'll be right back!"

Levi was inflamed, his face was red with anger. He despised that I was going, but he couldn't tell me not to. I turned back toward the crowd, popped in an Altoid, circled my lips with peppermint lip balm and didn't look back. It was a rare occurrence when I got to be alone with Grant for more than a quick minute and I wasn't about to pass it up now. Grant was the type of person who when you were alone with him, made you feel like you were the only woman in the universe. He didn't look at anyone else and gave me his full attention.

"Thanks for sharing your tickets," I said.

"You're welcome."

He flashed me a charming smile.

"I'm glad you could come."

I nudged him playfully, "Me too."

I huddled close as we walked, my body naturally magnetized to him. I imagined what it would be like if I was his girl, if he was my guy. What it would feel like to have his masculine hands holding my face as he kissed me, or how it would feel to have the strength of his body hovering over mine as we made love in the dim candlelight.

We stopped under a large white canopy filled with free food, drinks, and belligerent rich, old, white men sipping Crown on the rocks.

Good, no one will know me here.

We toasted, clinking our plastic cups.

"To VIP," he said then glanced over my shoulder at the walkway. Then glanced again a few minutes later I knew who he was looking for.

"I'm sure he can't get back here." I said. I was several drinks in and my threshold for inhabitations was decreasing rapidly. "Aren't these tickets really hard to come by? And security seemed pretty tight at the gate."

My words seemed to make him fidget. He shifted from side to side, took a sip from his plastic cup then looked at me with a gorgeous smile.

The mood changed between us. I'd called forth the elephant in the room and it acted like an ice breaker. From then on our conversation flowed without him glancing over my shoulder and without inhibitions.

"I'd love to hear you sing sometime, Dylan told me all about your time in Georgia Summer."

"You have heard me sing, around the bonfire. That's as much as I'm willing to do anymore. I'd rather listen, I love concerts. Especially in VIP, this is my first time."

"Really? Then I'm so glad it was with me," he smirked.

My heart raced. "I guess you can consider yourself lucky then," I said with the utmost confidence.

"I am lucky."

"Quit it," I said, "unless you really mean it."

"I do mean it," He said. "These are great seats and I'm lucky to get to share them with you. I'm surprised Levi let you go."

"What choice did he have? What would be his reason I couldn't share second row seats for half a concert with a friend?"

"He hates me," Grant suggested.

"I think you're right about that. He does seem to hate you, doesn't he?" We laughed and I nudged him with my shoulder. "Of course he hates you, you're hot. All guys *should* hate you. Funny they don't, it seems like exactly the opposite, except for Levi everyone loves you."

"No they don't, quit it." He smiled shyly.

I was crunching on the last bit of ice from a watered down wine cooler when he grabbed my empty cup and tossed it into the trash.

"Follow me," he said, then set his hand on my bare lower back prompting me to move forward. I happily did what he asked. I had a feeling he was a man who got whatever he asked for.

We shimmied in between rows of pickup trucks and music trailers, making our way deep behind the stage. There were no lights and no people, only extra-large tour busses with their engines running.

I shivered from the midnight breeze.

"Are you cold?"

If I was, would you put your arms around me?

"I'm fine," I said smoothing the goose bumps on my arms, wishing I could have said, *yes please hold me and keep me warm.* Instead I huddled close enough to feel his warmth and be tortured by his scent. A masculine scent, probably just his deodorant but it didn't matter, I wanted to bury my face in his chest and breathe him in all night long.

A stalky figure in a cowboy hat stepped out of a bus and was instantly surrounded by an entourage of bodyguards.

"Come here, quick," Grant said as he pulled me in front of him, his body pressed close behind mine. "I think that's Kenny Chesney," he pointed over my shoulder, then rested his arm down on it.

I didn't care about Kenny Chesney. I cared about the electricity that pulsed between our bodies.

Holy shit, what is this? Does he feel it too?

Long after Kenny disappeared, our bodies still lingered close as we stared into the empty darkness. The silence was deafening. I quivered with anticipation, I wanted him to turn me around and kiss me, it felt natural—right even. I turned to face him, brushing against his chest so closely that my nose swept across his divine smelling shirt. Time seemed to slow and I fantasized that he would wrap me up in his arms and kiss me like I needed to be kissed. I was giving him a chance, making a moment. I paused for a flash of a second waiting for it. But instead of being enveloped and devoured by passion my whole body seized in terror and my heart pounded like thunder in my chest when a voice yelled:

"You can't be back there!"

"We're leaving!" Grant yelled into the dark night and we trotted away laughing. "Come on, let's go to our seats."

As we approached our seats, we found they were overrun by a mob of cowboy hats and sweaty, tan bodies. Without looking at me or saying a word Grant reached for my hand. He pulled me close behind him and led me through the rowdy crowd like I was his woman to lead. The roar of thirty thousand people fell silent in my ears and nothing else existed except his warm hand encircling mine. Long after he could have, he still hadn't let go. We stood with our hands interlaced for what seemed like hours, not moving, as if we both knew that once we moved, whatever this was would end.

"We should get back," he said after an hour of Kenny Chesney songs. I hoped that *back* to meant back to his place where we could explore each other until morning, talking and kissing, and bring my secret desires to life. Instead he let my warm hand slide away and back into the lonesome cold. I felt hollow inside as he let me go, I felt alone again.

Levi was going to kill me, he'd be waiting with a plume of red smoke funneling out his ears. On our way back we got trapped by the crowd, squished together in gridlock—the best gridlock ever and I gasped when he reached and wrapped his hand around mine again. The soft strength of his touch on my skin, knowing he wanted to touch me even in that small way, meant something. A spark ignited inside of me that night which could never be extinguished.

He let my hand fall away just before we reached the exit where Levi was standing in the same spot I'd left him, still waiting for me.

***

Ur gunna get it!
And I'm gunna give it to u :D

Chapter 5

"I MAY HAVE LOST MY HEART, BUT NOT MY SELF-CONTROL."

—JANE AUSTEN, *EMMA*

It was the epitome of a perfect summer day at the cabin. The sun was directly overhead warming our skin. The breeze was almost imperceptible, moving just enough to keep us cool so we could stay outside all day.

Grant stood in the shallows, waves washing over him as he fumbled with the water ski. He hopped on one foot while trying to stuff the other into the boot and whining about not having gloves.

"Suck it up! You don't need gloves." I yelled, "Let's go!" I strained to see over the windshield of the oversized wake boarding boat, I sat up as tall as I could on the top of the white vinyl driver's seat.

"I like gloves, it's easier to hold the rope. Please look for them," he begged.

"I did. They're not in the boat." I looked over my shoulder at him. "You're fine without them, big baby. Come on, I'm hot let's move and get some air."

That summer we'd developed a mutual fondness, a flirtatious banter that hadn't been there before.

There was so much I wanted to tell him.

I think about you all the time, how you held my hand. Don't you think about me? I need you in my life. I dread another winter without you.

"Hit it!" he yelled, from the shore.

I thrust the throttle forward, the Moomba growled and dug in. The bow lifted into the air and the tower tilted backward. The cherry red and patriotic white reflection of the boat wobbled across the water as we

33

skimmed along the shore. Grant flew back and forth across the wake with ease, slicing sideways through the liquid glass. Dylan sat lazily in the passenger seat, happy to relinquish the captain's chair for a short while. Besides Dylan and Grant, I was the only person allowed to play captain and I was proud of my elite status.

When Grant was done I beached the boat in the shallows and watched as the usual gang of svelte, oiled bodies trickled toward the water. One-by-one bright colored beach towels floated into place and claimed their spot on the now-crowded dock. A blue cooler filled with Mexican beer sat permanently perched in the corner.

They were Dylan's friends, my acquaintances. I didn't have many friends. I had a child, a dog, a rising career, and a stressful relationship. I didn't have the time to keep meaningful friendships. Instead, I had a hundred acquaintanceships. I knew people, people knew me; we could do lunch, send flowers to the hospital, but I couldn't tell them my secrets.

Grant stood in the water next to the boat dripping wet, tan, and ridiculously handsome. I held up a half empty jug of V8 and two Coronas. No words were necessary, he nodded and grinned, and mixed us drinks as I flipped on the music. *Bob Marley's Greatest Hits,* the only music allowed in the boat. It was a pact we'd made earlier that summer and thus far, it had been strictly enforced.

The tone was set for an indulgent and memorable day as we clinked our frothy crimson bottles together.

"It's our thing, right?" he asked.

"You mean the music or the bloody beers?"

"Both," He said with a smile.

"Yes. Our thing."

Everyone trusted Grant. He was the one you wanted behind the wheel of the car, boat, or plane, the one you could trust to get you home safely, the one everyone looked to in a time of crisis. He was the alpha leader of our pack who could make a calm and rational decision midst total chaos.

I was happy when he was around, unusually happy. A fact that illuminated just how wrong I felt staying with Levi, and how different I was with each of them. Grant felt right; he was someone I could laugh with and laugh at, and someone who wasn't scared to laugh at me. He was extraordinarily intelligent, and would engage me in conversations about the origins of the earth and how humans came to have opposable thumbs. We had an infinite number of things to talk about. He was never boring, and I concluded that like me, he was someone who lived life on purpose. With Grant, not even the ocean was deep enough to fit all of the things we had to talk about. With Levi, the shallow hull of a shot glass would have sufficed.

I wondered, *would every day with Grant be exciting? Or would a life with him eventually become monotonous and dull in a year or two?*

My experience was that the excitement and deep well of conversation wouldn't last. I'd slowly lose respect, become uninterested, and not want to have sex. I'd complain about his shortcomings and eventually land in the exact place I was in with Levi.

Why would I throw one dull relationship away just to have another? Besides, it's me who's the problem and needs to change, right?

"Relationships are hard work and sacrifice."

"The grass isn't always greener on the other side."

"You'll trade one set of problems for another."

Those were the phrases I knew about marriage and maybe those things were true. I didn't know. What I did know was that a still small voice kept nudging me, telling me that great love did exist and wasn't so difficult after all.

I was more myself with Grant than I'd ever been with anyone else. Levi unleashed a monster, whereas Grant reminded me of who I was, and how far away from my true self I'd wandered. Grant unlocked the best parts of me. He made me want to be a better person and keep moving toward my goals no matter how impossible they seemed. With him I was courageous, and playful, and together we laughed with the innocence of a child. Yet there was no way realistically or logically that I could back out of what I had with Levi. Even if I did, what solid evidence did I have that Grant would really want me if I was single?

"You want to take it out for a while?" Grant nodded toward his shimmering silver Jet Ski swaying in the waves.

"Not alone, but you can take me."

Grant stared into the clear water with a wary smile and I braced for rejection. He sloshed his foot from side to side then lifted his chin. "Sure" he said, "I'll take you for the ride of your life."

He oozed sexual confidence. A playful confidence that made me want to tackle him and wrestle a few rounds slathered in hot oil. He snapped shut the buckles on his life jacket, patted the seat behind him and curled his index finger telling me to *come here.*

I grabbed the nearest girl's life jacket, a baby blue and pastel pink thing with "HO" in capital letters on the back. When I put it on, my boobs had nowhere to go except plunging out the arm holes like the center of a jelly donut—it was three sizes too small and two decades too old, a relic from my childhood. I shrugged off the embarrassing look and wrapped my arms around his chest. I clutched the straps of his life jacket, and in one mighty thrust I yanked hard, throwing both of us into the water. It was a refreshing plunge that was met with roaring laughter from the dock.

"Good one HO," Dylan said in his usual calm manner as he applied sunscreen to his biceps tattoos. Tattoos that made his bulging muscles look even bigger and added another level of intimidation to his already overpowering presence.

When Grant stood up, water dripped down the bridge of his nose, "You know I'll get you back," he smirked.

"That's not fair! You've already gotten me back many times," I whined as we shimmied back into place, poking and flicking at each other.

I settled in behind him and began to fantasize that he would take me to a secluded part of the lake and tell me how much he wanted me. *Be with me,* he would say, *leave him, I will love you better.* I would confess my long suppressed desire to devour him whole, and tell him he was the most extraordinary man on the planet. I would tell him that I was *the one* woman for him.

But that didn't happen. Instead he drove like a lunatic—zigged and zagged, throttled and jerked, and whirled us in the same circle until it formed a supermassive black hole that threatened to suck me in. I refused to let go, I would never let him go. I squeezed his hips between my inner thighs tight enough to squash a watermelon, and clenched my fist around my wrist securing myself to him.

I put my lips close to his ear, "You'll never get me off."

He turned his head toward me and in the most seductive tone he said, "I'll get you off, baby."

Did he just say that? Yes! Finally some real fun.

"I hope you do—but I think you're too chicken," I yelled into the wind.

His sneaky laughter told me that he enjoyed our inappropriate innuendos.

I wrapped my arms around him like I was saving an oak tree and laid my head on his shoulder. I moved with his movements, in-sync with every turn and tilt. It was the first time we'd been that close, the first time he'd allowed it, or maybe even encouraged it. I would have crawled inside his skin if he would have let me.

When the water pressure finally tore our bodies from the slick machine, we floated like bobbers in the waves.

"I have to pee," he said with a devious smirk, then thrashed through the water making a beeline toward me.

"No Grant don't! Please, please!" I yelled as I swam away. Then stopped and realized two could play that game. "I have to pee too," I said with a smirk.

"Well, go ahead then,"

"I will then. I am then."

I scooped up a handful of seaweed that was floating next to me and flung it at him. "That was in the water where I just peed."

He swished it around, "Yep, and now it's in the water where *I* peed." He flung it back at me with ridiculous accuracy.

He helped me back onto the Jet Ski, but not before he pushed me back into the water another time. I pouted and started swimming toward the shore.

"I'm sorry, I was just kidding. I won't do it again. I promise," he said. "Come back...please," he reached out his hand. "I'm not going to push you. Get up here." Then he reached down and clasped my arm pulling me from the water with ease. When he wrapped one hand around my lower back tiny hairs all over my body stood at attention, and I waited for him to do something, anything. Anything that would tell me how he felt so I didn't have to live in agony any longer wondering if it was only me who felt something between us.

He did nothing.

Water dripped from the stubble on his face and landed in the large chasm between my breasts. We looked at the drop simultaneously. I reached down and wiped it away.

"Ew," I said. He rolled his eyes and threatened to push me back in the water.

Our tomfoolery went on for hours as he kept us away from watchful eyes, staying in a secluded bay on the opposite side of the lake.

Is he hiding us intentionally? Do we have something to hide?

I wanted to believe that our privacy was by his design, but I couldn't be sure how he felt. I was only sure how I felt, and my feelings were intensifying by the second.

On our last wipe-out of the day, we surfaced to find the Jet Ski half a football field away and upside down.

"Oh shit, that's bad isn't it?" I asked with a crooked grin.

"It's not good," he said.

The downed machine gurgled and gulped in water. I secretly hoped we'd be stranded and have to swim to shore then walk back. That would take at least another two or three hours. So when we finally managed to flip the huge hunk of metal upright, I was disappointed. I was disappointed again when the engine choked and coughed and struggled back to life.

The sun had already circled past its midday point. We'd been out the entire afternoon when it hit me. I knew Dani was fine with my mom and dad but— *Shit! What if Levi showed up while I was gone?*

My fear was real but fleeting, snuffed out by much stronger emotions.

I sat down shivering and huddled behind Grant. Then a familiar gray gloom descended on me as I realized he was taking me home. The chances of us doing anything like this again were slim, and the prospect of having to watch him do these things with another woman were great.

As we skimmed the surface of the smooth water I peered into the woods, I understood their eerie calm, it enveloped me too. I set my head on his cold, padded shoulder and closed my eyes—I was an infinitesimal speck in the universe, and I felt it. Yet somehow with him, my insignificance was bearable. Whether it was reality or not, in some small way I felt significant to him.

The wind blew through my skin and my body trembled, I cowered behind him, tucked in my arms and disappeared in his shelter. Then a comforting heat covered the outside of my leg, surprising me. The length of his arm stretched out against my body, his palm and fingers covering as much of my cold skin as possible. Where our skin touched tension pulsed. The warmth of his arm remained unchanged as we took an unusual route home. I couldn't help but wonder if taking the long way back confessed what he couldn't say.

I wrapped myself tighter around him hoping to emanate how I felt without words. I embraced him whole heartedly as if somehow I knew he was the great love I was waiting for. Tears formed on my eyelashes. I wanted to tell him how I felt, but the consequences were too grave. I might wreck our friendship, and he might lose respect for me. I could lose Levi. The fear of being rejected and losing the only life I knew kept me as silent as the trees around me.

As we approached the cabin, a tall thick figure stood at the end of the dock. Dylan was looking over the water with binoculars, searching for us.

***

I miss u already baby :(
Remember, I'll be watching over u.

Chapter 6

"I WILL BE CALM. I WILL BE MISTRESS OF MYSELF."

—JANE AUSTEN, *SENSE AND SENSIBILITY*

7 months later

At the edge of the world I desired him less.

Warm sand squished between my toes, turquoise water hypnotized my soul, and the sound of steel drums filled my mind.

Blue sky mind—blue sky mind.

I reminded myself as I looked up, aspiring to be as simple and necessary as the pale blue uncomplicated sky. As I indulged in that simple moment standing by his side, I somehow became reset, wiped clean of my wandering intentions and ready for a new start, with Levi.

Just like it has appeared in the magazine, Magens Bay was a perfect crescent shaped beach lined with postcard palm trees stretching out over the water, and waves that crumbled imperceptibly over my toes. A lone waitress with ripped calves and a ponytail that whipped from shoulder to shoulder patrolled the beach selling overpriced diluted drinks. I imagined what it would be like to be her. To live every day in a bikini and bare feet. *I could do that.* Live at a slower pace, immerse myself in a simple existence with no greater meaning, and thrive in a world where the most difficult decision was coconut or mango.

Magens Bay was third on a list of the ten most beautiful beaches in the world. A list I vowed I would start checking off. Although Levi didn't care about being a global traveler or seeing the natural wonders of the world, experiencing all that our majestic planet had to offer was born in me. I had no choice other than to go alone, or drag him along.

Taking Levi to Magens Bay, spending time together without the temptation of Grant, gave me the time and distance to get some much needed perspective on my love life. What I found shocked me. I didn't feel as deeply for Grant as I thought I did, and for the first time it was easy to let him go.

Leaving our daughter with grandparents, vacationing with Levi came with no complications or obligations. It was just he and I, the rum, and the sun. I was enjoying myself with Levi again, enjoying his laid-back style.

Levi was born into a simple family with meager means. A family where togetherness and happiness were found without having a nice car, the latest pair of tennis shoes, or expensive jeans. His was a family that welcomed me into their home with a tender hug and a roast in the oven.

Levi was willing to do whatever I wanted, no itinerary, no alarm clock and no expectations. I could push us to scurry like tourists, or ask to do nothing on a beach. He was always willing to live life on my terms, and at the time he didn't seem to care. I took advantage of his easy going personality.

After Magens Bay, Levi and I strolled the emerald beaches of St. Martin, explored the au naturale beach Orient, snubba'd at Coki, snorkeled in Trunk Bay, and drank lime margaritas overlooking the lost city of Atlantis. When I cracked a Corona in Mexico, a pained and distant thought of Grant haunted me.

Would this moment be better with Grant or Levi? I asked myself.

Who would I rather be with right now?

Stop it—be content!

Make this work, Dani needs a real family, she deserves a real married family.

So...We set the date.

Chapter 7

I married Levi on a deadly cold night in December.

I invited Grant to the wedding. He was a friend and I would have felt bad not too. I sent the invitation through Dylan. It'd been months since I'd seen him, or even heard his name. I was certain he wouldn't show up—that he'd moved on.

Giving up Grant wasn't as easy as I thought it would be—not like giving up lutefisk for Lent, this was like giving up real food during a famine.

Even with my wedding approaching, I was still consumed by an internal melee. In the summer I knew I couldn't stay with Levi. In the winter I knew I couldn't leave him. Summer or winter, Grant or Levi, risk it or save it.

Whatever happened, the indecision just needed to end, and as soon as I put on that Cosmobella dress, it would end. I would be committed, and I would keep my promise. I was a woman of integrity who keeps her promises. Like that psychic said, it might be hard, but I could make it work. I had to. Besides, at the core of my being, my desire for Grant was just a biological effort to spread my genes—right? If anyone could overcome that, it was me.

***

The architecture was breathtaking. Sweeping views of fine art lined the walls on all four floors, and evergreen trees flocked with snow filled every corner breathing their fresh oxygen into the air. An art gallery by day and an elegant wedding venue by night, the building was a vintage marvel of exposed brick and polished wood floors.

The center atrium reached up through three stories surrounding the main floor with ornate wrought-iron balconies. Distressed wooden pillars wrapped in thousands of twinkling lights rose high into the cathedral ceiling. There were pink and white poinsettias air brushed with silver glitter to greet our guests, as Edwin McCain and Peter Cetera filled the air with love ballads. Wedding guests in black suits and sparkling dresses adorned the balconies like ornaments as they gazed down on the winter wonderland.

Lissy was my closest friend. She was ten years my elder, wise beyond her years yet still youthful in every way. She was the only one bold enough to ask me the question that no one else dared.

"Honey, are you sure this is what you want to do? It's not too late to change your mind," she said as she straightened the little white flowers that pinned up my long, straight hair.

"I have to," I told her, "it's the right thing to do and besides how could I live without him? How could I raise Dani alone? He's a good guy. He loves us, and I don't even have to change my last name!" I teased. But it was true, Ms. Summers was about to become Mrs. Summers.

"Honey, you shouldn't marry him unless you really want to be with him, don't do this out of obligation."

"Lissy, no marriage is perfect," I said. Regurgitating that and a few other clichés about marriage like, "What Levi and I have is better than nothing, we get along most of the time," I said.

I'd only known of marriages that were work and stress and compromise. So what I had with Levi seemed normal. It was the kind of marriage everyone else had. My clients bitched about their husband's, my mom had been complaining about my dad for twenty years, and my grandma about my grandpa for fifty. I turned to face Lissy, "I can't back out now," I said. "I'm already in my dress. And all marriages are hard work, right?"

She didn't respond with reassurance. "I was just asking," she said gently. "Divorce is hard. I would know, and I don't want to see you go through that."

"Honey, I love you for looking out for me and telling me the truth." I hugged her tight, shut my eyes and felt tears threaten to ruin my make-up. Tears I couldn't explain— they were neither happy nor sad, they were just tears coming from somewhere deep inside. Then with my chin on her shoulder, "I love Levi," I said.

"Then it's time."

I floated down two flights of stairs in a feather light ivory gown. Handmade with a heart shaped neckline, flowing fabric, and minimal embellishment. It was a simple and ethereal looking dress with long sheer sleeves that fluttered as I walked.

Dani was four, and old enough to ask why mommy and daddy weren't married. Now she was finally getting her wish and I was happy to give her a normal home life.

In pink chiffon, strappy sparkling shoes, and a chocolate brown ring made of coconut she'd refused to take off she marched unafraid down the aisle, then took her seat in the front row with our families.

I saw Levi's face as he waited for me. His skin was smooth and his sandy hair was in the perfect amount of disarray. He looked dashing in a charcoal suit with an ivory shirt and tie as he stood underneath a shower of white lights strung up like icicles. The love he had for me and Dani showed on his face. Peace and contentment filled his eyes where anger and contempt had often been.

I marched slowly along the promenade with my mom and dad on each side. Smiling and acknowledging our guests, I glanced through the crowd and for a moment, *he* flashed through my mind. I couldn't help but wonder if *he* was there, watching me.

I wondered what he would be thinking. Would he care, even in the slightest? My eyes scanned passed dozens of faces but there were too many and not enough time.

Do all women wonder if they're marrying the right person the very moment they walk down the aisle? I wondered, then dismissed my curiosity as just that, eternal uncertainty about the right or wrongness of my decisions.

Halfway through the ceremony we brought Dani up to stand between us. She was beaming from the united attention of her parents and a hundred pairs of watering eyes.

44

"Will you promise to raise Dani with faith, patience and love?" asked our female pastor. She was a woman of the Episcopalian faith, a religion I'd never heard of before I went searching for someone to tie our knot in the most secular way possible.

"We will," we spoke in unison, then latched a heart-shaped ruby necklace around her little neck, a symbol of our promise. As we knelt down and hugged our little girl, sniffles and whimpers emerged from the crowd.

Levi's hazel eyes were genuine and kind, and pooling with tears when he said "I do." Then it was my turn. With my emotions steady and my eyes dry, I repeated, "I do."

Dylan's band played four sets of classic rock that molested the posh walls of the art gallery. My boisterous father, a man of a million talents and the only person guilty of drinking more alcohol than me, auctioned off my "something blue" garter for a couple hundred bucks. I tossed a bouquet of white roses to a slew of tipsy girls, then true to my wild roots, I tipped back another bottle of wine, no glass required.

A few hours in, I was desperate for a moment of solace. I weaved through the remaining swarm of family and friends, exchanged pleasantries, told them I had to pee, and then quickly excused myself. In the full length mirror that was propped against the back wall of my designated dressing room I admired my whimsical gown and skinny silhouette, but was mortified by how much make-up had melted down my forehead and cheeks. I sifted through a mound of jackets, purses, and decorations to retrieve my make-up bag to paint my face back on. On the floor in front of the mirror, I blotted the oily mess on my forehead, wiped the orange looking bronzer from my brows and erased the smudged black eyeliner from beneath my eyes.

"I'm a fucking Zombie bride," I said to the mirror in a drunken slur.

When I was satisfied that I no longer looked like a rodeo clown in wedding dress I pulled out a tin of Altoids, ate three, smelled my armpits, and plumped my hair. I gathered up a wad of my dress, reached underneath and pulled out the mega wedgie I hadn't been able to get to with all those eyes on me. I was relieved, and annoyed. I liked wearing my yoga pants and gel sole Asics. I realized the formal wedding theme was not my style after all.

Exhausted, I sat at the large oval table in the center of the room, laid my head on my forearms and closed my eyes. I held in the unexplainable tears that tried to sneak past my lids, not knowing what exactly I was crying over. The room spun like a vinyl record and a shrill ringing from inside my head was painfully sharp in my ears.

That's when I saw him.

The next thing I remember was waking up on a bed in a motel room, still in my dress. Drunken amnesia shielded me from the extreme embarrassment I should have felt after vomiting in the hallway outside the honeymoon suite. And instead of making love to my new husband, he spent our wedding night sopping up my regurgitated spinach quiche as I lay passed out and drooling. I did regain consciousness for a brief moment, picked up my head and saw Levi and Lissy kneeling outside the hotel room door scrubbing the carpet with bath towels.

Eventually Levi removed my quiche and carrot cake spattered gown. I held in the urge to heave as he moved my limbs and wrangled with the dress. I was already a terrible wife—a dead, lifeless corpse. From day one he deserved better than what I could give him, he deserved someone who could love him wholeheartedly and without any doubt.

I apologized to Lissy later that week, thanked her for assisting on the vomit squad and asked her to keep my shameful secret in her vault. I never knew if Grant showed up or not. I didn't find out that he did until five years later.

***

Levi and I flew seven hours into the heart of the Caribbean. Despite my previous misgivings and drunken fiasco of a wedding night, I internally renewed my commitment to Levi, to Dani, to my little nuclear family. I felt thrilled to be married, to finally be able to say the word "husband" instead of "boyfriend." Then, only on this sick and twisted planet, in Bob Marley's country of one love and where "everything's gunna be all right," fate mind-fucked me again.

My excitement and fresh start faded fast when Grant showed up on my honeymoon.

***

I'm sorry it took me so long.

Chapter 8

"RESPECT WAS INVENTED TO COVER THE EMPTY PLACE WHERE LOVE SHOULD BE."

—LEO TOLSTOY, *ANNA KARENINA*

The water was glass-bottle green and I could see the island rising out of the ocean as we approached. A lush, prehistoric rain-forest blanketed the mountains over Montego Bay. *Ah...Jamaica, the land of no problems...?*

A man in a dirty island shirt and blood shot eyes lurked behind us as we walked through the airport. "You smoke?" he asked.

"No. No, thanks." I turned and smiled, then kept clunking my luggage across the tile.

"Aw, everybody smoke," he said, still following me. "How about some nice pineapple? You like pineapple? Everybody like pineapple." I walked faster. Levi walked slower, trailing behind clumsily like he was wearing socks with his flip flops. "I got the pineapple crush," the man said holding out his hand. As if I would touch his sweaty palm and get a closer look at his dirty fingernails. I kept walking. "You'll like the pineapple crush," he persisted, unscathed from rejection.

"No...No thanks." I dashed for the tropical air and eventually he gave up, trading us in for another young couple that looked like they too were on their honeymoon.

The unfamiliar heat penetrated my black yoga pants as soon as I stepped outside. It was a welcome feeling on my cold, pale winter skin.

"Damn, it's hot." Levi said, in his usual slow-talk style that not only showed up in his speech but in the way he walked and lived. Living slow was his lifestyle, and talking slow was his vernacular. It infuriated me and made me scream out loud *get to the point!* But also made us an instant targets for dozens of eager pot farmers looking for buyers.

"Hey…waz up?" A tall, black Jamaican man reached out his fist to Levi, then me. Without hesitation, he went right to his pitch.

"I'm a farma' you see." He shrugged his shoulders, and pumped his hands like he was jamming to reggae as he talked. "I grow the ganja—I grow the good stuff, not like you got back home. Where you from?" He lowered his voice and raised his eyebrows, "You like the ganja?"

"No." I said, which meant nothing because rejection was no deterrent.

"Yeah…you like the ganja…" He said to Levi in their shared slow talk then laughed and made gestures with their thumb and fingers as if smoking a joint.

"You like pineapple?" He asked me, unrelenting.

Who the fuck doesn't like pineapple? And when I say yes, he'll try to sell me some. Um…

"No. No thanks."

"Wha?" He said, too lazy to enunciate the "t." He took a step back, looked me over and dropped one shoulder as if to say *Damn girl, why you gotta be like that.* "Damn, everybody like the pineapple. You don't like pineapple?" He said.

I gave him a tight lipped smiled. "Nope."

He flipped his dreads behind his back, then turned to Levi. "Whaddabout you man, you like the pineapple?"

"Naa, I'm with da lady," Levi said, in his one-of-a-kind, molasses slow dialect. "She makes the rules you know." He continued, then he held up his palms and shrugged.

After the third hustle, and the fourth or fifth time being asked if I liked pineapple, I began to understand that pineapple didn't refer to my favorite golden juicy fruit, but that it was a pseudonym for the islands actual largest exported commodity.

We loitered around in Jamaica for a week. Most days consisting of nothing more than making a deeper imprint of the vinyl beach chair on my ass. We sampled the local fair and sipped the sweet libations of Appleton rum. I spent the week ferociously intoxicated and because it was Jamaica, an indiscernible amount of high.

Levi and I hiked up the slippery, moss covered rocks at Dunn's River Falls. The falls plunged hundreds of feet from the top of the rain forest into the mouth of the ocean. Mist lingered in the air and droplets of rain trickled down around us as we reached the thick canopy. It was one of the most romantic places on earth, and there, at the top of a spectacular waterfall was a *farma*, waiting for us like a hungry cannibal, needing what we had and willing to do anything to get it. He was ready for our rejection, so when we didn't buy any pot, he had something else to offer.

"Pretty lady," he asked, "What's your name?" His seemingly harmless pearly white smile shone even whiter next to his dark skin.

"C.J."

Then he turned to Levi for a quick fist bump. "What's your name brother?"

"Levi."

"Levi," he repeated, nodding his head, "A name for a king. King Levi and his queen C.J." He rummaged through a satchel looped around his neck.

"No thanks." I said preempting, refusing whatever shit he was about to sell us.

In the time it took for me to realize what was going on, it had already happened—he'd carved my name into a hunk of wood. A talisman like thing that resembled a Lincoln Log. I never saw it coming and apparently neither did Levi since his name was also carved into a second hunk of wood. We'd been duped, and the harmless looking man with white teeth and yellow eyes, was now demanding money for his carvings.

"Queen C.J and King Levi," he said looking at his work, "These are one of a kind, I can't sell these to nobody else. You pay me, and we both get something good eh?"

Fuck. I thought, next he's going to pull out a knife, stab Levi, steal my bag, and leave us for dead. I pulled out three twenties from my bag, his asking price, handed it to him, and he handed me the two juju voodoo dolls with our names carved into them. As I examined them closer, I realized there were other names that had been carved on there too, other victims he'd tried to trap, then covered their names with ours.

The tar asphalt burned the bottom of my feet when we reached the parking lot. "Hey, you need taxi? I get chu a taxi. You smoke? I'm a farma."

"NO!" We both yelled in frustration.

That night, my crimson skin stung as I took a shower. I looked at my bikini lines in the bathroom mirror and wondered how I could be so white all over in the winter. I was sitting on the edge of the bed, towel drying my hair, when the phone rang.

"I'll get it," I said. "Hello?"

A familiar larger-than-life voice yelled into the phone, "C.J.! Jamaica-me-crazy mon!"

I acted drab and boring, un-amused at his un-original joke so Levi wouldn't accuse me of having a better time with Dylan than with him, or accuse me of being nice to everyone else but him. Secretly, I was rolling with laughter.

"Hey Dylan, what's up?" I said.

Dylan exaggerated every word, "It's so nice here, seven miles of white sand. You gotta come see this. How is it where you are?"

"It's fine." I rubbed my wet hair in the towel, keenly aware that Levi was listening. "We've pretty much stayed on the resort, but we did go to Dunn's River Falls today and got fucking ripped off by some jerk who carved our names into Santeria voodoo dolls then made us buy 'em for sixty bucks."

"Same shit here," Dylan said. "C.J., you guys gotta come here. It'll be so fun for us all to hang out in Jamaica. We're going out tonight, come with us!"

"Dylan, it's my honeymoon."

"Bring Levi with!" Had I been alone, I would have swam to the other side of the island to be with him.

"Dylan, you're two hours away," I pleaded, hoping he would stop asking. "Any other time than my honeymoon...and you know we would, but we're beat for the day. Have fun, be safe, okay? Love you."

I loved being with Dylan, and it pained me to say no to him. We were bonded by the blood sausage and cooked brains dad made us eat when we were kids. We understood each other.

"Come on, when will we ever get to do this again?" He persisted.

"Dylan, I can't believe you booked a trip to Jamaica in the same week of my Honeymoon. What'd you expect? Maybe we'll come there tomorrow." I lied.

"You better come tomorrow," he said, his voice threatening. "Everyone's asking where you're at."

"Who's everyone?"

"Grant," he said, "and Paul, and Eric. C.J., everyone wants you to come here. I'll call you tomorrow okay?"

He's on my fucking honeymoon!

I couldn't go anywhere near the other side of the island, definitely not now. I listened for Grant's voice in the background. Catching flecks of his familiar tone filled every cell in my body with a nervous anxiety. My insides shook at the thought of Grant thinking of me or asking about me.

I cleared my face of emotion, hid any feelings that might have accidentally surfaced in my expressions. Levi was listening. "Who else is there?" I asked and Dylan confirmed what I'd wanted to know, it was just a guy's trip.

I didn't answer the hotel phone the rest of my trip and my cell plan didn't cover calls in Jamaica. I was unavailable to further temptation and turmoil. That night, I erased the thought of Grant with copious amounts of rum, and apparently I smoked a blunt too.

By three in the morning my new husband had the entire hotel staff looking for me. In a stupor, I'd walked away without telling anyone. Levi found me just before dawn, sleeping on a plastic beach chair a few hotels away, my head and body wrapped in navy blue pool towels. For the rest of our trip, he tethered me to a beach chair while I continued to drown myself in the all-inclusive drinks.

I thought about Grant, about the times we made up silly games and laughed until our stomachs hurt, and the way his hands felt against my skin. Mostly I pondered why he kept showing up in my life and why I had such an unbreakable attachment to him.

I saw a movie once, where a newlywed couple went on their honeymoon and the bride had sex with their scuba instructor with her flippers still on.

To make my marriage work, I had to avoid Grant.

I didn't trust myself.

***

We r so great 2gether and for 1 another.
I adore u so. Goodnight babe.

Chapter 9

"IF I COULD BUT KNOW HIS HEART, EVERYTHING WOULD BECOME EASY."

—JANE AUSTEN, *SENSE AND SENSIBILITY*

The following summer Grant was still single and all of my well-intentioned attempts to extinguish my attraction to him were epic failures.

I'd yet to see him with a girlfriend. So with Levi chronically absent from the cabin, Dani occupied with my parents each weekend, and Grant always around, our friendship flourished.

I whined as I handed over the air rifle, "Can we please just be done so we can jump in the lake now? I'm hot." Why don't you just let me win, isn't that what guys are supposed to do?"

"But you said not to," Grant shouted.

"Girls never tell you what they really want. Don't you know that by now?"

He smiled and swept his foot across the grass, ignoring my comment.

Our game of Horse was at a draw, we both had S's, and our pop can target was shredded beyond recognition.

"Let's call it a tie so we can go down to the lake and use those floaties I saw in the front yard," Grant said.

"Sounds great," I said. "As long as you know that I know it's not really a tie. I let you have that shot."

"Whatever! It hit the can."

"No, it grazed the can. I gave you that one."

We sat hip to hip on the cooler arguing about all the times he'd cheated when we played games and how superior he must have thought I was since he felt he had to cheat all the time. We drank our beers halfway down then began *our thing*. Just after we mixed the bloody in our Coronas, I heard a truck nearing the driveway. Before it registered that I should get off the cooler and move away from Grant, Levi's pick-up pulled up beside us. He didn't have to speak, his eyes revealed his fury. *I knew it! That's why I came here, you bitch!*

A thunderstorm descended on me, the sky turned an ominous gray, and the temperature dropped to a damp chill when he stepped out. Levi stared through me. I was guilty, and we both knew it.

Like a dog that had destroyed the kitchen cupboards and eaten the couch, I sat waiting for my punishment. Sensing how unwelcome he'd just become, Grant slid away almost undetected, headed for the dock and hopped in the getaway boat.

***

At the very least we were guilty of having a flirtatious friendship; at the most I was liable for an emotional affair. Beyond that, we hadn't done anything...yet. Levi made a few more surprise visits that summer to check up on me, but his unannounced drop-ins weren't enough to deter my forbidden friendship with Grant.

All summer we spent time in the boat and in the water, blowing up water balloons, or decorating the boat for the Independence Day parade. We played silly made-up games like who could balance on one foot on a tree stump or hula hoop while playing ladder ball, hula-ball, we called it. He cheated at scrabble, Uno and Battleship. I won at bocce, Horse, and thumb wars. We shared hours in the sun with friends and family and a few stolen moments when we were able to be alone. No matter where we were we gravitated toward each other; if anyone else had noticed, they didn't say anything.

Grant told me about his family, let me into his life, introduced me to his mom and her tiny toy poodles—baby gorillas, he called them. It was that summer when I came to know two things for certain:

> (1) I wanted to live, really live before I die. I wanted to know what it feels like to be loved by the man of my dreams.

(2) Levi was the man I couldn't live with, and Grant was the man I couldn't live without.

***

The sunset was spectacular from the lakeside patio and our friends and family had gathered to look at the shades of tangerine and pastel pink painted like a fresco across the sky.

"Hey..." Grant whispered, tipping his chair back, closer to me and out of earshot from Dani and Dylan. "My cousin Glen is growing weed out on the point."

My face twisted. "Really?" *Is he really going to ask me to smoke weed? Grant...smoke weed?*

I was sixteen the first time I smoked pot. When you're a teenager with no strong convictions about religion and God, smoking pot in the pastor's yard next door to our cabin was a perfectly acceptable thing to do. I tried it a dozen times or so after that, before I decided it that made me stupid, fat, and paranoid.

"Is this the Cousin Glen that was on that one trashy talk show because he looked like Jesus?" I asked. I'd overhead this story in a conversation before.

"Yes!" he laughed aloud, then retold the story of Glen's makeover from Jesus to regular Joe. A sneaky smile appeared on his face. "Why don't you give me a ride back to my cabin for the night so I don't have to take the boat, then I can show you."

I didn't peg Grant for the pot smoking type and although I'd dabbled myself, it was never going to be a lifestyle. Perhaps an occasional afterthought when vacationing in Jamaica, but never in my responsible life. In fact, it was a major turn off to think he might have a pot habit I didn't know about. It didn't make sense. Why would an intelligent, bipedal, modern humanoid be stuck in the stoned age? If he was a weed smoker, that was a deal-breaker for me.

Maybe seeing this side of him is what I need to let him go. Or maybe he just wants to get me alone?

We drove my car to the other side of the lake. "Turn here, turn here!" He threw his arm across my chest pointing toward the trees.

"Where? I don't see anything!"

"Stop! Turn here!"

"Oh...There." I said as I turned hand over hand down the near invisible driveway.

I'd been down that road hundreds of times and had never seen that turnoff. Lichens and moss overtook the dirt road and foliage concealed its entrance. It was an eerie hidden path that made me feel like we were already sneaking around.

I parked behind the vacant blue cabin where he told me to, then we walked toward the edge of the marsh. He parted the tall grass, making a small opening for us to slip through and as we did, we became instantly engulfed in a Darwinian landscape. Completely secluded, camouflaged from all sides, unusual plants and towering cattails encircled us.

The brisk evening air smelled of detritus, and all around were dragonflies bounding from one velvet cat tail to another. In the center of the marsh where it turned into a mossy bog stood an ancient oak tree barely clinging to its life. My body begged Grant to push me against that timeless oak, rip the buttons off my shirt and devour me passionately lips to breasts. Instead we gazed at a few spindly, pathetic pot plants. Amateur grown ditch weed, inside what looked like my mom's green plastic geranium planter. I was completely unimpressed.

Grant didn't ask me to smoke, not like there was enough to pack a pipe anyway, so I couldn't help but wonder why he brought me here? Was it a ploy to get us away from spying eyes? My heart beat in loud thumps. I wanted so badly for this to be the time he kissed me, or at least held my hand again. I wanted him to do something, anything. I needed him to numb the pain I felt from years of wondering if he felt the same.

We huddled close to one another on the only patch of dry ground and flutters of anticipation filled my stomach. Tension pulsed in the air between us and I thought I could hear his heart beating in his chest, but I couldn't be sure.

Make a move—please...don't you know how much I want you?

I was dying inside, impatient for something, for anything, to happen. "This place is amazing," I said, looking up at him, biting my lip, begging him with wanting eyes.

"Have you read *On the Origin of Species*?" He asked.

I shook my head.

"You should, I think you'd like it. See that red star?" He pointed to a twinkling red speck low on the horizon, eons from earth. I looked down the barrel of his arm, brushing my cheek against his skin. "That's Betelgeuse."

Then he gave me a long explanation of which I don't remember about why Betelgeuse is red, showed me Alpha Centauri and Sirius, then told me the real story of the Andromeda galaxy. All topics he enjoyed talking about, and I enjoyed listening to him talk, spending time alone with him. So I asked more questions like *why isn't Pluto a planet anymore*, and *do you think there are aliens?* To which he replied, "It's a dwarf planet" and, "of course there are other living beings out there. Though the distances between us are too massive, so it's highly unlikely we'll ever have an encounter. The real question is, if they do show up...who speaks for Earth?"

Who speaks for earth? I didn't have the faintest clue who should speak for earth or what that even meant but I indulged him in the conversation. His face lit up each time I asked another question. He seemed excited to have someone to talk to about all that geeky stuff he loved and I was excited to be learning. Sometimes he spoke in a language I could barely comprehend, using terms like "albedo" and "cumulonimbus." He tried to explain to me complex algorithms like the Drake equation and demonstrate how the Large Hadron Collider works. We discussed the implications of finding antimatter, which I thought only existed in a Dan Brown novel, and shared our views on the parallelism between Holy Communion and cannibalism.

I marveled at his intelligence and longed for those meaningful, interesting conversations to exist regularly in my life and in my marriage. Grant challenged me to think beyond this earth and pushed me physically to try new things; to not only get up on the wake board but also to look like I knew what I was doing. He didn't take any of my shit, he was always on cue with a witty comeback that rivaled my wise cracks. He was someone who could teach me new things about life and love and the human condition but he was also someone who wanted to learn from me. We had countless commonalities but enough difference to make things interesting.

We talked as a steady speckle of stars made their appearance in the night sky. We talked until his blue eyes seemed to glow iridescent in the twilight. It was as if we'd known each other for a thousand years and felt like our lust would linger for another ten thousand.

We emerged from our secret rendezvous then stood in the cool darkness next to my car, not wanting the night to end.

"Why are you still single?" I boldly asked.

"I guess I just haven't found the right one yet. How about you?"

"How about me what?" I said, "I'm not single."

"I know that." His voice was calm. "I mean, did you find the right one?"

I hesitated, "if you found a wallet in the Target parking lot, would you take it inside and return it?"

He laughed at my response. "Yes."

"So would I. I did the right thing. I did what I was supposed to do."

He nodded and smiled in agreement, understanding my predicament. "I did the same thing," he said. And since he eluded to it, now was my chance.

"What happened with your ex-wife?"

"She's not my ex-wife," he said, "we'd only been married for three months so marriage was annulled. It's like it never happened."

"So it's like she was erased from your life?"

"Yes. Her cheating was the best thing that ever happened to me. I was miserable before we were married. But I was young and didn't want to disappoint anyone. I would have made it work, I committed to that it wouldn't have been fun or easy, but I would have made it work."

"Do you think marriage *can* be fun and easy?" I asked.

"I think so. If you wait for the right person, be picky and don't settle."

"So that's what you're doing?"

He shrugged, "I guess."

"Is there someone you have in mind?"

A shy smile grew on his face. "Maybe?"

"Who?" I asked, my heart racing.

"She's from Seattle," Grant said. "She's from a wealthy family, grew up privileged, but still stayed normal...you know?"

No. I don't know, we were poor.

"Yes. I know."

"We live so far away from each other, we never really had a chance to see what might happen. She's coming up here to visit soon. You should meet her and tell me what you think."

I died inside as he told me about Molly.

Chapter 10

Where's the gun? Where is the fucking gun? I'll fucking kill him.

I ransacked the cabin while mumbling insults and listing all the ways I fucking hated him. I'd slipped into a temporary psychosis. I was a wife pushed over the edge of sanity by her dumb-fuck husband.

There was a gun somewhere I knew it. I searched the rack above the television but found nothing, only air rifles. I wanted *deer* rifles.

Nanook snuck up behind me to see what all the ruckus was.

"Go back to bed boy, go lay with Dani...go!" I shooed him. Then headed for Dylan's room.

"What the fuck are you doing?" Dylan whispered through the darkness.

I ignored him and continued my blind hunt through his bedroom closet scouring the far back corners on my hands and knees, feeling my way around in the dark, searching for a long cold barrel. I frisked the floor and walls, nothing—not even a baseball bat hiding in that musty closet only moldy wet suits.

In the top drawer of Dylan's dresser, there was a box of bullets, I'd seen them. Shells of some sort that he and Dad used in their deer rifles. There had to be a gun somewhere.

Dad's closet.

Four Hours Earlier

"You treat *everyone* better than you treat me! You treat me like a dog, worse than a dog. You fucking hate me. Just say it. I know you do. Just Fucking Say IT!"

Levi threw his arms up and yelled so close to my face we were nose to nose. I stood like a stone statue, unbending and nonreactive. My arms folded across my chest, and my feet cemented into a fighting stance.

The outdoor concert at We Fest stopped at midnight and thousands of people were herded like cattle toward the exit. It was a stampede of shivering bodies running for the shelter of their campers or cars, seeking relief from the torrential rain. Floodlights lit up the night sky, and illuminated the millions of shimmering drops pouring down around us.

Water gushed off my cowboy hat like rain pouring from a gutter and every thread in my clothes was sopping wet. My shoes squished and sloshed as I shifted my weight from side to side unflinching as I stood there, taking my punishment.

Levi circled me, flinging his arms, taunting me. He was drunk and when he pressed his face to mine I wanted to gnaw off his nose, kick him in the nuts, and gouge out his eyeballs. But any reaction from me, verbal or physical, would only escalate his madness. So I just went numb.

"You're a cold bitch. Heartless, you know that? You never loved me." His face twisted in disgust, "I gave you everything! Anything you wanted. What more do you want from me?" He shouted but I didn't react. "I've given you all I have. I've loved you. I've taken care of our family. I've worked my fucking ass off for you! For us!" He was soaked from the rain, but I could still see his tears.

He was right, he had worked his ass off for us, so much that at the end of every evening there was nothing left but crumbs. His lunatic rant was the by-product of big-gulp-size beers, mixed with years of unresolved resentment and anger toward me. Events ranging from my refusal to have sex, to arguments about who does the dishes, or picks up more dog poop had coalesced into one very large eruption.

We were a spectacle. A pretty girl in a cowboy hat standing in the middle of a muddy field, while her berserk husband circled her and ranted furiously. I thought of Grant, wondered if he was there somewhere in the sea of bodies.

Would he help me if he was? What would he do? Would he use his lethal martial arts skills to fight off my drunken husband? Or would he walk past me and leave us to sort out our embarrassing white-trash argument?

A man walking by with no shirt and a cowboy hat said, "Hey lady, you okay?"

No. Yes. I don't know.

If I said no, there might be a fight, if I said yes, it was an obvious lie and he still might intervene. I stared blankly as if I hadn't heard him and stayed silent.

The man shrugged and kept walking as if to say, *Okay you stupid bitch, stay with him then.*

"You're not gunna talk?" Levi shouted at me stumbling and slurring, "You're just gunna stand there and act all innocent? You really are a cold, heartless, bitch you know that?"

"Hey, leave her alone, you dick!" some girl yelled from the passing crowd.

"Shut the fuck up. Stay out of it. She's my wife!" Levi yelled back, as if the fact that I was his wife was justification for his behavior.

There was a cold callousness about Levi sometimes. He was easily provoked and not scared of a bloody fist fight. Levi was the guy in high school who stood in the middle of a circle of headlights waiting to fight anyone who dare enter. He was a dirty street scrapper who usually was the victor, but I'd also seen him the victim.

A few years before Dani was born, when our lives were one big party, I watched him take a dozen hits to the face as two thugs used his head for a punching bag while a third restrained me. The beating ended when Levi hit the pavement chin first, unconscious. The assailants quickly fled the scene and were never caught. It was a brutal attack that shattered his jaw into three pieces and left his mouth wired shut for months. The whole ordeal could have been prevented had Levi just kept his mouth shut for one minute. As Levi circled me, I had flashbacks from that night and prayed no one would intervene.

When Levi just wouldn't shut up, I could only funnel away the insults so long before they collectively caused an explosion. "I'm leaving! You insolent fucking jerk! I can't believe you wrecked another night." I got close to his face. "Know what?" I said in the most snide tone, "I do fucking hate you."

Then I turned and sloshed my way toward the gate, trying to lose him in the crowd. Levi followed close behind, mumbling and ranting among a flock of strangers.

When I got to Dylan's truck, our only ride home, I begged him, "Dylan, please take me back to the cabin, we have to go now. Please leave Levi here." My voice was strained. Before Dylan could answer, Levi strolled up and was intercepted by our friends. Each trying to talk him down, and keep him away from me. Insults and endless put-downs kept spewing from his filthy mouth. I recognized an evil in him that was also in me, it was an evil that only we could bring out in each other. I was as toxic and lethal to him as he was to me.

"Let him go, just ignore him." I said to our friends, fearing Levi would turn on them. When they stopped holding him back Levi approached me trying to be as intimidating as he could. I wasn't scared of him, I just hated him.

He put his lips to my ear.

"Wanna fuck?" he said then tried to cup his hand around one of my breasts. "Come on, let's fuck," he said again as he tried to fondle me.

I gritted my teeth and shoved him as hard as I could.

"No? You don't wanna?" He said. He was acting; putting on a show and I knew it. He was only doing those things to rile me because he knew it would. "Why don't you tell everyone you never wanna have sex with your husband? Why don't you tell them that I practically have to fucking rape my own wife!" He yelled into the crowd of onlookers.

Rage began to grow in me and I started boiling inside. Levi was the only being in the world that could provoke me enough to want to kill. In all other areas of my life, I was peaceful.

"She won't even kiss me!" He yelled toward our friends. "My own wife, won't even kiss me. I'm your fucking husband!" He screamed into my face so close I felt him spit. Then he started to cry. Real or fake, I didn't care.

I felt nothing for him. No empathy, only hate. I was humiliated and belittled. Broken so badly that sociopathic thoughts of violence flooded my mind as I stood there and watched him sob

Then, as if my mind hadn't issued the order to fight, and my body acted alone fueled solely on rage. I shoved him. Then ferociously kicked him. He didn't fight back which only made me even more furious. He stumbled, then found his footing and started to laugh sending me into a murderous rage. I pounded him with my fists in every way and every place possible.

"Oh, it's like that huh?" He pounded his own fists to his chest harder than I could hit him, showing me that my hardest hit didn't even phase him. A smirk grew on his face, he was happy to have finally awakened me in this way.

"Get in and shut the fuck up! Both of you!" Dylan finally yelled, and we obeyed.

I jumped out the moment we got to the cabin.

This is not the life I want for Dani and I...I'm done.

I spun around and lost all control when I realized he was following me up the driveway as if he was going to come inside.

"You fucking loser, I hope you die. I hate you." I scrunched my eyes and flared my lips, "I don't know why I ever married you. You're a fucking freak with no friends and no life." I walked toward him unafraid. Backing him away from the cabin. "Get out of here!" I flung my arms toward his face. "I don't want you. Can't you see that? Can't you take a hint? No one wants you here. This is *my* home, not yours." Abuse came pouring out of me. "You're not welcome here. You never have been. I've never wanted you here! I'll call the cops if you even try to step one more foot up this driveway. Get the fuck out of here!"

Levi's voice was calm now, "go ahead, call 'em. I didn't do anything." He shrugged, "I'm your husband. I don't have to leave."

His sudden calm demeanor enraged me, but what enraged me more, was when he stepped forward and wanted to make up. That's when I decided to kill him. That's the moment when I remembered there was a gun.

"Don't you dare touch me, and don't you dare try to come in the cabin."

"Stop it," He said in such a condescending way, my blood began to boil. "Loser huh? So that's what you think of me. Well, at least you're being honest now."

"Get out of here!" I lunged toward him, shoving him, every cell in my body quivered with maximum rage.

"No. I'm not leaving. This is my house too."

"Take a fucking hint loser! Get out of here!"

"Fine. Go fuck yourself." He said. "Oh...I guess you're probably used to that since you never want to fuck me."

He turned and walked to his truck.

Shocked and relieved that he was actually leaving, I watched him drive away and prayed he wouldn't hurt anyone on the road. I thought the night was over.

I crawled in bed next to Dani and was thankful no one in the cabin had witnessed our fight. My hair was dripping wet, my lips trembled, and my ears rang loud as I laid in the dark, unable to sleep. My head was heavy and throbbing in pain, but it was nothing compared to the weight and pain in my heart. I was drifting in and out of consciousness when I woke up startled by headlights shining through my bedroom window.

I knew instantly who it was. I threw back the covers and ran out of the cabin. There was Levi, standing in the dark, as if nothing had happened. He wanted to talk, wanted to apologize, and wanted to come inside. His inability to live in reality, to comprehend that people don't just come back from the places he and I had been, made me want to kill him even more.

The audacity of him coming back sent me on an irrational rampage. "How dare you come back? Did you really think I would let you in? I hate you!" I yelled so loud my voice cracked. "I will never forgive you. I will never sleep with you, ever again. I wish you were dead! And if you don't leave, I'll fucking kill you myself."

"Come on now," his antagonizing tone intensified my hysteria. He took a step forward wanting to reconcile.

My eyes narrowed and evil transformed me into something maniacal, I became possessed. Every attempt he made to quell me, touch me, or insinuate that I should forgive him, only sent me deeper into hell. Then, like the sky turning green just before a raging storm, I became eerily still.

"That's it," I said emotionlessly and calculated, "I'm going to kill you."

Unaffected by my own demonic words, I didn't blink. I stated the following facts like I was reading an instruction manual.

"You'd better get out of here. If you're in this drive way when I come back, I'll kill you."

"Stop it," his voice dragged out in the slow manner I so hated. He reached for me. I didn't move.

"You're fucking dead."

Then like a Stepford wife gone mad, I robotically walked into the cabin and methodically searched for the gun. After coming up empty in Dylan's room, I walked into my parents' bedroom. On my hands and knees, I pulled things from their closet floor, searching for the back wall, scouring the corners. It wasn't there. *Fuck.*

"Honey, what are you doing?" Mom whispered in the kindest tone.

"Nothing mom, I'm just looking for something, I'm sorry to wake you."

"If you're looking for the root beer sweetheart there's a new two liter bottle under the microwave, and more ice cream in the deep freeze."

"Okay, thanks momma."

I abandoned my search for a shotgun and lifted my favorite air rifle off of the rack in the living room. The moment I stepped outside, I cocked it as fast as I could.

This is perfect, better than a deer rifle. I can shoot him a bunch of times.

66

By the time I got to the end of the driveway, loaded and ready to light his ass up, he was gone.

***

Of course this is real.
2 people enduring misery 4 so many
years deserve this. :) Mwah!

Chapter 11

"A WOMAN SHOULD LEARN IN SILENCE WITH ALL SUBMISSIVENESS."

—TIMOTHY 2:11

I stayed with Levi because that's what women in my family did, I stayed because I loved him, I stayed because my problems with Levi were not really about Levi, they were about me. *I* was unable to change to accommodate what our marriage needed. *I* was the crazy, abusive one. If marriage is hard work and full of compromise, then it was me who failed us.

Everybody argues, his behavior is a reflection of yours, divorce is not the answer. I didn't know of a marriage that was perfectly happy. All of those hand-me-down expectations I'd been told about marriage seemed completely logical. If all marriages are unhappy and take work, then mine was no different.

I stayed because I was foolish enough to believe those things were true.

***

I met Molly later that summer.

She was like Grant described her, she reeked of family money.

I was unimpressed with her generous bosom and dried out blonde hair, but he seemed quite smitten. It was awkward in the boat, sitting close to her, pretending to enjoy a sunny day, watching her listen to *our* music and drink *our* beers. Grant was unusually silent, talking and laughing only when it would have been weird not to and he didn't make eye contact with me, like I had a third eye or something abhorrent he couldn't bear to look at. Over one short summer month, Grant had become someone I used to know. His playfulness was gone and he gave me nothing more than a polite, obligatory smile.

Somehow I'd become the crazy ex-girlfriend, the person in the group who made the situation awkward and less fun, the girl whose presence prevented him from having a good time. So I stayed away, I didn't want to see him with her anyway.

He eventually stopped coming around altogether, not even to see Dylan. He was with Molly now. I'd lost him. I'd lost the chance at what might have been true love because I was too afraid to reach out and grab it.

That gloomy summer turned into a dark cold winter. In December when the fierce snow storms rolled into the valley, they brought with them the blues. I was officially depressed, hollow inside, an empty shell where a once vibrant woman lived. I needed one of those rare nights out to see Dylan's band, I needed laughter. I hoped to find solace in the company of my summer friends and reminisce about warmer weather. I hadn't seen Grant in six months and I was curious if he was still around or if he'd moved to Seattle with Molly, or if maybe she'd moved here. Either way, I forced myself to be numb and hoped I wouldn't see them together.

Stale smoke hung in the air and marinated the old wooden panel walls of the run down bar. A grungy, patch wearing bouncer burnt his stare onto my ass like a cattle brand as I walked past, and the concrete dance floor in front of the stage writhed with intoxicated outcasts and women tonguing one another. Deafening music pierced my temples, and the kick of the bass felt like thunder in my chest.

"Hey C.J.!" Dylan shouted into the mic from his hidden spot behind the drums.

Dylan gigged with a heavy metal band now. It'd been years since we'd toured together with Mom and Dad and it still felt out of place to hear him play Metallica and Alice and Chains. He would always be Johnny Cash and Waylon Jennings to me. He'd also become a gargantuan beast, a workout-aholic with a scheduled day off from the gym once every two weeks.

The oversized girth of his back muscles made his arms hang unnaturally far away from his sides. They swung oddly stiff as he walked toward me, and I noticed that his eternally swollen biceps bulged with a new round of abstract, tribal looking tattoos. But his hardened exterior melted away when the deepest, most sincere brown eyes looked at me from under his tattered cap, eyes that mirrored an exact reflection of my own.

"Ew don't hug me," I said as he got close, dripping with sweat.

"C.J., I'm glad you came out," Dylan said, then flipped his drink straw down and took a sip off the rim. He nodded his head in the direction of the door, "let's go."

I followed him outside, hiding behind him but the snow still pelted my face and instantly froze the inside of my nostrils. I tucked my head down into my jacket and ran to the bar next door. Dylan pulled open the door and a familiar rush of welcome heat blasted me. The dim bar lighting, the clamor of people talking over the music, and the sound of his velvet voice flooded my senses.

I knew immediately that I was about to get some of my sweet addiction.

The Dot, I presumed, was a reference to the bar's infinitesimal size. Yet ironically it was a place filled with predominately oversized people whose asses all seemed to hang over the edge of the black vinyl barstools.

"Hey Larry," Dylan shouted over the music to the three hundred pound bartender. "Bloodies," he yelled, holding up two fingers. I heard Grant broadcast our names over the mic in between riffs of "Life in the Fast Lane."

"Dylan, C.J.!" He yelled, and by the smile on his face he seemed delighted to see us.

I instantly missed him, and when I saw him it hurt. It hurt like seeing a long lost love in a busy crowd, the one you compared all others too, the one you loved more than you'll ever love anyone again, the one you lost. I felt a whimper emanating from deep within me. He was my greatest loss, yet I hadn't even had him yet.

Dylan and I listened to Grant sing a few more Eagles songs and a rendition of "Werewolves of London" before he set his guitar down and stepped off the stage. That's when the first estrogen strike hit. A group of females surrounded him, and I understood their frenzy. What woman wouldn't want that body around her, and that voice serenading her in the bedroom after making heavenly love?

Before Grant was able to crawl out from under the cat pile, Dylan tipped back the last of his watery drink, "Gotta go, last set," he said. "You coming over tonight?"

"Not sure?" I shrugged. He set his gorilla-like hand on my shoulder.

"You should, it'll be fun. Let yourself in. Let Peanut out. I'll be there as soon as I can." He flashed me a closed lip smile then started walking away, "love you."

"Love you. Thanks for the drink." I said.

Dylan yelled to Grant over the chatter of the crowd, "Good job bud, sounds great, see you tonight."

For so many reasons I should have been leaving with Dylan, going home like a good girl. Yet the pull Grant had on my heart was unshakable. Grant looked at me with desperate eyes, asking for my help to escape the cougar mauling, I shook my head and crinkled my nose.

Nope.

He sighed then pushed his way through the female fanatics and hurried toward me with an unexpected fervor. He was happy to see me and it showed. He smiled and opened his arms for me to fall into.

The world became flat and everyone toppled off the edge as I fell off my barstool and into the shelter of his arms. When I tipped my head back to look at him, his pale blue eyes knocked on the door to my heart, then let themselves inside. Just being near him dissolved any residual pangs of guilt I had over going out that night, leaving Levi behind.

"It's so great to see you," Grant said as he sat down on the barstool next to mine. "I didn't know you were coming tonight."

"I know. It's rare," my voice quivered and so did my insides. "You sound amazing," I said. "I loved 'Werewolves of London.'" He shrugged off my compliment. "Seriously, you sound great," I rolled my eyes, "like always."

He changed the subject, he didn't like talking about himself. It seemed to make him uncomfortable. "Lake season is coming," he said. "I can't wait to listen to Marley and do our thing."

"It's December. Summer's long ways away."

"So what? I dream of lake season all year, don't you?"

No, I dream of you all year, and lake season only makes it worse.

"Yes...I dream of lake season too. Are you going anywhere warm this winter?" I asked.

He called to the bartender and ordered us *our thing* then turned to me, "I'd like to go back to Jamaica."

"I loved Jamaica," I said, "and just think, this time you won't be on my honeymoon."

"Yes. That's right," he dropped his head recalling and laughing to himself. "I *was* on your honeymoon...wasn't I."

"You were definitely on my honeymoon," I said and the tension grew thick between us.

"How about you? Are you going anywhere this winter?" He asked, changing the subject.

"Nowhere fun, just work, fitness stuff. Grant, is it just me or are these drinks just not the same without the sun and the Moomba?"

"Something's definitely missing," he said as we clinked our long necks together then toasted: "To a short winter and another hot summer."

As we took a sip, one of the band members yelled and waved for him to get back on stage. Grant gave him the one minute finger but kept his eyes on me.

"Are you going back to your brother's tonight?"

"I haven't decided yet. You?"

"I'll go if you go."

He stared at my lips, waiting for my response, holding up his one-minute finger again. My heart raced toward an unshockable rhythm.

"Well that's an offer too good to pass up." I said with a sly smile.

"Good. I'll make an excuse so I don't have to tear down tonight. I'll be there as soon as I can." Grant bounced with energy as he walked back to the stage. He was the Grant I knew again. He was happy to see me and it showed.

I'd fallen for him so long ago, and being with him again confirmed that it would never go away. Having to live the rest of my life wanting him so badly was cruel and unusual punishment, even for *my* wandering heart.

As he walked away, the same cluster of bitches stared at me from across the bar. I knew what they were saying…*What's so great about her? Magic pussy or something?* I bathed in their jealousy and sent over a polite *fuck you, he's mine* grin.

I sat on my barstool and finished my drink, declined a few requests to dance, and fantasized about what it would be like if the ring on my left hand was from Grant. I walked up to the stage, smiled and waved good-bye. He moved to the side of the mic, "See you soon?"

I gave him a half-hearted nod then waved goodbye to the rest of the band.

"You better be there!" He called out to me as I turned to walk away.

I was confused by his eagerness to be with me, wasn't he still with Molly?

Even though I knew Levi would be furious if I went to Dylan's, I was powerless over my obsession. Seeing Grant in the winter months was rare and thrilling, and I was incapable of turning down any opportunity to be next to him. There was always a chance that Levi might show up at Dylan's, throw a huge fit, break something or someone, but even that wasn't enough to keep me away.

Hey, going over 2 Dylan's.
Don't wait up. I might stay overnite.

When I stepped outside, snow fluttered in every direction swirling in blustery gusts. I tucked my nose into the faux fur lining of my winter coat and slid into my car. My poor summer VW Beetle was frozen to the ground like a tongue to a pole; the tires ripped off the ice leaving behind a little skin as I pulled away.

A quick vibration buzzed in my pocket. It was Levi.

Do what u want. That's what u
Always do anyway, isn't it?

He was right. I always did what I wanted regardless of him. *He just let me off easy,* I thought as I stuffed my phone back in my coat, resumed shivering, and then punched my mukluks to the floor.

The anticipation of seeing Grant made me quiver with excitement. Once I knew I was going to see him, I became scared to lose him again. I'd missed our friendship and I needed to tell him that, didn't I?

Yes, tonight, I will tell him how much I've missed him.

***

Baby, I miss u 2:) I'm here.
I'm always here :)

Chapter 12

"SOME CUPID KILLS WITH ARROWS, SOME WITH TRAPS."

—WILLIAM SHAKESPEARE, *MUCH ADO ABOUT NOTHING, 3.1.104*

Be bold, take risks for what you really want, do it tonight. I told myself on the car ride over to Dylan's.

Find the courage to tell him I think about him, that I don't know why but I dream of him every Sunday night, and that I couldn't bear to see him with someone else.

I pushed through Dylan's frozen garage door and was blasted by the hot coils of a propane heater, and greeted by the sight of a dozen pairs of perfectly sculpted silicone breasts. Posters of waxed kuchies and tight asses clung to the walls.

Dylan's garage was a man's lair with a fully stocked mini fridge, surround sound, and plush carpeting that cradled a meticulously polished new Corvette that shimmered with golden flecks. The over-sized chair hiding in the corner, and the worn out blue couch had each hosted their share of indiscretions.

I peeled off my winter layers and was kneeling down to greet Dylan's little mutt Peanut when Dylan burst through the door. Grant was behind him holding a bag of fast food.

Gross. He eats that shit?

He held up the grease soaked bag as if to say hello, then pulled out two folding chairs and motioned for me to sit down beside him.

"It's so awesome you made it out tonight," Grant said as he ripped into the thin paper sack.

"I'm glad I got to see you too," I said. "See you devour that crap so I can give you CPR when you drop dead from a heart attack."

A shameful expression grew on his face but he took another over-sized bite in spite of my comment. "But I'm starving," he muttered with his mouth stuffed full of cheap food.

"No. Children in Sudan are starving. That's just gluttonous."

"You're right, I shouldn't eat like this. Are you grossed out?" A morsel of meat sprayed from his mouth and landed on the table. "I'm sorry!" He shouted.

"Yes, I'm grossed out," I said, "but if you want to eat that shit, go ahead." I leaned back in my chair, "I'll miss you when you die an early death but go ahead."

"You'll miss me?" He said, in the softest, sweetest tone.

"Of course I'll miss you. Wouldn't you miss me?"

He nodded his head slowly. "Yes A lot."

Our eyes met, there was a trembling between us that could have been measured on the Richter scale. It was so intense we looked away from one another.

A small entourage of Dylan's groupies piled into the garage for a night of Das Boot and Hammerschlagen. *Good,* I thought. *People to distract Dylan, so I can be with Grant uninterrupted.*

"You should have come up and sang a song tonight," Grant said.

"You didn't invite me."

He scoffed. "You don't need an invitation. You know that."

"Grant," I sneered, "it's been a decade since I've been on stage. I'm not just rusty, I'm corroded."

"No you're not. I've heard you sing at the lake, around the fire. You're good."

"I'm not good. You must have had too much to drink those nights."

"Quit it. I'm serious," he said. "You should start singing again. We could do a few songs together."

I shook my head. I didn't need to think about it.

"I have no desire to be on stage again. That part of my life is over," I told him, and I meant it.

I was burnt out by the time I turned seventeen. Years of weekend traveling in a cramped van with my mom, dad, and Dylan, entertaining blue haired crowds with songs like "She's Too Fat For Me" and "In Heaven There Is No Beer," not exactly a teenagers idea of a rave weekend. I felt like a damn Partridge kid. I didn't willingly giving up underage drinking and all night bonfires to travel every weekend with my bickering, semi-talented musical family. I did it because I was expected to and I was still bitter about it. I hadn't plunked a key on the keyboard or bellowed a single note on stage since the day I walked away. The day I moved out of my parents' house to get away from a life of music that I didn't want to be a part of anymore.

Though when Grant asked me if I would come on stage with him, for the first time in more than a decade, I was secretly delighted at the thought. For the first time, I was thankful that I had that rare experience from my childhood. The pressure of continually having to learn new music, enduring the grind of endless practice sessions, and the wear that loading and unloading an entire stage of sound equipment had on your body, was something we had uniquely in common. It was an unusual life that I understood, a life he could tell me about, and I could relate. Music was a passion that ran through his blood, and he needed the right woman to share it with.

Then it happened again, like it always did when we were together, everyone in the room disappeared. Dylan's friends eventually shuffled out and the noise died, leaving nothing but my beating heart pounding loud in my ears. Every word in our conversation turned awkward, like it was all just a diversion to mask the things we thought but couldn't say.

Be brave.

I nudged myself, digging up the courage to say something meaningful. I leaned my elbows forward and rested my chin in my hands. Then I took a leap:

"I could stay up all night talking to you...it's so easy with us."

He hesitated, took a strained breath, and then nervously brushed his hand over his mouth as if to remind it to be cautious. "I feel the same way," he said. Then he looked into my eyes in a way he hadn't before.

77

Finally, he was letting himself fall, he was about to let me in and show me his real feelings.

It's now or never, keep going. Tell him how much you think about him!

He spoke before I could mobilize the courage to say something.

"I can't believe how late it is, I'm tired. I think I'll crash on the couch in the house for a while before I drive home."

What?!

Disappointment slapped me across the face with an open palm—the mood between us changed instantly. Once again we were back to that place of familiar gray distance—and I was angry. He was holding back and I knew it. I felt it. It pissed me off. Everyone had left the party, Dylan was in the house, and we were finally alone. But instead of having an honest conversation about what ever this was between us, we tossed cans and bottles into the recycle bins and picked up the party trash without saying a word.

When the cleanup was done, I followed him to the door ready to leave. My heart pounded furiously with anger at his cowardly silence—a silence that rang shrill in my ears and made me feel like I was about to implode.

Grant please, say something! Do something!

"Ready?" he asked, "Are you sure you're okay to drive home?"

I rolled my eyes. "I'm fine."

Then he turned off the lights, reached for the door knob...and stopped.

He froze in place.

He wasn't even breathing.

I wasn't breathing.

The electricity between us seemed to ignite my skin. I cowered behind him in the darkness, waiting...

Why did he stop?

Shit!

Levi?

Grant turned around to face me with his head hung low. It wasn't Levi he stopped for.

It was me.

My eyes were fixed on his silhouette, I could feel his reluctance fading. I stared, waiting and wondering...*what is he going to do?* He lifted his head and took a slow step toward me. Our bodies were illegally close and an immense tension throbbed between us. My senses became acutely aware of everything him; the faint smell of spearmint gum on his breath, his chest rising and falling rapidly now, and the dark shadow of his masculine form enveloping me. My mind raced.

Am I going to cheat on Levi? Is this it?

Then a warm, unfamiliar hand slid across my bare neck and my head fell slowly into his palm. His fingers buried into my hair and I let out a pleasure filled *Mmm*...when he pulled me gently to him.

My breasts pressed hard against his chest. I wrapped my arms around the contours of his lean torso and he laid his head softly down on my shoulder.

He'd surrendered.

I vanished beneath him, filled with sensations of belonging, connectedness and finally, home. He warmed my body and my soul. Though one feeling trumped all the others. The one I'd been searching a lifetime for but had never felt. Contentment. With him, if only for a fleeting moment, I felt content.

No more searching, no more wondering, just absolute security and contentment. He was the one. It was the feeling I'd longed for, the one that always seemed just out of reach. Now, it was calling me home, he was calling me home. We held each other, consumed with one another for what felt like hours before I broke the silence.

"We should crash on the couch out here for a few hours."

A swell of anxiety filled my chest as I waited for his reply. But he didn't need to speak, his actions spoke louder than any words. He loosened his grip, let his hands fall away from my body, took a step back, and he was gone. Just like that. Where a warm shelter had just been now stood an empty shell, a body without emotion.

The man I longed for, the only man I'd ever felt fully alive with had just retreated, again.

Why did I suggest such a foolish thing? What a stupid thing to do! Maybe he thought I wanted sex? Or maybe he didn't feel the same? Why would he want a cheater anyway, after what happened to him?

He was doing the right thing and I knew it. I was the dirty one who had just suggested an adulterous nap. I didn't care, my heart needed him.

"I don't think that's a good idea...I'm sorry," he said.

I don't want your fucking pity.

Cold, emotionless, and not expecting to ever feel his hands on me again, I was breathless when he grabbed me with both arms and pulled me close, "Don't you see!" he forced the words through gritted teeth, "I don't want to leave you."

"So don't." I carefully touched my forehead to his chest, breathing in his scent and absorbing his embrace.

"I have to," he whispered. "You feel so good, what am I supposed to do?"

His words were laced with confusion and pain.

I was laced with confusion and pain.

Then I heard the click.

With one hand interlaced in mine and the other behind his back, he'd locked the door.

This is it. Is this what I really want? Oh shit, I don't know, I don't know. I don't want to be a cheater, but...

I stumbled as he tugged me along behind him toward the couch. With his back pressed into the cushions, I took shelter in the space in front of him and nestled into his warm body. His masculine legs intertwined with mine, a strong hand gripped my hip, and the other he offered me as a pillow. His touch was foreign, everything about him new, yet somehow he felt more familiar than anything I'd ever known.

Sleeping was impossible and I feared the smallest movement might send him away. I laid still and silent and I could feel his heart beating wildly against my back. What occurred when we were together was undeniable and his racing pulse proved it. We had an unequivocal magnetism to each other. It was real, it was extraordinary, and we both knew it.

"I didn't expect this," I whispered into the darkness. "Being with you feels even better than I imagined."

"I had a feeling it was you," he whispered back.

What did he just say?!

I wanted to turn and kiss him—God how I wanted to kiss him.

"I need you to know I've never done this before—it's just with you and me—"

"Shh..." He whispered then wrapped his whole self around me, "You don't have to explain. I know. I feel it too."

Then he stuttered like he was about to tell me something, but held it back before it came out. His lack of courage or sudden change of heart shattered our moment of bliss. When he finally spoke, the way he said it was kind, but his words tore me open and left me to bleed.

"We shouldn't be out here like this. I'd better go in the house. You should wait a bit, then come inside so it doesn't look like we were together."

I couldn't move or speak. I knew we felt the same way, how could he just ignore it? His hot and cold streaks were so erratic no meteorologist in the universe could have predicted what he might do next.

He fumbled over my lifeless body then stood over me as I lay despondent.

"I'm sorry," he said.

I don't need your fucking sympathy, don't pity me, coward.

I didn't speak. I kept my wounded mouth shut since I too was a coward, and afraid to tell him the truth about how I felt.

A gust of freezing snow invaded the warm darkness as he walked out and slammed the ice crusted door shut behind him. Humiliation groped me like an unwelcome intruder in the night. I wanted to suffocate myself in the couch cushions, I contemplated it.

I laid there lonely and embarrassed, wounded by rejection and disappointed by my lack of self-control. Our friendship would never be the same, how could it be? And now I had a secret to keep, an actual secret. Not just a phantom emotional affair, but a real live secret. I'd crossed the line of fidelity. Snuggling, confessing, and wanting another man like I wanted him *is* cheating, right?

I once heard there are two types of people. Those motivated by success and those motivated by failure. I was neither. I was motivated by anger. For me, it was anger that released a massive store house of energy and motivation. I slammed the garage door shut behind me, hoping he would hear me leave.

I will never do this again. I swear. I will never do this again.

I was done with him. Done. Done. Done.

I was done with this self-inflicted sadism.

Chapter 13

He sat on the barstool, twisting the pool cue between his palms as I strutted past. My heart almost stopped beating when he wrapped his hands around my hips and pulled me down hard onto his lap.

6 Hours Earlier

Another sizzling summer was underway and Grant and I were instantly back to where we'd always been. My promise to be done with him lasted only as long as the remaining winter months. With Levi an hour away at home every weekend, and Heidi (the girl Grant had moved on to after Molly, who turned out not to be the one) in Australia, we immediately re-kindled our extra-curricular flirting.

It was a sunny, reggae Saturday as I dangled my legs off the side of the boat, skimming my toes on top the water and singing along with Marley's greatest hits—still on repeat. The absence of our significant others, several Apricot Brandi slushies, and a handful of bloody beers was the perfect cocktail mix to ignite our smoldering flame.

We were punch drunk and frolicking around the lake in the Moomba. Lissy was our sober chaperon and clearly annoyed with our unchaste behavior. Grant pushed the limits of her patience.

"Stay there," He motioned to me and I was expected to be his accomplice. It was a skit we'd done a handful of times on unsuspecting victims.

Undetected, he slipped off the bow and into the water, then swam lengthwise underneath the boat. His disappearance was my cue.

Lissy was sitting on the platform, sloshing her legs in the water when I hollered out to her. "Lissy, you should stay tonight, we can build a fire." I was employed to be her distraction. I swam toward her holding my drink in the air with one hand, treading water with the other. "Come on," I said, "let's hang out this evening."

"Nope. And when you're done with that beer, you can take me back." I felt bad for what had already happened and was about to happen, she might never come back.

A terrified scream bellowed from her mouth and she clutched her hands across her chest holding in her frightened heart. Grant yanked her ankles so hard he nearly pulled her off the platform.

"I'm sorry," He said laughing—not actually sorry at all.

Grant's energy was contagious, his laughter charming, and he was quickly forgiven for his prank. He pulled himself onto the platform dragging a large swampy bog of green gunk covered in slimy algae. It reeked of some rank unidentifiable funk.

"Let's play with it!" He clamored.

"Swamp thing?" I crinkled my face. "Gross, get that thing away from me."

I swam to the front of the boat, out of his throwing range but he dove in and raced toward me with his muck in tow.

"Get that stinky thing away from me, you play with it." I pulled myself back into the boat escaping whatever he was about to do.

I dug out my camera and started filming. He stuffed swamp thing down the back of his shorts and swam across the top of the water displaying it like tail feathers. Then he moved it from his shorts to his head and wore it like a wig. He displayed it on his chin as if it was a five foot beard, then hid behind it as if it was a bush. I was thoroughly entertained by his uninhibited antics, but I was pretty sure Lissy had had enough.

He tossed the green slime aside, climbed to the top of the tower then catapulted himself into a backward somersault. He was larger than life, exuberant every moment of the day, bursting with delicious male potential. It was impossible for me not to fall in love with him.

I set down the camera, slipped back into the water and swam to him, leaving Lissy in the boat alone again.

"Happy birthday Grant," I said, pumping my legs to stay afloat while holding my beer bottle above the water as he did the same. "I hope this is an okay Birthday for you."

"This is a *great* birthday. I get to spend it with you."

It was cruel of him to say that.

Lissy looked over the edge of the Moomba, "Hey lovebirds—"

Ohshitohshitohshit...

"When you guys are done down there you can take me back to the cabin, I need to go home." Her face said what she didn't dare say out loud: *what the fuck are you doing! You're married!*

Numerous intoxicating drinks, hours of immature behavior, and a plethora of sexual innuendos would have been disturbing for any sober friend to tolerate. Grant and I had enjoyed a full day of cannon balls, back flips, and a one legged water-treading contest while Lissy looked on and made sure we didn't drown. Our naughty chemistry was unstoppable and my friendship to Lissy unbreakable. No matter what happened, I knew she'd be on my team.

Lissy waved goodbye then disappeared down the winding lake road. As soon as her shimmering silver car was out of sight, I felt his breath behind me.

"Let's go to Willy's." He was so close to my skin the hair on the back of my neck stood up.

"Sure," I shrugged. "I'll sober up, have dinner, and hang out with Dani for a bit. I'll pick you up at your place?"

I turned around and found his meandering eyes looking over my exposed shivering body. I opened my mouth wide as if to be offended but was actually delighted when he flashed me a naughty little smile and quick raise of his brow. The un-said was ever present between us.

"My place?" He smiled. "I can't wait."

I didn't want that day to end, and I got the feeling neither did he.

Debonair and delicious, he sauntered toward my car. He was freshly showered and wearing clean, fashionable clothes. He carried himself like a dashing, modern gent. The neighbors had often speculated about his sexual orientation, because surely such an intelligent, well dressed, and talented gentlemen couldn't be straight.

His clean appearance made me look like I'd just gotten out of the ocean. I was an air-dried, wavy haired, beach bum. Though we shared the same ruddy glow from the sun, the same overly white Visine eyes, and the same unspoken hunger.

His masculine scent filled my car as he slid into the passenger seat and once again I was forced to fantasize about wearing his shirt, nothing *but* his shirt.

Unable to control myself, I burst out, "You smell so good."

"I do? Oh...stop it." He looked away, bashful, ignoring my compliment.

"No. Actually you really stink because you're so old now. I forgot to ask, how old are you today?" I fidgeted with the stick, grinding the gears into reverse.

"Twenty-nine." He grumbled.

"Twenty-nine. Single. No kids. Hot." I flashed a *you-know-you-are* grin. "And your girlfriend? Is she the one like Molly was the one?" I kept my eyes forward on the winding road and glaring sunset.

"I thought so right away."

"And now?"

He hummed, "not so sure."

"That means no. Well, I'm glad she's not here. This way, *I* get to take you out for your birthday."

Willy's was a lakeside bar perched on the top of a steep hill overlooking our small, pristine lake. A regular gathering place for passing bikers and weekend beach bums. It was Dylan's favorite place to go, but on this weekend Dylan was a hundred miles away gigging at a small town street dance. The cosmos had aligned perfectly so that Grant and I could spend time alone together. A reddish cloud of summer dust circled my car as we pulled into the gravel parking lot.

"What if someone sees us together...alone?" I asked as I yanked the emergency break and turned off the ignition.

"We're friends," he said. "It's my birthday. No big deal."

We sat on barstools next to the pool table and ordered another drink. Not that either one of us needed another drink after our already indulgent day, but if all that alcohol had not been swimming through our blood, what happened next might never have happened.

He raised his bottle, "What should we toast to?"

"Your birthday of course and um...how about...to our first date?"

Did I just say that?

He nodded his head slowly, smiling, acknowledging my sentiment but not saying a word. We clinked our bottles together and took a refreshing sip, then he motioned for me to follow him.

"I've got some cash for the jukebox, let's go pick out some songs."

He stood dangerously close behind me, looking over my shoulder as I scrolled through songs and artists. "Are we breaking our pact if we play something other than Marley?" I asked.

"Of course not, that's just for the boat." I could feel his hot breath on my skin, his lips close to my ear. "Pick something good. I'll get a game of pool ready."

"You mean you wanna get your ass kicked in pool too?" I said bluffing.

"It's like that, is it?" He stepped back, "you're on."

He ran a few solids, nothing too impressive. We listened to *Michael Jackson* and *Sublime,* and I watched and laughed as he did wildly accurate impressions of *Slim Shady* and *Shaggy.* Being with him was more fun and more right than anything I'd ever known.

I strutted around the table, tempting him, luring him, that's when he grabbed me, one hand on each hip and pulled me onto his lap.

I was shocked. Shocked!

He held me down, his fingers wrapped around my hips. My skin tingled as he brushed his nose lightly across my shoulders and I could tell by the soft whirl of his inhalation, he was breathing me in.

In a hungry growl he said, "I can't keep my hands off you any longer."

***

"All I Wanna Do"
Is playing right now &
Made me think of u. :)

Chapter 14

We were in public! In a busy bar, on a tiny lake, with a small towns' worth of residents. Everybody knew everybody!

After all these years, why here? Why now?

His courageous move made me want him even more. Even if I was nothing more to him than a forbidden adventure—I would be *his* forbidden adventure for as long as he would have me.

Thrilled by his attention, but mortified someone might see us a nervous excitement fluttered through me. I nestled into him, fitting perfectly on his lap. Our sunburned cheeks pressed together and our lips pulsed with desire inches from one another. Then, as if nothing had happened, I stood up and positioned myself to take another shot.

His eyes followed me in disbelief.

I punched the cue ball and missed, "Your turn."

"So that's how you want to play," he gave me a slow, confident nod, "I'll play along." He chalked his cue with the little blue square and peered at me with his handsome grin. "Excuse me," he said then playfully nudged me aside.

I elbowed his ribs just as he was about to shoot. "Oops...sorry," I said when he scratched. Seeking retribution, he walked behind me and dragged his fingertips across my bare lower back.

The thrill of our game, the thrill of him wanting me, lit me on fire. I traipsed in front of him, expecting a witty crack, or inappropriate innuendo. Instead, he wrapped his arms around my torso and pulled me back down onto him again.

A sound slipped like velvet past his lips. "Mmm..." His heart thumped against my back and his fingertips caressed my bare waist. "I'm sorry," he whispered, gripping my arms, pinning me to him. "I'm so sorry."

"I'm not."

His forehead dropped against my shoulder with a thud, "I shouldn't be doing this."

Silence hung between us for what felt like an eternity before I spoke and when I did, my voice cracked with desperation. "Please," I said. "Don't stop. I don't want you to stop."

Grants lips lingering near my ear, "Then we should go."

It was hard to get off his lap, I could have died there and been happy for all eternity. He threw some cash on the bar and we both hid our faces as we hurried for the door.

The car door shut and we were sealed in, exiled from the outside world and instantly his warm, welcome hands sought my body and began to wander. I drove aimlessly, staring at the white line, unable to focus on anything but him touching me. Winding highways and lake shores blurred past as his hands respectfully, lovingly drifted along the contours of my body. I would've kept driving forever.

"I'm sorry," he apologized a fifth time, pulling away his hands then immediately putting them back. A low rumble resonated from his throat, "I should be more responsible."

I stared at the center line, "No you shouldn't. You should keep your hands on me forever."

It was as if he'd waited a lifetime for permission that had just been granted. He feverishly explored my body in places he'd never been. From my collar bone to my navel; then my waist to my thighs, he touched me in the most sensual way. He caressed my every bend and turn, my every freckle and bony joint. From the veins in my hand, to the knob of my elbow, from the ridge of my hips, to the scars on my stomach, he examined, cherished me—all of me.

His fingers traced the sun faded ink on the back of my shoulder. "Dani Jean," he read aloud, touching the deep rose and sun burnt colored tattoo. "You're a great mom," he said, then tucked my hair behind my ear.

His words melted my maternal heart and held me captive. He'd watched me raise Dani, he'd been there in the background, driving the boat and filling water balloons every weekend since she was a baby. He knew me, and he knew her. He'd been watching all this time, more than I knew.

I was forever under his spell and I never wanted to be without him, ever again. And if being with him, like this, turned out to be a mistake, it would be the best mistake I'd ever make.

The sun dipped behind the trees and the pavement became an ocean of black ink.

"I shouldn't be driving."

"I know. I'm sorry," he said. "Pull over, I'll drive back."

"No." I snapped. "Keep your hands on me. Don't you know how long I've been waiting for this?"

"You've been waiting for this? No, I've been waiting for this." I looked over and saw his growing smile.

My pulse raced as we approached the hidden driveway behind his cabin.

Was I dropping him off? Is it over? Or is this just the beginning?

Thoughts of what was happening and what was about to happen raced through my mind. I parked where he told me, behind the blue cabin, then turned off the headlights, but kept the reggae music on. The meaning of the words, the syncopated beat, the gospel undertones of love and unity; it all seemed to set the mood for the beginning of an incredible love story.

He scrolled through the songs, stopping at one we'd heard equally as many times as the others. Smooth and nonchalant, he sang to me, "Could You Be Loved".

"This is my favorite Marley song," he said then kept singing and looking at me.

I almost had a heart attack right there in the driver's seat of my tiny Volkswagen Beetle. His silky voice singing those lyrics penetrated the deepest part of my desolate heart, awakening it from a long, lonely slumber and making it feel something it'd never felt before.

The tips of his fingers traced my collar bone back and forth, then he set his palm in the center of my chest. I'd never felt anything so fateful...so alive as his hand covered my heart and radiated an emerald love into me. A love I knew he felt too. He closed his eyes and hummed a hum of delight.

"You have no idea," he said out of nowhere.

It was the start of him holding back and I knew it. "Then tell me. What do I have no idea about?"

He traced a single line down the length of my arm then slid his fingers between mine. Our interlaced hands brushed across the honey tone of my skin. "You're so beautiful," he said. His eyes locked with mine. I tumbled into the moment, falling fast without a parachute.

"I've thought about you for so long, and I dream of you every Sunday," I said.

"Sunday?"

"Yes, Sunday. After being with you all weekend my mind dreams of you every Sunday after I go home. I guess I miss you." I unbuckled my seat belt, slid over the console of my little Beetle and straddled his lap.

I hadn't had sex in months, but it wasn't sex I craved. I craved him. I needed him, I was myself when I was with him. I had married the wrong person, therefore I'd become the wrong person. Now ironically, I was having an affair that was turning me into the right person.

His hands slid under my shirt, up my bare back and into my hair. He tugged it gently back then pressed his lips into mine.

Our first kiss...

Was intoxicating. He was intoxicating, more than I'd imagined he would be, and in such a different way. My physical body was drunk on him of course, but the invisible union of our souls felt like destiny, like we'd been meant for each other since the beginning of time.

I'd been starving, desperate for emotional love, begging for it like a dog begs for crumbs. Now what I felt with Grant illuminated just how lonely and isolated I'd been in my marriage.

The sensual kissing escalated in to a steamy enthusiasm for something more and my already tiny car became too small to contain our fire.

With his hands in my hair pressing me to him, he whispered on my lips, "Follow me."

I stepped into the moonlight, not more than a second passed before I was crushed against the cold metal as he hungrily devoured me. My body arched in pleasure as he made a trail with his lips from my neck to my chest. Then without warning, he whisked me up from the hood and tugged me along the shoreline behind him.

The moonlight shone down on us like a spotlight targeting an escaped criminal, giving away our coordinates. We were already on high alert so when his phone rang loud from his pocket, we both jolted stiff like we'd been shocked. He reached in to silence it, then pulled it out. The screen glowed bright with hues of blue and green, blinding my night vision.

It was her.

On the screen of his phone her face was giddy with a new love glow that crushed my heart in a single glance. He stuffed his phone back into his pocket without saying a word.

"She's not here, is she?"

"I hope not." He said befuddled, "she's supposed to be in Australia."

"Maybe you should answer it? Just to be sure."

He shook his head. "No way. I'll call her back."

Her phone call reminded me of his predicament and that I wasn't the only cheat. We tiptoed along the reedy shore, looking into the warm glowing windows for signs that someone might be watching.

"Shh…" he put his finger to his lips as we approached his cabin.

"You shh…" I said louder, then slapped his shoulder.

Playfully, he yanked me along harder, up the creaking steps and into his cabin. Then we snuck down a narrow hallway and into a back bedroom.

The bedroom door creaked shut, I heard the click of the lock, and my senses became acute. A visceral awareness of just exactly where I was, and what I was about to do came over me. I felt his labored breath on my skin and heard his wildly thumping heart.

He stood inches in front of me in the darkness and for a moment there was reluctance—then just as quickly as it had arrived, all hesitation melted away as he swept me into his arms. Through the years I'd known him his body never changed, it seemed immortal. His strong hands sprawled across my back, then gripped the bottom of my shirt and lifted it off. I tugged at his and he was instantly bare. I set my forearms on his shoulders and pressed my bare skin against the warmth of his body. Silently begging him not to stop, I hummed in pleasure. He silenced me with his lips.

For hours we became acquainted, kissing, touching, and tormenting one another. There was a clear unspoken line neither of us were willing to cross. So on that night, shirts off, jeans-on, was as far as it would go.

It was four in the morning when I asked to look at his watch. If I didn't leave soon, the sun would be up. I couldn't risk being seen but I didn't want to leave. I wanted to stay with him forever. Going home, getting caught, not getting caught, being stuck in my life, stuck without him, they were all intolerable options. I was too scared to ask him *what now*, and too insecure to tell him how I felt, so I agonized in silence.

"I have to go." It was painful to whisper those words as I lay draped against his warm bare skin wanting more.

He encircled me in his arms, wrapping me tighter then nudged me to move on top. I laid my head on his firm chest, over his heart.

So this is who he is? I thought as I listened intently to the miraculous nature of his heartbeat. I longed to be inside it.

He reached for my hand, opened the creaky door and peeked out. We ran quickly from his cabin across the wet grass and back to my car.

I looked up at him before getting in, needing him to say all the right things, wanting him to ease my mind about what would happen next. My eyes begged him to tell me that I had not cheated for nothing, that what we had was magnificent and lasting, and that he felt it too. Instead, he looked even more confused than I felt. His eyes were pained and seemed to apologize for the reassurance he couldn't give. My head fell into his hands as they surrounded my face. Then he pressed his soft lips to mine.

It was a sweet kiss with a clear message.

Every girl knows when she's being broken up with. Whether it's a direct dumping or the round-a-bout way a guy starts to ignore you, and that kiss was no exception. It lacked the passion a man conveys when he can't wait to see you again, it lacked the fervor of a man in love who refuses to let go.

That kiss was a kiss goodbye. A let-me-down-easy, I really do care about you but this was a mistake. I promise it will never happen again, I'm so sorry...goodbye.

Chapter 15

"...IF TRUTH WERE EVERYWHERE TO BE SHOWN,

A SCARLET LETTER WOULD BLAZE FORTH ON MANY A BOSOM."

—NATHANIEL HAWTHORNE, *THE SCARLET LETTER*

It was a cruel kiss goodbye and a sobering drive home.

I slipped into the cabin just as the sun was revealing the morning fog on the lake then crawled into the bottom bunk, still in my dirty clothes and day-old mascara. Dani slept next to me, her plump face exuding innocence, making my sinful existence feel even more despicable. I laid my head on her pillow and stared at her porcelain face.

I'd failed. I wasn't showing her what a good mom and wife should be. I'd just cheated on her dad when I should have found the courage to leave instead. It was hard to sleep with the morning sun shining bright in the room, but sleep would have eluded me regardless. Stomach wringing guilt and flogging shame had teamed up to keep me awake.

It was nine am when I heard tires on the pavement outside my bedroom window. It was Levi making a surprise Sunday visit. I leapt out of bed and locked myself in the bathroom before he could make it to the front door. I brushed my teeth twice, washed my face, and neck, sprayed perfume in my hair, and dropped in Visine. I slipped on fresh clothes, rolled up last night's attire into a crumpled ball and stuffed it deep down in my duffle bag. I popped in an Altoid, slipped on my sunglasses and stepped out to greet my husband.

The rest of the day I clung to Levi like a leech clings to its oblivious host. Silently I was begging him not to leave me yet I really didn't know why. All I could think about was Grant, but all I wanted was for Levi not to find out. I was panicked, terrified of what my consequences might be. I didn't want to lose Levi, I didn't want to be alone. Without actually coughing up a confession I did everything I could to apologize for what I'd done.

I tied our floaties together with twine so we could be near enough to hold hands. I sat beside him on the dock, went for a dip in the cool lake water when he did, leapt into his arms and asked him to jump into mine. I got him a beer when he wanted and rubbed sunscreen on his back when he asked. I was a passive, good little wife. I offered him a neck rub, lunch, and anything else he might want, all of the things I didn't typically offer. In addition to my peculiar, clingy, needy, servant like behavior, I was out-of-character silent. My mouth was gagged, stuffed full of lies.

Levi was annoyed and suspicious of my unusually meek behavior, "What's wrong with you?" he barked in a harsh tone.

I just fucking cheated on you and I feel horrible, that's what's wrong with me!

"Nothing. I just don't feel good."

I feel like I might throw up, and all I can think about is Grant, and last night, and kissing him and cheating on you!

"What did you do last night? Drink too much?" Levi asked in the most condescending way.

"No."

"Where'd you go?"

Shit, shit, shit, where did I go?

"We all just went to a few bars. Nothing crazy." Hung-over and quivering with anxiety, I stood up and held back the urge to heave. "I just need to eat. I'll be right back. You want anything?"

"No," Levi said uncaring and suspicious of my sickness.

He knew something was up. I had to start acting normal or he'd keep asking questions. I had to ignore him, or argue with him, or be nice to everyone but him—all the things I normally did. But I couldn't, all I could do was hang on him. My cheating heart raced and thrummed loud in my ears, threatening to expose my secret. I needed more time to prepare my defense, to sweep my car for evidence, to wash my skin and conscience clean. I needed to make sure no one saw me last night, or saw my car parked on Grant's side of the lake.

That's when it hit me...*Shit! Where's my purple shirt?*

When I got out of bed, I was wearing my white undershirt. Where was the pale purple burn-out tank that went over it? *Shit!*

I searched for it under the bed and between the sheets, nothing. I slipped on my flip flops and clicked out to my car. I rummaged around in the back seat, the hatch, under the driver's seat, under the passenger seat, in the glove box...nothing. *Shit!*

Levi was insidious as he crept up behind me. "What are you looking for?" He asked.

Before I could respond or stand up from my stooped over position, he pressed against me. "I'd like to get some of that later," he said, antagonizing me. I shoved his hands away in total disgust. "Figures." He huffed, then walked away. I went back to my search and continued to retrace my steps.

Did I come home with it?

I wasn't sure.

Did I leave it at Grant's?

I wasn't sure.

I couldn't call him or text him, it was too risky. I could only hope he'd find it before someone else did or that it would turn up somewhere I'd have an explanation for.

At home later that evening, Levi and Dani were at the kitchen table coloring with crayons when I overheard their conversation.

"Did you have fun at the lake this weekend?" Levi asked her.

"Yes. But I cried when Mommy didn't come home last night."

I gasped then flung myself off the couch. "What?! Yes, I did, honey."

"No, Mommy," she was angry, "I woke up and you weren't there," she said with her head down, sulking. "Grandma laid with me and I cried," she tilted her head and examined her picture.

"Honey," I said in the sweetest most convincing voice I could, "it was late, but I did come home. I snuggled in next to you."

Levi was staring through me now, his mind working on overdrive making connections, piecing it together, examining all the possible reasons behind my odd behavior and Dani's accusation.

"Dani," I said, "we woke up together this morning...remember?" It was half question, half leading the witness.

I'd wondered if my feelings toward Grant were so obvious, they might be detectable by others. Now, by the scorned look on my husband's face, I guessed I was right. If it was true I didn't come home, he knew who I was with.

He'd pieced it together, figured it out.

He knew.

I wouldn't lie—I would just omit. I would tell the truth, but leave out a few hurtful details that would be best left undisclosed.

Levi threw down the crayons, stood up, then stomped up the stairs without saying a word. I ran after him.

"I fucking knew it," he'd turned around at the top to confront me. "You were with him. Weren't you?" He was more livid than I'd ever seen him.

I held my ground, stood by my lie. I looked at him with a blank stare, uncomprehending, "What are you talking about?"

A red-hot, raspy voice gurgled from his throat. "You know what I'm talking about. You were with him weren't you," he said in such a satanic tone that my bones shuddered.

He didn't believe my dumbfounded expression. I tried another tactic, invoke my right to defend against being wrongfully accused.

I showed him an equally enraged face then yelled, "I don't know what you're talking about! How dare you accuse me!" Then rambled through my lie, "a bunch of us went to Willy's for drinks, we stayed out till midnight."

"Who's a bunch'?" he asked, and by the confident look on his face, he knew I couldn't answer.

I couldn't say the name of one person. If I gave anyone's name, he could call them and check out my alibi.

"You know, the usual crew, there were a lot of us." I walked away, hoping he wouldn't follow.

"Who?" He snapped.

"Everyone!" I shouted, not knowing what else to say.

"Grant?" He said calmly.

Shitshitshit.

"Was Grant there?" he demanded.

"What? What are you talking about?" I was fucked—I didn't know *what* to say.

Levi stepped closer, "He was, wasn't he?" He said, backing me down the hallway.

My heart pounded in my throat. "Yeah. So what? I don't know why you're being such a jerk?"

"Oh, I'm a jerk?" He pointed at his chest.

"Yeah, you are," I said. "*So what* if I go out with friends for one night. I go out twice a year at most! Big fucking deal." I shook my head in disgust and tried walking away again. He followed me.

What I said next was a below the belt shot, a desperate attempt to divert guilt away from me and onto him. "At least I don't go to the strip clubs and jerk off to other women when I go out."

"You bitch," He said, shaking his head. Fed up with me, he walked into our bedroom and started packing.

"What's new, I know you think I'm a bitch. I'm used to it, it doesn't hurt me anymore."

He shoved clothes from the top drawer into a dusty old duffel bag.

"I knew it," He mumbled. "I fucking knew it, I knew you wanted to fuck him. You did fuck him, didn't you?" He stopped packing, looked at me, and waited for my response.

"No. Do you want me to?"

"I really don't care what you do," Levi said.

I should have fucked him then. Maybe I will next time.

"Then why are you with me?" I said in disgust.

"Why are you with *me*?" he snapped back.

Evil expressions unconsciously formed on his face as he fought back the urge to strangle me. I found him hideous, it was easy to hate him. "Good question," I replied, "Good question."

The anger between us reminded me of how much I hated him, how dysfunctional we were together, and how horrible it was of us to fight with Dani sitting downstairs. I *wanted* him to leave, I welcomed it.

He couldn't. He was just as codependent on our dysfunctional marriage as I was. We were perfect for each other in that way, both too cowardly to leave, too selfish to change, yet too wounded to be happy.

***

A week later I was still mulling over Grant's every touch, the smell of his skin, his hand over my heart, his liquid voice when he sang "Could You be Loved". I re-lived each caress in slow motion, committing every second of that night to memory. It was a week filled with torture and obsession in equal measure.

I had to talk to Grant, tell him I couldn't stop thinking about him, tell him I couldn't breathe without him. But if I called Grant or texted him, and Levi found out, he would have all the proof he needed to leave.

I didn't want Levi to leave, in a heated moment I did, yes. But if I couldn't have Grant then I didn't want to be alone and being with Levi was better than being alone—I couldn't bear to be alone. As much as I wanted Grant, and as much as I hated Levi at times, I was still clinging to a dysfunctional life with someone, rather than a life without anyone.

At eight o'clock on a Monday morning I sat in an empty parking lot staring down at my phone. I composed a text, erased it, and then re-wrote it again. Not knowing what the ramifications might be, I forced myself not to care. I closed my eyes and hit send.

U don't need to respond.
I just wanted u to know
that I don't regret 1
minute with u.

Then I deleted the sent message, and agonized for days wondering if and when he would respond. But getting a response from Grant was like finding the Hope Diamond in a Walmart parking lot—it just wasn't going to happen. It didn't happen. Days went by, then months and my phone was still silent. It was over.

I needed to get away from him, get away from the dream of a life with Grant so I could live my life with Levi. There was only one way to do that.

I would move.

Yes.

I would move.

Chapter 16

North Carolina—no, Maine—no, Maryland—no, California? I channeled my obsessive energy into a project...we would move.

I was qualified, educated, talented, even. I could turn a fifty pound overweight woman into a size four bodacious bombshell or give a skinny white chick a booty like a Brazilian beach model. I'd built up a large clientele, I was traveling, teaching workshops, and working part time at a local university. I was hired by corporations to help their employees get healthy, and every day people who just needed accountability. When it came to weight loss, breaking habits and establishing new ones, I knew what I was doing and I knew how to get it done.

I sent my resume out, blanketing the lower forty-eight looking for something new and exciting. I took a few trips, received a few offers but none of them felt quite right. Then, when I least expected it, my opportunity arrived heavenly and sprinkled with gold. It was like finding my very own north star, a ray of golden light pointed the way home—inviting me in to explore its secret gardens that longed for my return. I went deep into the hills of Southern California, to explore this new land and make it our new faithful home.

It was a sprawling mountainous village of solitude for the ultra-rich. A getaway for celebrities like Oprah Winfrey and Barbara Streisand, CEOs, and business tycoons—the one percent. I read an article in a San Diego newspaper that said, "A millionaire is not enough, we're talking about the super-rich, they're the ones that go there."

It took six months of strategic planning just to get my resume through that shimmering door and truthfully, I never expected a call. So when the call did come in, I was thrilled that all of my planning and schooling had paid off. Within a few weeks, I was on a plane from the frozen tundra of Minnesota to the sun drenched San Diego valley.

I rented a car and drove through miles of unfamiliar winding hills. Then, tucked away from the main road, I found the entrance. Just like I was told, if you didn't know what you were looking for, you'd never know it was there. I pulled up to the black iron gate and looked into the security camera. A pleasant voice greeted me through the speaker.

"Can I help you?"

"Mrs. Summers, here for an interview."

"Welcome Mrs. Summers. One moment please." Then without another word, the gates clicked open then closed behind me.

I parked where I was told, took the walkway I was directed to.

That's when I saw it:

The Golden Door.

A stunning symbol of wealth and luxury, peace and new beginnings and I walked through without looking back.

It was a health and fitness resort of magnificent grandeur, a purported six thousand a week. For someone like me, staying there even for one night, was unfathomable.

A lone coyote howled at night outside my bungalow, songbirds sang unfamiliar tunes, and the sound of trickling water from the endless streams in the Japanese style gardens was ever present day and night. There were endless boardwalks, fruit tree orchards, organic vegetable gardens and private trails with sweeping views of the mountains or the ocean. It was an exclusive community where people, animals and nature existed in harmony.

Each day was dedicated to a string of simple pleasures: sipping matcha, sitting in the lemon grove, walking the labyrinth, or going to a meditation class. My personal favorite were the miles and miles of unadulterated hiking trails.

My soul could thrive among the organic vegetables and uncomplicated life of a Yogi. I would dwell within the golden walls, drag a rake through the Zen garden, and sit for hours contemplating the perfect placement of three rocks. I would teach restorative yoga, and salsa dancing, and lead hikes at six am. I would do what I did best—I would make women skinny and in the process, and I would forget about Grant. Erase him from my memory and get so far away from what I had done, that I could live like it hadn't even happened.

I spent several days auditioning, interviewing and I never expected to get offered a job, there was a line of applicants wanting to get it. Most of them were willing to work for free just to make the kinds of contacts that stayed there.

I returned home with stars in my eyes and plans to start as soon as possible. But not long after I left that golden valley, the haze wore off. The magical spell a place like that casts upon you had disappeared. I realized that it might not be a good idea to move my family three thousand miles from home, where we knew no one, and had nothing.

It turns out that if you want to work in paradise, they don't pay you in cash, but rather you are given three magic beans and a hand full of dirt in exchange for your services. It wasn't enough to stuff my life into a U-Haul, drag Dani, Levi, and Nanook thousands of miles from home, hoping to grow a magic bean stalk. I rescinded the offer as quickly as I had accepted it.

It was late winter when I came back from California and another summer was approaching. Another summer of temptation and confusion. I had to stay away from Grant. I promised myself I would and that's what I did.

I avoided the lake that summer. Instead I broke my back, literally broke my back pouring every last drop of energy I had into my work.

I had no idea our night together would find a way into his heart forever.

It wasn't over, it hadn't even begun.

***

Oh God, ur so worth it.
What time can I have u?

Chapter 17

"EVERY HEART HAS ITS OWN SKELETONS."

—LEO TOLSTOY, *ANNA KARENINA*

I stuffed ice packs into the fold of my yoga pants wearing them like Band-Aids everywhere I went. The pain hadn't gotten any better and it'd been months since the first episode. Everyone I talked to had a remedy to fix me, but nothing worked. I was deteriorating. My usual spirit which generally overflowed with conquest and curiosity was now drowning in pain.

The pain was persistent-sharp-dull, nagging-stabbing-throbbing, multi-dimensional, bone-pain. It was everything and nothing I could articulate when someone asked what was wrong. Except to say that it gnawed on me like a flesh eating bacteria. No words seemed catastrophic enough to describe it,

The first time I heard a "pop", I was teaching *Pilates for Dancers* to a flock of teenagers who resembled pink flamingos.

"Inhale, exhale, circle-and-sweep, lift-and-point," Pop—Pop!

A searing pain pierced through my lower back like a lightning bolt. My knees buckled, and I fell to the floor in the front of my class.

I'd been teaching ten classes a week. Yoga, Pilates, Latin dance, and half a dozen other formats, in addition to seeing clients, speaking, and cooking. It was nothing new or strenuous, it was just my job.

"C.J., are you okay? What's wrong?" The flock surrounded me.

"Um…I'm not sure, I need a minute." I clung to the ballet-bar on the front wall as the aftershocks hit me in waves and charlie-horse cramps seized my body. "I need a breather. Let's take a quick break," I muttered as I lay draped over the cold metal.

I didn't want to lose my job because of an injury and sixty bucks an hour teaching at a dance studio wasn't something I could afford to give up. I couldn't get hurt, I had no time for an injury.

A pair of look-a-like teens in snug pink shoes helped me to my feet. I hobbled across the polished wood floor and into the hallway where I could be alone and assess what-in-the-hell had just happened. The pain was an eight out of ten.

I can still finish class. I have to.

Besides, I was acclimated to punishing pain, chronic sprains and never-ending tendonitis. It was the plight of a fitness instructor, the dark side of working out for a living. Taking time off work to heal an injury was not an option. I dug out an extra-large bottle of ibuprofen and sloshed back another eight hundred milligrams.

I clapped my hands, took a step back into the classroom and secretly winced, "Ladies," I barked, trying not to show weakness. "I must have sprained something in my back, I'm going to take it easy tonight, but let's keep going. Do what I say, not what I do."

Any weight on my right leg made the lightning bolt strike and caused me to make a hideous grimace. I stood in one place for the remainder of class trying not to show the pain on my face.

Whatever it was got better over the next few months, dropped from an eight to a four, but never fully healed—only hibernated under the surface, threatening to club me if I did too much of anything.

As the months passed, physical pain turned into emotional pain, then emotional pain turned into depression. The injury that never healed was the catalyst that sent my already fragile emotional-balance plummeting into a bottomless chasm.

An inherited proclivity toward severe depression had turned on like a genetic light switch. The right combination of emotional stress and physical strain had formed the perfect storm and now a black plague of depression was allowed to thrive indefinitely and uncontested within my mind.

I slowly became a recluse, an emotional shut-in, masquerading like bamboo—green and fit on the outside to hide the hollow within. I further abandoned my marriage. Incapable of contributing anything positive, we'd become nothing more than a complete and total shit storm.

When I expressed my unhappiness, "I can't live like this anymore. We don't get along, all we do is argue and nothing changes."

Levi's response was always the same, "It's not that bad, you're over-exaggerating."

My every feeling, every opinion, every expression, concern or emotion, was thoroughly invalidated. What I felt and thought didn't matter, and thus, I didn't matter. Levi remained oblivious and in denial of our dysfunction as my discontent, depression and pain metastasized at an unprecedented rate.

My brain hurt, my body ached, my back felt broken, I was a human calamity who lived in dirty clothes. I stopped taking my vitamins, plucking my eyebrows or cooking healthy food. I was truly, utterly depressed and convinced I'd stay that way for the rest of my wretched life.

"What more do you want?" Dylan asked when I complained about the general malaise of my existence.

"Happiness?" I said, but wondered if such a fantastic fable actually existed.

I went to a counselor to see if I was crazy.

Jane was a stout, spiritual woman in a lavender office, with lavender books, and a lavender blanket that I wrapped myself in as I sat on her matching lavender couch.

I babbled and cried, week after seventy five dollar week but eventually her wise, understanding, old-soul taught me three very important lessons:

(1) I needed to get on and stay on my fricking medication!
(2) No one and nothing can make me happy. I'd have to figure that out on my own.
(3) Any one of the three A's could justify a divorce; addiction, abuse or an affair.

"One more thing," Jane said, "write a letter to your back."

"Write a letter to my back?"

"Yes, write a letter to your back."

I obeyed lesson one. When Wellbutrin finally showed up at my doorstep holding a pair of shoes in my size, life became more comfortable. So together, my shoes and I hiked from the bowels of depression back into my life.

Lesson two meant that I had to unravel every thread on which my life was woven. Only then, when I was irreversibly undone, could I rebuild anew.

I began to consciously deconstruct every negative thought, habit and behavior I'd ever adopted knowingly or unknowingly. I meditated, journaled, took workshops and read a plethora of self-help books. I took baths, got Rolfed, cleaned my closet, and cleansed my colon. I made juice from every green or purple vegetable I could find then abstained from food for fourteen days. I smudged my home until the evil presence that lived within the walls stopped tormenting my sensitive spirit, cleared my mind until I was an empty cup, and burned incense until I reeked of patchouli.

As for lesson three, I was still too cowardly to confess my sins, and too co-dependent to leave. And as for the letter? I showed up at her office and handed her my assignment. It read:

Dear C.J.'s Back,

You fucking suck, she wants to do so many things, but because of you, she can't. She complains about you all the time, how you're a constant nag, poking, kicking and stabbing her. How could you! How could you have gone ahead and given her the back of an old lady? What's she supposed to do now—huh?

She says she wants a divorce and she will find a new back since you have not supported her when she needed you the most. She also says to tell you to go fuck yourself, and that you took away so many things she loved to do and that you stole her career. You really suck, you, you...grandma back.

Oh, and one more thing...she loved yoga and you fucked her out of that too. Thanks a lot asshole.

-Me

She looked at the letter, and without reading it handed it back to me. "Now write a letter from your back to you," she said. So I did.

Dear C.J. you fucking bitch,

How dare you blame me? It was You who abused me all these years! A decade that you spent fucking me up! How could You! I gave you signs. Signals and pain, and told you years ago that I needed a rest. But nooo you had to keep going, and going, and going you crazy bitch. Who do you think you are—accusing me? This is not my fault.

Get your shit together, find other hobbies and stop blaming me for your unhappiness. You are the one who sucks. I would have carried you, supported you for a lifetime, but you screwed me. You abused me, and over used me, and I'm done with you.

I'm going to abandon you for a while and let you suffer like you did to me. It's your turn to be ignored you crazy cunt, call me in a few years and I might pick up the phone. In the meantime, don't bother trying to fix me, it won't work. Oh—and one more thing, fuck you!

-Me

***

I'd been nine years since I met Grant, five years since I married Levi, and two years since my sinful indiscretion. Two years since I'd sent Grant that text and I'd yet to hear back from him. I never knew if he got my message.

It felt like the magnetosphere that had once pulled us together had faded into a weak, depolarized glob of nothing. I'd seen him only in small sips with awkward eye contact. Our encounters were superficial and too guttingly painful for me to stick around and be tortured by so I stayed away. I gave up. I was certain he'd given up too.

Then on a starry winter night as the lazy snow drifted to the ground—it started again.

****

I so feel the same way. :)
My beautiful woman!

Chapter 18

"OUT BEYOND IDEAS OF RIGHT AND WRONG,

THERE IS A FIELD, I'LL MEET YOU THERE."

—RUMI

Ad·dic·tion:

The state of being enslaved to something psychologically to such an extent its cessation causes severe trauma. —Dictionary.com

Yep. I was addicted.

The moment I saw Grant on stage, my abated desire regenerated its severed limb. The years I spent trying to evict him from my mind were futile. I'd wanted him since the day we met, and still I wanted to wrap myself around him and relish him for all eternity. More than anything, I wanted him to have a burning desire for me. No matter how many years had passed or how committed I was to leaving him alone, fate kept bringing us together.

I had no ulterior motive on that winter night other than to see Dylan. I knew Grant might be on stage next door, but I wasn't there for him.

As we always did on his break, Dylan and I walked next door to catch a glimpse of the band. Through the reddish glow of the stage lights, we formed an unbreakable stare. Seeing Grant again made me ache, it was a tormented feeling of emptiness, a hollow that only he could carve out or fill. He sang a lonesome song that floated over the crowd and haunted me to the core. It was called "Bittersweet," a simple tune with an acoustic ring and clear message that foreshadowed what was, and what was to come. He'd been watching me all along, waiting, hurting, wondering if it was love.

Anxiety twisted my nerves as Grant walked toward Dylan and I. His smile was big and gorgeous and a small scar on his upper lip made it the tiniest bit crooked. I stared at his lips while I waited in line behind Dylan, and when it was my turn to greet him, Grant opened his arms like he'd done so many times before. I wanted to surrender, to fade into him, but I wouldn't let myself go there again. It would only cause me to relapse and need him.

I resisted the instinct to press my breasts into him and lay my head on his warm chest. Instead, I gave him limp hug and light two finger tap on the back as if he had a contagious disease. Holding back was laborious and the tension between us was glue thick.

Grants eyes strayed from our three party conversation and met mine in awkward glances, each one more confusing than the last.

What the hell is this? He's had his chance, I'm done. Stop looking at me.

His obvious interest in me was regressing and painful, and I wanted to leave so I could check back into rehab and start over before I fell too far off the wagon.

"You good?" Dylan said to me as he stood up.

His assertive voice zapped me back to life. "I'm fine. I'm going to finish this beer then go home. Love you."

"See ya bud," Dylan said to Grant, then walked back to his gig next door.

The chill of Grant's ice blue eyes staring at me made me shiver.

Don't even think about it. I'm done.

I was going to hold my ground no matter what he said.

"It's so good to see you. It's been so long."

Really? He's going to be adorable and charming and make me want him again? Precisely why I shouldn't see him and exactly why I can't resist him.

I gave a slim uninterested smile.

He leaned in close and spoke over the bustling bar, "My mom says she sees you and your new dog walking by her house. She really likes you—she talks about you. I heard about Nanook, I'm sorry."

"That's nice of her and thank you," I said with a solemn face, not wanting to think or talk about my dreadful last day with Nanook. "I stop by to see her baby gorillas when they're out."

And sometimes when I'm weak and see your work vehicle parked in her driveway I weave up and down the block like a stalker hoping to get a glimpse of you.

He laughed, "Yes, the gorillas. Don't let them lick you, they eat shit, you know."

"Gross!" I slapped his shoulder as he tipped his head back and laughed.

"Well, they do," he added still chuckling. "You should stay for the last set. I'll buy you a drink. Bloody Corona?" He asked just before he hit me with a two ton bomb. "I miss you."

Did he just say he missed me?

The words seemed to float from his mouth and idle in the space between us waiting for my reply.

"Please, stay awhile," he said.

I fanned my hand through the empty air next to me, "You mean me and all my friends?"

"I wish I could join you. Why don't you come up and sing a few songs? Then you don't have to sit here alone."

"Um...no thanks." A bloody beer landed on the counter in front of me. "You trying to get me drunk again?" I tilted my bottle toward his.

"Maybe?" He moved in close, commanding my full attention, "Meet me at Dylan's?" he asked with a bashful smile.

Why, so you can use me for a make out session then leave me again? What, no girlfriend this year? No, thanks.

I shrugged and didn't respond.

113

"It'll be fun. I promise," He insisted. "We can play cards or battleship or do anything you want."

"You really think you'll win at either of those?" I raised an eyebrow. "Oh, never mind, you will win. Cause you cheat!" I said then playfully pushed him. He exaggerated and fell off his barstool, then pointed at me with a wild grin as he backed away.

"If you change your mind and want to sing a song, just come up, okay? But you really should come to Dylan's." He said.

"I won't, and I'll think about it."

I sat alone at the bar and listened to the next set. Every song foretelling something, every glance filled with meaning.

C.J! These are only songs! Not how he actually feels!

I set my half empty bottle on the counter and slid on my winter coat realizing that I was slipping fast into a Grant induced coma again, where nothing else in the world exists. I didn't trust myself, I had to leave. I felt his eyes on me and was careful not to make eye contact. As much as I wanted to stay, wanted to be with him, I didn't want to consent to anything imprudent, I'd done so much to distance myself.

I walked toward the stage, smiled and waved, and mouthed *goodbye*. His head swung to the side of the mic and he stepped toward me as the band kept playing.

"You're going to Dylan's right? Wait for me, I only have a few songs left..." He was strumming and leaning over the stage waiting for me to respond. There was no time for a conversation, I had to decide.

I was weak and unable to say no, "I'll meet you there."

"Promise?" He tilted his head, skeptical.

I exaggerated a huge nod and rolled my eyes, acting annoyed, "Yes. I said, I promise.'"

When I walked into Dylan's garage, I had Déjà vu, only this time Levi and Dani were out of town and I wouldn't have to explain where I was, or when I was coming home, or *if* I was coming home. Unlike last time, I wasn't thrilled to be there. I had successfully distanced myself, it had taken nearly two years, but I'd done it and I didn't want to start over.

This is a bad idea, I need to leave.

I shut off the lights and went into Dylan's house to use the real bathroom instead of the five gallon piss bucket in the garage left out for anyone too drunk to make it inside. When I opened the front door to leave, Grant was standing there with a gorgeous grin and obvious glee. I became paralyzed.

"I was looking for you." His voice was calm and inviting, and true to my bipolar emotions, I was instantly glad I hadn't abandoned the chance to be with him.

I stuffed my shivering hands into my coat pockets, "I'm right here. But I can't stay long or drink too much, I need to be able to drive. I have to let Bodi out."

"Can't Levi let him out?" It was so wrong to hear Grant's voice saying Levi's name, it made me shudder.

"He's not home. He and Dani are in Minneapolis for the weekend."

A moment of silence stepped between us as we processed the implications of what I had just revealed. The tingling that spread into every part of me when I was with Grant had begun.

He waved me into the garage. "I can take you to let Bodi out."

You can? Why?

I looked at the carpeted garage floor and swept my foot across it, stalling, pondering what to say, deciding what I was going to allow to happen. "We can hang out for a little while then I'll take you whenever you want," he insisted.

He walked toward the fridge and just the act of him walking away turned on some biological switch. The threat of not being near him snapped me to life, and prompted me to follow him.

We sat next to one another, in the same folding chairs, at the same card table with the same blasting propane heater as last time. Then it happened again, like it always did when we were together—the walls came in close, people around us disappeared; and the Earth stopped its orbit to allow us extra time together, to fulfill our destiny.

Our attraction to one another had always stemmed from meaningful conversation, and that night was no exception. We filled in the blanks about the last two years. He schooled me about the historical significance of the Hofbrau house and walked me through his somber trip to Dachau. Places that I later had to Google to find out exactly what we were talking about.

I told him about my attempted move. We shared a good laugh over a mishap with a small family of deer, and the barbed wire fence that entangled his car so he could save their lives. He informed me of his healthier food choices, and tried to convince me he'd changed his ways. For reasons not yet known to me, although there were people around us, inside and out and everywhere in between, not a single one of them tried to infiltrate our conversation.

"Where is Heidi?" I asked.

"I don't know where Heidi is," He replied.

"Grant. Why are you still single? You must want to be a bachelor, because if you didn't, you could have anyone you wanted."

"Not anyone. I'm waiting for the right one."

"That's good, most of us don't wait for the right one and end up with a miserable one instead." We shared a laugh at the unfortunate truth of my comment. He deserved to have the right one not just anyone, and not a marriage like mine.

We'd re-connected as if no time had passed—but so much time *had* passed, and I was no further from wanting him than I was five years ago. He was the itch I could never scratch. He was always there, just under my skin, in a place I'd never be able to reach.

"I should go. I need let Bodi out," I said. "You don't have to drive me, I'm fine." I tossed my mostly full bottle into the recycle bin.

"I don't mind, I can take you." He tossed his bottle in too and followed me.

I slid into his passenger seat and blew my warm breath into my hands. "I'm sorry, it'll get warm quick," he said as heat blasted the floor boards. "Where do you live?"

Am I really going to take home the man I cheated on my husband with? Let him onto our driveway or into the house? Levi would kill me...kill US.

"Twenty-two fifty-six Garrison Street." I replied.

He dug in the center console, pulled out his IPod and plugged it into a small hole in the dash. I looked at him and grinned when I realized what it was. Recognizable reggae transported me back in time to that night—our night.

"Hey," I said, "It's not summer and this isn't the Moomba."

"I listen to this all year, don't you?"

"Could You Be Loved" filled the dense air around us.

The chemistry between us had endured. It was undeniable and intense, and exactly how it had been since our first summer together.

"There's only one thing I think of when I hear this song," I said, biting my lip.

"What's that?" He asked all shy, like he didn't know.

"You know," I said.

He shot a devilish smirk at me and confirmed we were reminiscing the same delicious memories. He turned up the volume and we sang along to every song.

"One Love"

"No Woman No Cry"

"Stir it Up"

The decibels of our singing voices climbed a few notches with each song as we got comfortable with each other again. We filled in with mumble-jumble where we didn't know what words were said, and laughed at each other when we sang the wrong ones.

"Are you sure no one's home?" He said before committing to the driveway.

"I don't think so," I shrugged. "They're supposed to be in Minneapolis, I haven't heard anything otherwise."

117

Stopping in what usually is Levis spot, he clicked through the gears and into park. I was uneasy about him being in my driveway. What if the neighbors saw? What if they said something to Levi? Levi would know instantly who it was.

I didn't care. I was mentally exhausted from Grant's hot and cold, emotionally fucked-up from my own toxic marriage, and crippled by debilitating pain. I didn't care. All I wanted to do was exist and try to be happy from moment to moment.

"You want to meet Bodi?" I asked.

He retreated into his seat, "Is that a good idea?"

I shrugged, indifferent, "Its fine, everyone's gone."

"I don't think I should."

I didn't care if he did or didn't. His waffling made me frustrated. "Whatever, I'll be right back."

The wind blew through my winter jacket when I stepped out.

"Okay, I'll come in," I heard him yell from behind me, "I have to use the bathroom anyway."

He turned off the car and followed me up the sidewalk to my front step then stood close behind huddling into his jacket as I fumbled with my keys in the lock

"I hope a murderer never chases you into your locked house."

"What?" I wiggled the knob, my fingers stiff and clumsy.

"You would've been dead minutes ago," he teased.

"I'm going to let Bodi bite you." I said. "He won't bite me."

"Yes, he will. Bodi doesn't like men."

An image of Levi waiting for me on the other side of the door flashed in my mind and sent waves of fear through my blood. I paused with the door cracked an inch. The house was dark, Bodi was barking, I walked in and flipped on the foyer light. Grant squeezed in behind me, I was acutely aware of how close our bodies were.

Bodi stood proud and stout at the top of the stairs. "Don't talk to him or try to pet him. And don't look him in the eye." I said as I kicked off my boots and leapt two steps at a time up the stairs past my little brindle Shiba—who was so fixated on killing Grant he didn't even notice me.

"He's little," I yelled as I ran in to the bathroom, "so if he bites you it won't hurt that bad. Just don't try to touch him!"

Bodi barked ferociously as I sat with my yoga pants around my ankles. "Just ignore him and walk past!" I hollered through the bathroom door. Then I heard a new rabid anger in my little Shiba's growl.

"What did you do to him?" I said as I walked out of the bathroom tugging and adjusting myself. Grant paused and eyed me with that aroused look only a guy could have from seeing a woman fiddling with her clothes.

"I didn't do anything. I just reached my hand out and he lunged at me."

"I told you not to look at him or touch him. Don't you watch Cesar Millan—no talk, no touch no, eye contact? Bodi, come on boy—let's go outside." I patted my leg and walked him to the patio door.

"Nice piano," Grant said as he looked around my house.

"Thanks, I just got it."

"You should play me a song." He said excitedly.

"I'm just starting to play again so I suck. Why don't *you* play a song?" I leaned my elbows on the black granite island and stared at him in my home. I never imagined him in my home, in Levi's home.

"You've heard me many times," He said, "Now it's my turn to hear you."

"I've never heard you play piano though." I said.

"I'll play, but you go first. I'll listen from the bathroom," he said as he walked away.

I sat down in front of my new polished onyx piano and returned to music after a thirteen year anger induced hiatus. Deciding to play music again was part of reconstructing myself; abolishing residual bad feelings and learning to enjoy singing and playing on my own terms. For the first time in my life it didn't feel forced and I was enjoying playing for myself. Until Grant, I hadn't wanted to play for anyone but myself.

The cushioned bench welcomed me; I pressed my foot onto the damper and began with the most recent song I'd been practicing. A dull ache spread in my chest as I realized why I was singing that song. Why I'd picked those particular words to reignite the musician in me. Why I'd been practicing it for weeks with tears in my eyes for no particular reason. Now I knew.

I'd been longing for him like a lost soul longs to go home. He was my *Home,* my place of refuge that I always longed to go back to. No matter how many summer seasons had come and gone, no matter the distance between us or impossible circumstance, somehow we'd always found a way to each other again.

When I reached the chorus, he approached me slowly, listening as if he'd never heard me sing before. "You sound so good," He whispered in my ear, sat down on the piano bench beside me and stared at my lips.

"You're making me nervous."

"Don't be nervous, keep playing," He laid his head on my shoulder, nestling into me. A soft *murrr* vibrated from his lips.

My heart skipped into an irregular rhythm when he slid his hand onto the top of my thigh. It felt shocking but it felt right—like we'd been together for a lifetime and his hand should be on my thigh.

I ached for red silk romance, and carry me away passion, and I ached for it with nobody else but him. He was a breed of charming I couldn't resist.

***

Hi, huny. :) I'm waiting
patiently for u. Everything's
in order 4 tonight.:) Call
when u get close, so I can
get the garage door 4 u.
Kisses!

Chapter 19

OVER THIRTY-FOUR MILLION USERS

—AshleyMadison.com

"I didn't know you could play like that," he said as I lifted my hands from the keys, "You're amazing."

Then he went silent, his face wilted and his shoulders slumped. It was the expression your body makes when you're too afraid to show who you really are, or have to live without saying what you need to say.

I laid my head onto his shoulder and we melted into one another, unmoving and barely breathing. I wanted so badly to kiss him, or to have him kiss me. All I had to do was tilt my chin up and his lips would be right there. But I couldn't, not in my house, not in Levi's house. Cheating was inexcusable, but cheating in your husband's home or bed seemed just plain evil.

"C.J., play another song."

"What do you want to hear?" As if I could actually take requests.

"I'm sure I'll love anything you pick."

Grant was far more accomplished so playing for him was unnerving. But his encouragement awakened something within me, something that I used to love, and something that disappeared more than a decade ago that hadn't surfaced since. My memory started to flood with lyrics and chords and inspiration and for the first time in as long as I could remember, I wanted to play for someone, I wanted to play for him—and only him. It was as if I'd been practicing for this moment.

His fingers splayed across my lower back and radiated warmth into my skin. "I've never done this one for an audience," I said as my fingers searched the slippery keys for the unusual C flat diminished, "but I'll try."

Somber tones of minors and flats oscillated through the air as I began to play. Small strokes of his thumb and fingers across my flank were a colossal distraction during an already difficult classical piece. Nervous and excited, I fumbled through the notes then stopped abruptly, "I'm the queen of half-songs. That's all I know."

He applauded my mediocre talent, a generous compliment. I was a fair musician at best.

"Your turn," I stood up to switch spots. "How long have you been playing the piano? Can you read notes?" I asked, assuming that like me, all road musicians learned in their basement and played by ear without any formal education.

He smiled like he was hiding a secret, "a few years," he said modestly, "and yes, I can read notes." He fiddled with the settings, stopped at the sound of orchestra strings, then after a few trial plunks he began to sing...

"Never Tear Us Apart."

I almost leapt off the bench and whirled around, "I love this song, I can't believe you know this one." The expression on my face matched the expression I'd seen dozens of people make when they spent time with him. It was a shocked pause that clearly stated, *is there anything he can't do?*

Nope.

The breadth and variety of his talent was immense, he never stopped surprising me. Not only could he play the piano, he was a pianist. He continued to sing, I was captivated by his serenade and couldn't help but feel he was singing those words about us. Telling me a story about how he'd been waiting for me, that we'd be together for a thousand years, we'd drink wine, we'd fly, and nothing could ever tear us apart.

Over the next hour our impromptu karaoke date turned into an eighties hair band battle spectacular. We sang as many obscure, one-hit-wonders as we could think of. Songs from bands with names like, Flock of Seagulls and Bananarama. After half a dozen songs it was like we'd come to the end of a playlist. The music stopped. The room went silent. All I could hear was the ringing in my ears and the hum of the refrigerator. Our obnoxious impressions, belting vocals, and cough-inducing laughter hushed.

I wanted to say something about *that* night. I felt like he wanted to say something too. Instead he blew a disconcerting draft of cold air into my face when he spoke.

"We'd better get back. Dylan might wonder."

I plopped into the passenger seat and sulked over his lack of gumption.

Just say something! Anything!

I wanted to scream at him! I felt his attraction to me, tonight more than ever. An enormous swell of tension filled the air between us, and the car shrunk smaller and smaller as we got nearer and nearer to Dylan's. I was drowning in anxiety over everything unspoken. I turned toward him, about to speak, then didn't. He turned toward me, took a breath, and then sunk backward. I stared at him, my distraught expression begging him to tell me...but still nothing. Scooping out my heart with a rusty spoon would have been less brutal than enduring the empty silence between us.

I went from vulnerable to angry, then angry to furious—yet another let down from his epic hot and cold head games. Grant lived in slow motion, every moment calculated and deliberate. He did things on purpose. So when the car slowed then came to a stop a mile before Dylan's, I froze, I knew something was finally about to happen.

He pulled over, clicked the gears slowly into park then turned off the headlights. Heat blasted through the vents sending billows of hot air up my legs. My senses became acute like a wild animal and time became viscid slow. The click of his seat-belt unfastening,. The rustle of his clothes. The sound of my shallow, rapid breath, everything was zoomed in and crystal clear as I waited for him to say something.

His face was no longer able to hide the way he felt, "Since that night..." he said, gripping the steering wheel hard with both hands as I gripped my heart, ready to give it to him. "I've never stopped thinking about you. You're always on my mind."

His words seared through my veins like a hit of heroin. Waves of heat and ecstasy pulsed through my body as I sat unmoving and unable to speak for what felt like an eternity.

"C.J? Did you hear me?"

He deserved that long silence while I absorbed what he'd said, for all the years I'd waited to hear him confess something real, I deserved a moment to let it soak in. When I finally spoke, I committed to not holding anything back. I would say everything I needed to say, I would be honest no matter what the consequences. Whatever this was between us, would be resolved tonight.

"You mean...that night was real?" I said.

"Yes, of course it was real."

"It's just been so many years, I began to wonder if I'd imagined it." I looked down and fidgeted, circling my thumbs. "That night meant something to me. It wasn't a mistake."

"It wasn't a mistake for me either. I knew what I was doing. I still know what I'm doing." I could almost see his heart beating out of his chest like a pop-up valentine's card. "After that night, I didn't know what to do, I didn't know what to think. I wanted to talk to you, I wanted to see you, but what was I supposed to do?"

I shrugged. "I don't know...maybe call me? Tell me how you felt." He tipped his head as if to say...*really?*

"I think about you all the time C.J, more than you'll ever know."

I needed to know and I needed him to tell me. I was done with vagueness, I needed resolve. "I need you to tell me then, cause I don't know."

He hung his head, "I want to tell you but...I'm not the kind of guy who takes another man's wife."

"You didn't take me." I snapped, "I wanted to be with you."

"You know what I mean."

"No, I don't know what you mean. You didn't steal another man's wife. I wanted *you*, remember?"

"It so feels good to hear you say that," he said. "I didn't want to cause problems for your marriage, I just couldn't help myself, with you it's just..." he hesitated, I feared he would retreat again.

"It's just what?"

Grant looked at me with unassuming eyes, "It's just always been you. I can't resist you any longer, I've tried."

An enormous smile grew on my face, "I've waited so long to hear you say that. I don't want you to resist me any longer."

He let out a breath, and with it any residual hesitation, allowing himself to feel for me in a way guilt hadn't allowed him to feel before. His desire was unbound and his blue eyes seduced me when he said, "It's been torture having you right there in front of me all these years."

"Why didn't you say something?!"

"I wanted to, I just couldn't."

Time idled between us as I tried to absorb what he was saying. It was so surreal that if there was ever a time I wondered if I was living on the fringe of reality or fantasy, this was it.

"Maybe we should kiss?" I suggested. "You know...just to see. I mean, we were both pretty intoxicated last time, so...I think we owe it to ourselves to see if there really is something there." He invited me toward him with enticing eyes and a subtle, sinuous smile.

"That, is a great idea."

The gap between us slowly narrowed, our lips seemed to pulse for one another and when they met, it was a perfect seal, muting the outside world, allowing us to savor and cherish our long awaited reunion. Sensual and soft at first, our kiss evolved into an intense rapture. He slid his fingers through my hair and pressed me harder against his full lips. The thrill of kissing him, the fear of getting caught, and the intoxication that came with him wanting me was euphoric. I needed him in my life like I needed air to breath.

This time when our kiss ended his eyes weren't vacant, he wasn't kissing me goodbye, he was begging for more and I found myself crushed into him once again, engulfed in a wildfire that couldn't be extinguished. I was love struck, and for the first time in as long as I could remember, the deep empty well that had become me didn't feel so dry and deserted after all.

I shifted back into my seat, tugging at my bottom lip with my fingers and smiling an uncontrollable smile. "What the hell are we supposed to do now?" I blurted into the silence.

We erupted into a tension breaking laughter.

Then without warning, like he'd done so many times before, he switched, retreated, cowered back into the hole he'd come from.

"I'd better get home," he said. "Do you want me to give you a ride back to your house? Or take you to your car?"

What!

I went from euphoric to dejected in three seconds flat. I wasn't done, my questions weren't answered, this wasn't resolved! I was desperate to know what was going to happen next.

He shifted the car into gear and started driving. He was taking me home.

How can we just leave each other like this—unfinished, unanswered?

"I don't want to go home. I want to be with you," I said abruptly.

"I want to be with you to, but...we can't." He let out a sigh of frustration.

"What do you mean we can't? We already have. I thought you said...I thought you wanted this? Don't take me home, I'm not going there."

"Do you want me to take you to Dylan's then?" His voice was gentle. He knew I was red-hot angry but he didn't know that I'd never felt so unloved and abandoned by his on again off again bullshit.

"No," I said like a stubborn toddler and crossed my arms. "Take me to your place." I cringed at hearing how desperate I sounded, but the freight train of abandonment had started rolling and I couldn't stop it.

He ignored my plea and kept driving.

"I don't want to have sex if that's what you're thinking. I just want to be with you." He didn't respond, he just kept driving toward my house.

How could he do this to me? How dare he tell me those things, kiss me like that, then take me home!

126

I was furious as we approached my neighborhood, unable to stay composed or silent, I snapped.

"I can't fucking believe you are taking me home! You—you liar."

He looked confused. I was confused. He shrugged his shoulders, "What do you want me to do?"

"Take me home," I insisted, "to *your* home."

He stared at the road, "I can't."

I threw my hands up. "Why not?"

"You know why," he said politely, never riled by my rude behavior.

"No, I don't know why. Cause I'm married? That didn't stop you before." He gave me the only expression anyone could after that insult, but I didn't care. "I won't do this again, I can't." I said. "If you don't take me with you tonight...I will never, ever, speak to you again. And I'm not kidding. I will move this time for real, I'll erase you from my life and we will never be friends. You will never see me at the lake, I will be forever dead to you." I waved my hands in the space between us and raised my voice even more, "I can't take this anymore!" Then I laid my vulnerable heart out there for him to stomp on and discard. "I feel something between us, and that kiss...I know you felt it to. I don't know what this is, but it's not normal and it hasn't gone away after all these years. If I'm wrong and you don't feel the same way about me then tell me now and I'll leave you alone forever. I just can't keep doing this."

I waited for him to say something, anything. I waited for him to throw it in reverse, whip a U-turn and take me with him. Or at least step on the gas, push me into oncoming traffic and put me out of my misery. What he did, was so much worse.

He did nothing.

Nothing but stare into the blackness, detached and stoic. I was infuriated as he pulled into my driveway and put the car in park. I waited for him to speak, to at least say goodbye. Then after what seemed like an hour, I realized he was just waiting for me to get out.

A tear rolled down my cheek. I was about to lose him forever and he didn't even care.

127

I'd been so duped, how could I have been so stupid?

I sat at the edge of the seat looking at him, "Tell me you never want to see me again. Please, just do me that favor and make this easy for me."

He was silent, vacant.

I bowed my head, wiped a single tear from my chin and felt a slice of the crushing pain that would hit me as soon as he pulled out of my driveway. I'd cry for weeks, maybe years, maybe another decade.

"I get it, I get the hint," I said. "You don't need to say anything." Then with a fake strength I said, "I'm sorry it had to be this way......I'm sorry you had to see me like this. We can't be friends, I can't be friends. You won't see me again I promise. I won't put myself in this situation ever again, I'll make this easy for both of us."

I shifted in my seat, getting ready to step out but waiting for a brief moment, giving him one last chance to stop me.

Please stop me. Please! It hurts so badly.

Then I turned to him to say a final goodbye. With tears in my eyes I said, "I wish we could have been together in a different lifetime, I have a feeling we would have been really amazing. You are the most incredible man I've ever known and I meant everything I've said. Goodbye."

I opened the passenger door and stepped out into the freezing cold.

Chapter 20

"THESE VIOLENT DELIGHTS HAVE VIOLENT ENDS."

—WILLIAM SHAKESPEARE, *ROMEO AND JULIET*, 2.6.9

A bitter wind sent snow blustering into the car as I stepped outside, and a damp trail of tears across my cheek turned instantly to ice. Whatever this was, it was over. I would keep my promise.

The driveway was polished into a slick skating rink from the fierce winds. I gripped my hands around the frozen roof so I wouldn't fall, then just as I was about to slam the car door and complete my grand tragedy, I felt his warm hand wrap around my inner thigh and tug me back.

Grant leaned over the passenger seat. "C.J.," his voice cracked. "I'm sorry. I never meant to hurt you—I don't want to lose you. Please, come back in here." He tugged me toward the seat and I fell back into the warm leather. I shut the door and sobbed with my face in my hands.

"Don't cry, please I'm sorry...I'm so sorry." His consoling arms surrounded me and he buried his head into the nook of my neck. He stayed there, gripping me tight until I had no more tears to cry. Without saying another word he clicked through the gears and headed toward the other side of town.

We crept into the darkness of his double stall garage.

"I'm sorry for my rant," I said. "I'm so embarrassed. I just..."

"You don't need to apologize or explain anything. I should apologize for not telling you how I felt sooner." He slid his hand into my hair, "I *want* you to stay with me. I'm sorry I didn't tell you sooner. I wasn't lying, I meant everything I said too, I meant everything I have ever said."

I stepped out of his car and stumbled through the darkness until he found my hand. He led me through a maze of unfamiliar belongings then through a doorway. I slipped off my shoes and followed him up a narrow stairway...*to heaven?* I thought, *or is this the ascent before a fatal fall into my own personal hell?*

He didn't show me around or offer me wine—instead he splayed his hands around my hips, pulled me into him then crushed me against the wall. He lavished me with exactly what I needed—him. Our lips moved in sync, tangling soft and deep, ravenous and sensual in just the right moments. Then his strong, forceful grip lifted me from the floor.

I wrapped my legs around his lean waist and slid my hands through his hair, tugging and clenching as he carried me to his bedroom. I was trembling as he set me on the edge of his bed—then, as if I was as light as a silk scarf, he slid me into place gently guiding my head onto his cool sateen pillow.

The insecure girl in me allowed a fleeing jealous thought, or two.

I wonder how many women he's had in this bed. Stop it, C.J.! Don't ruin this, you've probably had more.

I wonder if he still loves any of them? Stop it!

He hovered over me, kissing my bare neck, moving slow, and taking in the contours of my female form. With feather light fingertips and impressive restraint, he respectfully caressed my breasts. He was cherishing me like I was an exquisite silk, careful and attentive, his touch gentle and considerate. He was a mature, sensual man who lingered over my exposed body with his eyes open, taking me in, savoring the moment. In my most desperate hour he bathed me in adoration and desire. He filled my empty well.

A warm glow enveloped me and I laid motionless when he pressed his palm to my chest, holding it there over my heart. He felt it too. He had evolved specifically for me, and apparently I was created only for him and this amorous gesture affirmed those fateful facts.

Streaks of moonlight shone through his bedroom window illuminating our silhouettes as we explored each other deep into the night. Captivated by his masculinity, I was fatally attracted to every part of him—the smell of his skin, the stubble on his face, his sweet breath.

I drug my hands across the landscape of his sinewy back and stroked his flawless bare skin for hours. He joyously teased me, tugging my black-cotton-spandex down below the peaks of my hips, exposing a trim bikini line, then he stopped. He enjoyed watching me wanting him and exerted his dominance just enough to let me know he was enjoying himself as he devoured my female form.

My thighs quivered with excitement and disbelief as he moved slow and deliberate, but respectful not to go too far without permission. And although it would have been easy to fully consummate our affair, we instinctively understood that it could wait. That it would be better if we waited.

Through a long and enchanted night, we laid side by side, our warm bodies intertwined in as many places as possible. I drifted in and out of sublime consciousness until the honey glow of the morning sun peeked into the room. I had to go, before the town woke up, before Dylan saw my car, before we got caught.

***

There was no crossing the center console that morning for a goodbye kiss, no—I'll call you later, no—what should we do now? There was just silence. But it was not a confusing and cold silence like before. This time it was a peaceful silence, filled with calm and certainty and warmth. A warmth from his hand that stayed on me without breaking contact, and a certainty that came from his eyes as he glanced at me from the driver's seat.

There was no going back to our old lives.

When the car stopped, I stared at his blue, blood shot eyes. "Goodbye," I said with a pout and pushed out my lip. He brushed it lightly with his fingertip.

"Not goodbye," He said. "See you later."

I took a deep breath and stepped out into a whirl of blinding snow. As I turned to close the door and look at him one last time, he leaned over the passenger seat and puckered his lips with an audible smack.

"Mwah!"

The moment my Volkswagen gasped to life, Grant waved good-bye, then was gone. I sat on my hands, shivering and watching my breath fog the windows, shaking inside, but not from the cold. My mouth was dry, my hair and clothes were rumpled and my clumped eyelashes from yesterday's mascara irritated my eyes.

I hope to God Levi isn't home.

***

Ur all I ever want. :)

Chapter 21

Grant's fingerprints covered my skin and I smelled like the masculine scent of his sheets. I stripped off my dirty clothes and stuffed them into the washing machine. A foreign, giddy smile gleaned across my face as I stood naked in the laundry room trying to fully comprehend what had just happened.

I impulsively searched for and collected any and all out of place hairs or fibers, any speck of forensic evidence that might have clung to my skin, clothes, or hair. Then I frenzied through a mental check list of what I needed to do to not get caught.

I wiped away fingerprints from the piano and door knobs; I lifted the toilet seat and checked for evidence of over-spray. On my hands and knees I wiped the bathroom floor clean of any hairs or sloughed off skin cells, then scrubbed my own skin until it was raw and sterile.

Wash my clothes—check. Shower—check. Shave, brush my teeth, and examine my skin for scratches or bruises—check, check, check. Search my house for anything he might have dropped—check. Vacuum the carpet, wipe the foyer floor, shovel away the tire tracks and footprints in the driveway—check. Call Dylan to see if it sounds like he suspects anything—check.

Thank God Bodi can't talk!

When my checklist was complete to an OCD level of satisfaction, I collapsed into bed, physically and mentally exhausted. I felt as if I'd been awake for days. My head throbbed as it sunk into my familiar pillow and my body shivered under the cold sheets in my bed of lies. Heavy eyelids forced me into darkness, but restful sleep was not on the menu. A million images of him flashed through my mind, preventing me from slipping into the unconscious world. I'd only been resting for a short time when the vibration and loud ring of my phone jolted me back to reality. It was Dani.

"Hi baby, how are you? Did you have a fun time?" I tried to sound normal, like I wasn't still in bed at noon on a Saturday after an all-night scandalous affair.

"It was fun," Dani said, her voice virtuous.

"When will you be home?"

"I don't know," she moved the phone away from her mouth. "Dad—when will we be home? Dad says we'll be home about three o'clock. I gotta go mom, we're playin' a game."

I hung up then looked at the clock on my phone. I had three hours to figure out how to hide the love struck elation and simultaneous guilt that was surely apparent on my face. First, I scrolled through my contacts just to look at his name. My pulse raced at the sight of it, *Grant E.*

I changed his name to Adam G, held it up, looked at the white lettering with the unfamiliar name and felt as if I had desecrated something sacred. I changed it back, needing to feel connected to some tiny shred of him and I vowed I wouldn't change it again unless I needed to.

The shades were pulled tight, making my bedroom a dark cold den. Huddled in my king size bed with the covers pulled up to my chin, my mind replayed every single moment of what happened the night before. My emotions swung from ecstasy to remorse and I tried to rationalize why what I had done is justifiable.

Married women cheat when they aren't getting what they need at home.

It's just as much Levi's fault as it is mine. I tried to tell him how unhappy I was, I tried to make it work. It takes two people to have an affair.

Although I did feel horrible for cheating on Levi, I wasn't going to let him find out what I had done. *Some things are just better left unsaid, right?*

As three o'clock approached something prodded me to do a triple check for contamination. When I was satisfied that there was no physical evidence of my marital breach, I devoured and entire box of mac n cheese, and then half a tin of Altoids.

"Mommy!" Dani yelled from the foyer.

"Hi sweetheart," I ran to her and knelt down, then glanced up at Levi with artificially white eyes. "Hi. How was your trip?"

"Fine. How was your night, enjoy your time alone?"

"Yeah, I guess," I shrugged, then quickly took Dani downstairs into her room for a few games of Candyland.

The rest of the evening I avoided Levi, terrified that he'd see the thrill of passion hidden just behind my eyes. I stayed silent to conceal the thick layer of lies on my tongue. At bedtime I made my nightly wall of pillows between us, wiggled in my ear buds, and clicked play on "C.J's wooby"—a playlist of dreary songs that could make me cry or put me to sleep.

I felt Levi crawl into bed on the other side of the wall and I knew it would only be a matter of time before he created a fissure in my defensive barrier. I could feel his frustration seeping through the pillow wall then I felt the first unwelcome touch. He gently slid his hands over my skin then rocked me, trying to wake me. I groaned, pretending to be in a deep and grumpy sleep.

Levi punched the bed with his fists, enraged by yet another rejection. Then stormed out of our room mumbling something like, "God! You never want to be with me. You fucking hate me!"

I didn't react, I played dead. He was right. I didn't want to be with him, not sexually or otherwise, and I was making both of us miserable. He didn't deserve a cheating, abusive, neglectful wife, but as hard as I tried, I couldn't be anything but those things for him.

My continual rejection must have been devastating to his self-esteem and I felt terrible for the anguish I caused him, but I couldn't change. I couldn't force myself to love him and desire him like a wife should love and desire her husband. I couldn't force myself to overflow with respect for him where there was only an empty well.

***

Sunday

When is he going to contact me? Am I supposed to contact him? How does this affair thing work? Do I get a divorce right away? How will I afford to live on my own? Who will get the house? Will I have to pay Levi? What about Dani?

Within a few hours, I drove myself nuts asking what-if questions that could not be answered. In an attempt to clear my head, I walked until my back couldn't hold me upright any longer. With Bodi by my side, I stayed on the bike path near main roads hoping that by some miraculous chance Grant would drive by and see me, so we could talk.

I didn't hear from Grant on Sunday and the frightening prospect that maybe, just maybe he'd changed his mind, hit me like a tightly packed snowball to the face. I cried in bed that night.

Monday

It was Monday, and to get to Monday I had to go through agonizing Sunday and he still hadn't contacted me. We didn't have an excuse to see each other, or call each other. I had to talk to him, I had to see him, I could hardly breathe. I was obsessed at a whole new level of mentally ill. I'd become that crazy-girlfriend-stalker that was convinced it would be okay to show up at his work, or wait outside his house for him to come home. I mean, after all, I had earned those privileges after what we'd done, right?

After two irrational and compulsive days I'd already driven myself berserk, so I made a decision, a conviction really, so I wouldn't have to contemplate whether or not I should contact him.

Since I was not thinking clearly or rationally, I would not contact him. If the things he said to me were true, then he would find a way to me.

Tuesday

It was Tuesday! And to get to Tuesday, I had already gone through agonizing Sunday and discombobulated Monday. Drinking Rex Goliath Syrah at three o'clock on a Tuesday was not something I normally did, but on this particular Tuesday it seemed like a perfectly acceptable thing to do.

As I was waiting for a white Owl to fly through my window and deliver my secret letter from my mister, I sat at the dinner table with my laptop and Rex. I decided to Google him but I found nothing. Nothing. It was like he didn't even exist. Then I Googled my own unpopular self and found a dozen links—not one of them important or exciting, but at least I existed. *Why was he a cyber ghost?* I wondered. And, *When IS HE Going TO Contact ME!*

Wednesday

By Wednesday at nine o'clock p.m., I was nearly water boarding myself with Cabernet. Dani was in bed, and Levi lay comatose on the couch downstairs. With my arms draped over the tall mahogany kitchen table and my cheek squished against the cool wood, I over-dramatically felt sorry for myself, moaning and rolling my eyes ad nauseam.

When IS HE Going TO Call ME!

Since I couldn't tell or talk to anyone about my quandary, pent up frustration and impatience manifested itself in the form of over-exaggerated body movements and odd compulsive dance moves in the kitchen.

I checked my e-mail for the fourteenth time in three hours.

That's when I saw it! *Holy shit it's him! It's him!*

To: summerscj2256@gmail.com

From: grant@spyonyou.com

I opened the e-mail that had arrived from heaven. With nothing in the subject line it read...

Dear C.J.,

I am wondering if you sell gift certificates? I would like to get my mom some private sessions with you for her birthday. Maybe pilates or yoga personal training? Let me know what you have available, you can e-mail me or call me on my cell phone 212-555-0975.

Thank you!

Grant

I took a very long pull straight from the narrow opening of the wine bottle, read it again, took another swig, then hit reply. I typed "I spy you" in the subject line.

Dear Grant,

I would love to have your mom as a client. Yes, I do have gift certificates available. I will call you on Saturday so we can discuss.

Looking forward to it, thank you,

C.J.

He replied to my e-mail that night but took "I spy you" out of the subject line.

C.J.

That would be great, I'll keep my phone on me. Call when you get freed up.

Grant

From that Wednesday night through Saturday morning I lapsed into a state of transient global amnesia. I remember nothing. It was like my mind had left the country on sabbatical. When I woke up on Saturday morning I was four pounds lighter, couldn't remember where I had been, and was miraculously, pain free.

Saturday

I circled the Target parking lot like a dog sniffing for the perfect spot to do my deed. Heat blasted through the dashboard slots, drying my eyes and mouth and as I pulled out my phone, pangs of anxiety swirled in my stomach. My heart raced like a champion thoroughbred as I scrolled through my contacts.

Grant E. Just the sight of his name in my palm made me sweat.

He answered on the second ring. "Hello, this is Grant." He sounded scrumptious.

"Hi, it's me."

"What are you doing?" he asked in an all-business voice that was unfamiliar and aloof and I didn't like it.

"Calling you from the Target parking lot." I barked.

I heard him talking to someone in the background. *Yes, I ordered it, all right, sounds good, see you later. Bye.* "Sorry about that, I can talk now. How are you?" He said, his tone softer now, the way it was when we were alone.

"Well, I'm definitely not having the most productive week," I said.

"Me neither. If I get any more distracted, my business will go under." He laughed. There was a small awkward pause as we each searched for something to say. Then to my delight he said exactly what I needed to hear: "C.J., I can't stop thinking about you."

I was awestruck.

"I can't stop thinking about you either. I knew I was attracted to you. I knew we had something. But I didn't expect to feel like this. I can't think, I can't eat, I can't even work." I was so nervous my lips trembled as I spoke.

"I didn't expect this either," he said. "I feel the same way. I need to see you again."

My heart felt like it was about to explode from excitement. "I want to see you too," I said. "You're all I can think about. But if...if *he* finds out," I checked to see if Levi was lurking outside my car, then I whispered into the phone as if someone was listening. "He'll freak."

"I know," Grant agreed.

"Grant, I need you to know that I've never done *this* before. And I never would have but—but it's just...you."

"I've never done this either," he said. "I tried not to think about you, I tried to stay away. I tried not to let this happen, but—" I could hear a quiver in his voice as he spoke. "I've thought about you and wanted you for so long...I can't stay away any more." There was shyness when he spoke and I felt his reluctance to bare his soul to a married woman. I didn't blame him.

"I don't want you to stay away," I said. "I was so happy when I got your e-mail. I was scared you'd never contact me."

"You know I could never do that."

I wanted to trust him, but disbelief loomed inside of me. Grant had left me before. He sensed my reluctance, and from it, he opened his heart to me in a way he had never done before.

"I was scared to send that e-mail," he said, "I hoped Levi didn't check your e-mails, but I had to get ahold of you. I thought about showing up at your work, or waiting by your car, or leaving you a message using an alias."

"I thought about doing all of those things too." We laughed out loud at our similar neurotic compulsions. "Levi doesn't check my email," I said. "He doesn't even know how to use my computer. You can e-mail anytime, it's safe. I thought about contacting you too, but I didn't know if I should..."

"Of course you should," he said. "I wished you would have, I was waiting for you."

"So what do we do now?" I asked.

"When can I see you?"

"Come to the yoga studio after my class tonight. No one will be there."

I heard his rapid breathing, he was still on the line, but he was silent and contemplating my suggestion, analyzing the risks of the proposed rendezvous.

"Are you sure it's safe?"

"Yes. Levi never comes there. Besides, Dani will be in bed and he can't leave her home alone."

"What about your coworkers? Isn't there anyone else who has a key?"

"Yes, but it'll be late, they won't be there. And we'd hear if someone came in anyway. I would just tell them you're one of my clients."

They would know he's not just one of my clients. I don't take clients that late at night, nor do any of my clients even remotely exist in his caliber of man-hot.

"I'll be there. What time?" he said with an enthusiasm that delighted me.

"Eight-thirty. Text me when you're close, and I'll open the door for you."

"I don't know about texting…" he said sheepishly.

"I know. They can be traced right? Like on Dateline when the husband kills his wife and gets busted because of a text message he sent to his mistress after the deed was done?"

He laughed and confirmed my suspicions. "Everything can be traced."

"I pay my cell bill every month, I don't get paper statements and his name is not on my account so he'll never see it anyway. I'll change my passwords too."

"That's a good idea. Do that," Grant said.

"He won't see them. Trust me. He doesn't even text. He's still got a flip phone."

"If he suspects something, he'll figure out how to text."

"You're right." I felt paranoid that somehow Levi already knew about Grant. I scanned the parking lot to see if he'd followed me. "I'll keep my phone on me twenty-four seven, I'll be really careful. You know I will."

"I know you will," Grant said, "We wouldn't be having this conversation if I didn't trust you."

"See you tonight," I said in the most seductive way possible.

"I can't wait."

"Oh hey, I just remembered, did you want me to bring that gift certificate for your mom?"

We burst out laughing simultaneously, then said goodbye and hung up the phone.

***

I meticulously prepared for the ancient ritual by placing a single drop of sensual jasmine into each candle. Then I mindfully lit each wick while sending up a request to make this night unforgettable.

Like tiny earth-bound stars, one hundred warm glowing flames reflected off the windows, illuminating the Yoga studio.

***

*Let's kiss? That would
be great! Missing u, babe.
Ur always popping into my brain. :)*

Chapter 22

"AS A LOTUS FLOWER IS BORN IN WATER, GROWS IN WATER

AND RISES OUT OF WATER TO STAND ABOVE IT UNSOILED,

SO I, BORN IN THE WORLD, RAISED IN THE WORLD

HAVING OVERCOME THE WORLD, LIVE UNSOILED BY THE WORLD."

—BUDDHA

Warm vanilla candles created a blurry line of twinkling flames in the window sills of the second floor yoga studio. I set out the little silver tins until every last one in the bag was gone.

Enchanting sounds from an ancient time reverberated through the great room as the Gayatri Mantra hummed on repeat. Heat billowed into the sacred space from the corrugated vents in the ceiling, we stripped away our clothing—allowing our bodies the freedom to undulate and rediscover their natural suppleness.

My hair was fastened loosely beneath a thick headband while Ganesha sat perched on my earlobes wishing me good fortune. Shiva was ever present to assist me in dissolving that which I no longer needed, to make room for those things that were my true destiny. I folded myself into siddha yoni asana then struck the meditation bowl three times with a worn-out wooden mallet. Like a stone being tossed into still water, the sound of Om rippled through the room, creating a contagious calmness.

"Good evening yogis, welcome to candlelight yoga." I said in hushed voice.

I'd been a yoga devotee since I was nineteen, my practice was traditional. I didn't just do yoga, or go to yoga. I lived a life inspired by Yogic philosophy. I understood that Yoga was never meant to be a workout for your butt. Rather its ancient pathways are a blueprint for living life to its fullest potential. I understood that the physical movements were only one small spoke on the wheel, and that I would have to practice clean eating and non-stealing and contentment more than I would have to work on my physical strength.

On this particular night, my enlightened self could hardly remember how to teach the ubiquitous salutations, or speak the Sanskrit words I had spoken a thousand times before. My mind had deserted me. My calm, centered, yogi core had unraveled.

I cheated my class out of a full savasana, stopping uncharacteristically early to shoo everyone out the door. I expected him at any moment. My phone was stuck to my palm anticipating the quick buzz, but I looked at it every sixty seconds anyway, *just in case.* When the screen finally lit up the darkness with its bold white lettering, it read...

Can't wait 2 see u!
B there in 5. :)

I leapt down the stairs when I heard the knock and there he was, standing outside the glass door without a winter jacket, his hands stuffed into his jeans pockets. He turned his face away from the passing cars, and we exchanged muffled laughter through the glass as I fumbled with the keys in the lock.

"Could you have picked a place with more windows?" He asked as he stepped inside rubbing his cold hands together.

I shrugged, "Its fine, don't worry."

The fact was that I hadn't thought that one through. I'd just led him into a house of glass. Windows from the ground to the wooden ceilings covered the entire studio, and where there were no windows, there were mirrors. Mirrors that reflected our images in several locations, making us quadruple visible.

"Come on," I said, then pulled him by his shirt up the stairs and into the center of the candlelit studio.

"C.J, this is amazing. I wanna do yoga," he said, circling around, taking it all in.

"I would love to teach you yoga, I have a special kind just for you," I said with an eyebrow raised and naughty intentions.

"I hope you do," he stepped toward me, examining my garb and wild haired yogi look.

"You're so sexy, baby. I've missed you," he said, pulling me close, procuring me. Like a bodyguard, he enveloped me and made me feel safe when I was with him. I wrapped my arms around him and pressed my ear to his chest. With my eyes closed I listened to the unique rhythmic thumping that belonged only to him; a heartbeat that became etched into my memory forever

"So, this is what you do." He said.

It was his first glimpse into this side of my life. "Partly," I said. "Mostly I see clients in private sessions for weight loss or I teach people how to cook healthy."

"Can I be one of your clients? I want to get healthy."

I sucked in a deep hesitant breath, tilted my head and grit my teeth, "I'm sorry, I'm not taking any new clients at this time. I can put you on my waiting list though."

He gave me a sly grin, "Show me something," he said, then stepped back to give me room like I was about to give him a strip tease.

"What do you want to see?"

"I want to see that one thing you do on your hands with your legs out to the side. Like in the picture."

I furrowed my eyebrows. "What picture?"

"You know, that one on your website."

He went to my website?

I took a step back, "Are you stalking me?"

"Yes," he said playfully, pulling me close. "I've looked at your pictures many times."

My mouth fell open, "You have?" I was secretly thrilled.

"Yes. I love that one of your big, beautiful brown eyes. The one where you're hiding behind a book." He pulled me in tighter, then swayed us side to side as if we were dancing.

"Well, I have a confession too," I said.

"What's that?"

145

"Two confessions actually. I Googled you."

"Find anything good?"

"No. In fact, I couldn't find anything." I pulled my head back and squinted my eyes suspiciously at him. "I'm not sure you are who you say you are."

"Quit it," he laughed. "What's your second confession?"

"Remember that day a few years ago when we played super-snipers and bocce ball at the lake?"

"Yes, of course I remember that day. I remember you looked hot in that little black bikini with your tight little tush." He slid his hands down my back and caressed my curves, a major distraction, that made it hard to finish my thought.

"After I developed the pictures we took that day, I had to hide them because we were inseparable and naughty, and it showed in the photos. In every picture we were glued to each other. My confession is that I couldn't throw them out, I hid them in a book and I secretly look at them."

"What about the video you took?" He said like a light bulb had went off. "The one from my birthday."

"Let me tell you what I did with that video.: I watched it as soon as I could, so I could see you again. It was torture watching it, seeing us having fun like that and not being able to be with you."

"Torture for you," he said, "this has been torture for me!"

"Anyways, I destroyed it, immediately after watching. It was way too incriminating. Hey, speaking of incriminating, did you ever find a shirt? I sort of lost mine on that one night I was with you." My face cringed, we both knew to which night I was referring.

"Yes."

"You did! I always wondered where it went. Where did you find it?"

"In my bedroom, on the floor. Thank God I found it before my mom did," he added, "She might have recognized it was yours."

"Your Mom?" I said, aghast. "Your parents were in the cabin that night, weren't they?"

He flinched, "Yes."

My jaw dropped. "Why did you bring me there then?"

"It's a family cabin, you know how that is, what else were we supposed to do?" He shrugged, "I can't believe how gutsy we were," he added, "so blatantly obvious in public. I thought for sure someone would see us, and that eventually we'd get caught."

"Me too." I said, "I've missed you every day since that night."

"I've missed you too. But I'm here now."

He looked down at me with eyes the color of Caribbean water. He was sumptuous in the candlelight and everything about him enchanted me. At the same time, everything about him caused a flutter of heartbreak.

"I wish it didn't have to be like this," he said, as he wrapped his arms around me in layers, each time squeezing me a tiny bit tighter. He laid his head on the top of mine. "I wish we could be together under different circumstances."

"I can't lose you again," I mumbled, my face fused to his torso.

"I'm right here, baby. I'm right here." He said, reassuring me.

"Grant," I pulled away to look at him. "I don't want to be with Levi. I don't love him and I should have left years ago."

"You don't have to explain yourself to me."

"I want to, it's terrible living with him and thinking of you. It feels so wrong, I hate it. I just…"

I couldn't finish my sentence, I didn't know what I was going to do, or where I would live, or how someone even files for divorce or what that even means?

We stood in the flickering shadows holding one another.

"What do we do now?" I asked, hoping he had a plan, a long-term solution to our conundrum. I hoped he would tell me what to do so I didn't have to decide on my own.

He didn't. "I don't know," he said, shaking his head, "I don't know. I just know I want to be with you."

Our web of less-than-desirable circumstances was complex and gut-wrenching to think about. There would be so many things to work through.

How would Dylan react? What would I tell Dani? My family would not approve of a divorce. Would his family ever accept me if they knew all of this? How could I ever look at his mom again?

Bam. Bam. Bam. Bam!

"Shit! Who is that?" Grant whispered. His face was mortified as he grabbed my shoulders and bore holes through me with his eyes.

"I don't know. No one is supposed to be here."

Chapter 23

"THE COURSE OF TRUE LOVE NEVER DID RUN SMOOTH."

—WILLIAM SHAKESPEARE, *A MIDSUMMER NIGHT'S DREAM*, 1.1.134

Bam. Bam. Bam. Bam!

Whoever it was, pounded on the door so hard it rattled through both floors. My mind swept the building for places to hide Grant.

Thai room—nope. Bathroom—nope. Out the window? Yes—out the window, onto the roof, he'd have to figure it out from there.

"You can go out the window," I said. "It goes to the roof, but I don't know where from there."

"It's below zero outside!" he said desperately, "Go look out the window, see if you can see who it is first."

I peeked out of the second story window looking down on the front door, trying to get a glimpse of the knocker. I pressed my nose against the cool glass and could hear my heart beating loud in my ears.

I exhaled a massive sigh of relief when I saw her wavy hair, "It's just my Russian friend, Galina."

Galina was a rebellious Russian with muddy red, curly locks and a black belt in Tae Kwon Do. "She's already walking away," I said as I clutched my heart and took a step back from the window. "She does stuff like this, holy shit my heart is pounding."

"Mine too." Grant said. "What time do you have to be home?"

I frowned, "ten-thirty. I told Levi I was going to the grocery store after I was done teaching. What time is it?"

Grant squeezed the tiny button on his silver, waterproof watch. The watch I'd seen him wear every summer for as long as I could remember; the watch that was somehow a part of him, like a tattoo. It hugged his tan, lean forearm just above his wrist bones. For some inexplicable reason, I felt privileged to be close to it, close to a small piece of his real life. I'd often wondered where he'd gotten that watch, and why he took such care not to lose it and why he wore it everywhere.

I wanted to learn about all the small details of his life, I wanted to be *in* all the small details of his life. I wanted to rent movies together and go through the car wash and kiss, I wanted to know if he liked his pillow soft or firm, or if he liked highlander grog or plain Arabica. I imagined what it would be like to be a part of that life, his real life. A life he let very few people into. I knew that if by some miracle it happened, it would be extraordinary.

"It's nine forty-five. You'd better go."

I whined and burrowed into him, "I don't want to go. I want to spend the night with you."

He pressed his lips to my forehead and took a deep breath, "I wish you could too...in time," he said, "in time." He gave me a tender squeeze then let me go.

I would have stayed with him all night, regardless of the consequences. "Just a few more minutes," I begged.

He laughed softly and pulled me back into him. "Of course, baby. I want to give you everything you need."

I tilted my head back inviting him into my lips, "I need you."

"I'm not going anywhere," he said, securing me in his gaze. "I need *you*." His words took my breath away, literally. Somehow him wanting me, made it hard to breathe, made my chest ache in pain and pleasure at the same time.

We blew out the remaining candles then walked through the darkness back down the stairs. On the bottom step he grabbed my arm, spun me around, then indulged me in a long kiss goodnight. A feverish kiss. The kind of kiss you get from a man indulging in the moment.

"Text me when you're in for the night, if you can, only if you can," he said. "Don't take any chances."

"I will, and I won't."

"Remember to delete any texts you send, and any you receive—then delete the deleted texts. Right?"

"Believe me, Grant, I will." And I did. But not until after I wrote each one of them down in a word document and saved them to my computer under the file name "favorite book quotes."

"Goodnight, baby." He kissed me one last time before he walked away.

As he disappeared into the blustery night I wallowed on the bottom step, overcome with emotion. Sadness, elation, hope, fear were mixed up into mess of feelings.

Then after what I deemed to be a reasonable amount of time for us not to be seen together I stood up, ready to leave, and found my lower body paralyzed from piercing pain.

Pain seared across my lower back and forced me to my knees, I gripped the handrail to keep from falling, and when I tried to move again, that's when I heard it.

Pop!

It was a pop like when you smack your lips together. Except this pop was much deeper, more muffled and dense followed by crunching and grinding sounds when I moved. It was a crackling noise you might hear at bonfire, not something normal coming from a living body.

I hobbled through the bitter wind and plunked down into my frozen car. Barely able to lift my left leg to push in the clutch, I drove in third gear most of the way home, coasting to the stop lights, praying for green so I wouldn't have to start over from first gear.

At the grocery store, I pushed a cart so I could lean on it, dug out my extra-large bottle of Ibuprofen and grabbed a water from the check-out stand. I twisted the seal and chugged, not caring that I hadn't paid for it yet. I gathered up a few items to make my trip legitimate then headed for home. The pain slowly subsided but after that night, it never went away again.

Going home to Levi felt like cheating on Grant. Had it been the other way around and Grant was going home to his wife...it would have been intolerable for my fragile female ego. I would have drove myself nuts thinking about them. *Would he have sex with her? Would he show her the same affection he showed me? When is he going to leave her?* I would have made a horrible mistress.

As my garage door shut, I took a moment to re-read, commit to memory so I could write it down later, then delete any incriminating data from my phone. I hobbled into the foyer with my plastic grocery bags and the fear of Grant's scent in my hair. The house was dark and silent, I put away my strawberries and Boca burgers, went into Dani's room, kissed her pale smooth cheek then retreated to my bedroom exhausted, ready for sleep.

When I opened the door I saw the familiar flicker of candle flames.

***

*Goodnite, baby. :) I wish
I were next to u right now.
We fit so fcking gr8 2gether!*

Chapter 24

"A WOMAN OF WORTH IS A CROWN TO HER HUSBAND;

BUT SHE THAT MAKETH ASHAMED IS AS ROTTENNESS IN HIS BONES."

—PROVERBS 12:4

Levi was sprawled out on top of the covers in nothing but his bare torso and boxers.

"Hi sweetheart," he said, "I've been waiting for you." The tone of his voice already trying to seduce me.

I let out an annoyed sigh then muttered, "hi," in the most irritated, *don't-even-try-to-fucking-touch-me,* way possible, then walked past him and into the closet. I pulled out an old T-shirt, a clean pair of panties, and the ugliest sleep shorts I could find, then went into the bathroom to undress and avoid an unwanted mauling.

Knowing he was expecting...*it,* I lolly-gagged in the shower, dilly-dallied brushing, flossing and whitening my teeth, tweezed my eyebrows and clipped my toenails. Then I sat on the ledge of the tub, turned off the audible click of text messaging and smiled at the thought of *him.*

> *I'm so glad I got 2 see u*
> *2nite! U make me melt.*
> *I'll txt u 2morrow. I'm*
> *going 2 bed. Don't text*
> *back. :) Goodnite.*

Then I deleted the message, then deleted the deleted message.

After what must have been forty five minutes I stuffed in my headphones, slipped my phone between my hip and the elastic of my shorts, then executed my plan: act tired, complain about being exhausted, listen to music, ignore him.

I walked around to my side of the bed, fluffed my pillow, then discretely slid it in-between us creating my nightly barrier. I laid on my side with my back to him and pulled the comforter up to my chin.

"Goodnight," I whispered into the candlelight and yawned, "what a long day, I'm so tired."

The flickering shadow growing larger on the wall told me I wasn't going to get off that easy. I felt Levi mosey closer to me, then drape himself over the pillow barrier.

"I thought maybe we could be romantic." He said in the most gentle, tip-toeing way, making me feel terrible for rejecting him for the trillionth time when he was trying to be sweet.

"I don't think so; I don't feel up to it."

Please, please, please, let that work.

"You don't have to do anything," He said as he slid his hand onto my flank. "You always like it once we get into it." His voice was optimistic, not yet laced with the tone of bitter rejection—but that would come.

"You're right I do. But I really can't tonight, I have to get up early tomorrow." I silently begged him to stop and resisted the urge to ask him to *please take your hand off me.* I pulled the barrier pillow snug against my back and wrapped myself tighter into the comforter. I sensed the looming freak-out.

"God! You never want to have sex, I'm your husband! What do you expect me to do?"

Jerk off?

"My own wife doesn't even want to touch me, do you know how that makes me feel?" He said as he pressed his face close to mine. He knew how to push my buttons, how to rile me. But on that night I just cowered into my pillow, wanting to go to sleep, trying not to get angry.

"I know, I'm really sorry, I just can't make myself do it when I don't want to," I pleaded.

He got out of bed, threw his hands up and yelled, "well why don't you want to? Do you think I'm disgusting or something? Why won't you even kiss me?"

154

"Levi calm down, it's too late to argue like this. Besides, you don't want to sleep with me when I'm not into it anyway, what fun is that?"

"You're my wife. You should want to!"

I sighed, annoyed by his comment, but I knew he was right. I *should* want to, but I didn't.

"You really are a cold hearted bitch, you know that?"

"Yes, I know that. But thank you for reminding me." I stuffed my head further into my pillow and started to cry, most of it fake, hoping it would make him go away.

"Oh great, now *your* crying when *I* should be the one upset—figures."

Levi rustled with his pillows then ripped the comforter from my listless body, leaving me cold and exposed. He mumbled something as he was leaving then slammed the bedroom door. I flung myself up, grabbed a blanket from under the bed, blew out the candle then patted the empty space beside me as I called for Bodi.

"Come here boy, come on. Come snuggle."

Bodi lept from his cool spot on the floor, wiggled his miniature rust colored tail, then curled himself into a circle next to me. He tucked his snout into the warmth of his hind legs and closed his eyes, unaffected by our outburst.

I pressed play on my iPod and tried to do the same. "Moonlight Sonata," again.

***

In order to avoid a catastrophe, Grant and I established rules for communication:

(1) He can't call me, only I can call him.

(2) He can't text me unless I text him first. I will let him know if he can or can't text back.

(3) If a text seems "off," it might be a trap and he'll respond with *I think I have the wrong number? Who is this?* If it *is* me, then I will respond with, "It's me, you Dingo."

(4) All text messages sent, received and deleted must be deleted after reading, as well as the call logs.

(5) If he needed to get a hold of me, he could send me an e-mail, which also must be deleted after reading, along with the delete folder and recycle bin, just in case.

I was reading and sending so many text messages and e-mails each day, I didn't have time to work. My clients got fat, I was late for appointments, and my brain was a jumbled up maze of racing thoughts, all of which looped back to *him.*

Going to the grocery store was my usual alibi so I could sneak away and call him. He answered right away, he always answered right away.

"Hello, this is Grant," he said in a serious tone, like it was a business call, as if he didn't know it was me.

"Hello," I said, in a faked voice. "Is this the Grant that likes to hook up with his best friend's sister?"

"Yes, it is true, and I need to be punished." We shared a giddy chuckle. "When can I see you again, baby?"

"Soon I hope. I miss you," I said.

"I miss you too. When can you get free?"

"How about Wednesday night?"

"Perfect. What will you tell Levi?"

"I'll tell him I have in-home sessions, he has no idea where my clients live or who they are, and he doesn't suspect anything anyway, so it'll be fine." Grant snickered at my deviousness, he wasn't thrilled to be sneaking around but he was happy I was thinking ahead and wiping our prints clean. "You pick the place this time."

"Hmmm, yes, I'll pick. Somewhere without glass walls. Come to my office, no one is there at night."

"I would love to come to your office."

"Great, I can't wait to see you and your tight little tush again," he said. "Do you think you'll have another chance to call today?"

"I'll make an opportunity."

"I'll keep my phone on me but I might not have a signal where I'm hiking, so leave a message if it's okay to call back."

"Aww, I want to go for a hike," I whined. "Where are you?"

"The Superior Trail near Duluth."

"Ugh...*fun*, I wish I was there," I pushed out my bottom lip, "will you bring me sometime?"

"Yes. Baby, you know we will go hiking many, many times."

"*Promise?*" I said, like an insecure teen asking her first boyfriend to never break up with her.

"Of course I promise." He spoke with a confidence I didn't yet have. "You should send me some pics today," he suggested in the most scandalous tone.

"I'll send one if you send one," I said.

"Um...I'll think about it."

"Come on, it's only fair that way."

"Okay, if you send me some really good ones, then I'll seriously consider it. Gotta go babe, Mwah!" He said as he smacked his lips.

After we hung up, I sat in my car with the windows sealed tight, cut-off from the outside world I basked in his attention, smiling and giggling to myself like I'd just been asked out by the cutest boy in school. I soaked up the feelings of being wanted by the most wanted man I'd ever known.

Later that day I sent the first sext. A pic of my nude legs from the top of my inner thighs to my toes, submerged in a steamy bath. It got an immediate response.

> *Oh God, babe. I almost*
> *choked! Sexy! More, more!*
> *I wish I were in that bath. ;)*

> *I wish u were 2. :0*

Then he sent one of himself. Not too daring, but admirable. His whitey tighties peaked out of his jeans and clung to his subtly toned torso. His arms and chest were firm, defined but not huge, just delicious. His phone covered his handsome profile, concealing his identity.

Now it was my turn again. I pulled open the top drawer of my dresser to find something to put on, only to be mortified that I didn't own lingerie in any other color than some shade of old-lady-beige. I immediately went to Victoria's Secret, bought a dozen colors of cotton thongs and a few lacy push up bras.

So that Levi didn't find my new, barely-there trove, I stashed all but a couple of the panties in my gym locker. Then stuffed a few of the not-so-obvious pieces in my underwear drawer behind the sea of don't-touch-me taupe.

Black lace bra, deep purple panties, face concealed, click, send...

So fucking hot, baby!
More, more, more!

Black lace bra, deep purple panties, *tugged down*, face concealed, click, send...Every picture received an immediate reaction.

Ur in so much trouble,
u hot sexy babe! Quit it.
Ur torturing me! Okay.
Send more. :D

I was eager to please, so I kept the naughty pictures uploading, each a little more risky than that last. I tried to send them during his most inopportune times, during work meetings, conference calls, while he was training in an employee, or solving some complicated mathematical equation. I tried hard to match up his every work obligation with a near nudie.

Ur gunna get it!

I sent him the most scantily clad picture when I knew he was having dinner with his family. No bra, no panties, cheeky shorts barely on one cheek, click, send...

U fucking hottie, wearing
my fave shorts. Maybe we
could slide them over and
slide me in. :0

I'm not sending another
Until u send 1 to me. And
it'd better be good!

I patiently waited for the chime, and when it came in, my mouth fell open. His handsome face was shrouded by his phone, and his package was concealed behind an army green duffel bag that sat on top of a bathroom counter. He was blissfully indecent and completely out did me with the full nudie. I immediately responded.

Holy shit, u r so hot!
Nice duffel bag. :) Im
so lucky!

No, I am the lucky 1. :)

Really? Did he really feel lucky to be with me? I read it twice, once out loud, but I still couldn't believe it.

I wasn't daring enough to send a full nudie so I had to figure out another way to one-up him. This weekend, when he was on stage, when I knew he couldn't answer his phone—I'd leave him a red-hot naughty voice mail. *After* I indulged in a few full glasses of Cabernet.

***

It was finally Wednesday.

As planned, I told Levi, "I have to work late tonight, I have in-home clients. I should be home around ten or sometime after."

"You sure have to work late a lot," he huffed.

"I have a client that wants to get in. Its good money, what do you care anyway?"

He spoke with disdain. "I *don't* care. I was just saying."

159

I kissed Dani goodbye, flung my bag onto my shoulder and walked out. I did actually see a client or two, but canceled my last session, spewing some lame lie from my unfaithful lips so I could free up an additional hour to be with Grant.

I made the forbidden call. "I'm free," I said. Wishing I was saying those words and referring to an entirely different context.

"Great, I've been waiting for you. Can't *wait* to see you. Pull around to the south side of the building, then park next to the big van so it conceals your car from the road."

I did what he said. I hid my little car behind the big van with *Spy2* on the license plate, next to a long rectangular warehouse. He was waiting for me at the side door and pulled me in by my sleeve.

A white box with glowing green buttons was mounted on the wall just inside the door. I watched as he punched in a few numbers arming the system, then turned back to the door and looked in all directions to make sure I wasn't followed. When he was satisfied that I was alone, he gave me a playful rough kiss then pulled me swiftly behind him. I found myself in a dark sprawling warehouse with boxes stacked on shelves to the ceiling.

"You look so good, baby—my sexy vixen," he said. Then tugged me into him, lifted the cheeky black mini skirt that clung to my yoga pants and inspected me, "I like this."

Then he slid his fingertips down the length of my arm then into my palm, brushing past my wedding ring as he interlacing our hands. Our palms pressed together tightly, and I was acutely aware of the cold metal wedged between us.

Taking off my wedding ring would be so final and I wasn't quite ready. Everything had happened so fast, I didn't have time to think through what my plan was. I knew I had to make some hard decisions, plan my getaway. It all felt so paralyzing, I didn't know how or where to begin. The only thing I knew was that I couldn't keep having an affair. I hated the way lies felt on my tongue and how guilt sat heavy on my shoulders.

"Is there anyone here?" I asked as I draped myself over him.

"No, baby, just us."

**

*Honey, u are so fucking
hot! Loved our time 2 gether. :D
Now, let's do it again. Yes, please.
Thank you. :)*

Chapter 25

BE·LO·EVD: A PERSON WHO IS GREATLY LOVED —DICTIONARY.COM

I remember that night at his office with a crisp clarity. It was the night that he told me he loved me.

I clutched his shoulders as he hoisted me onto a wooden work bench then nudged my knees apart. He stood between them without hesitation and gave me exactly what I needed:

An eternal blissful kiss.

The kind of kiss that even when it ends, your soul remembers, the kind of kiss that plays in your mind for all of eternity, the kind of kiss that a man gives a woman when his instincts to roam have been tamed. His breath was sweet, his tongue minty, and his intention was clear.

He was loving me.

I felt it, I heard it, I even believed it, at the time. But there was still a voice deep inside me reminding me that when it's too good to be true, it probably is. It was that voice that never allowed me to fully feel what he was offering. It was that voice that made me question his every word and touch a hundred times over. I laid my head on top of his shoulder and he wrapped me in his arms. Layer by layer, tighter and tighter until he enveloped all of me.

"Grant, is this for real?" I asked.

"It is for me."

"Sometimes I feel like you're still holding back. I mean, I understand why you would be, but...I feel like there's so much more to us than we talk about; I feel like we have something that most people only dream of but never get to experience. Do you feel that way too?"

"C.J.," he said quietly, "I feel it. Trust me, I feel it. And I'll keep showing you if you let me. I won't hold back anymore." He interlaced his fingers behind the sensitive skin of my lower back and melted into me.

"It's you baby," he whispered with his lips on my skin, "I can't believe it's you and that you're really here."

"I'm sorry I put you in this position," I said, my voice strained. "I wish we didn't have to sneak around."

"It's kinda fun," he said with a devious grin.

"Will you still want me when I'm not so taboo?"

"Of course," he gushed, "Baby, don't even think like that. I'll always want you. I don't like sneaking around either, but let's do what we have to so we can be together."

"Grant, I don't want to be with Levi. It was just too hard to leave. I know that's not an excuse to stay but..." I trailed off, I couldn't finish, couldn't admit to how big of a coward I was. How I'd stayed only because I was too afraid to leave. "I don't love him like a wife should love her husband," I said. "I haven't for as long as I can remember. In fact, I don't even like him anymore. I need you to know that when I go home, I don't have sex with him. I haven't had sex with him for months, and before that, it was just pity sex anyway." I shook my head, embarrassed at the dysfunctional marriage I'd helped to create and had been too afraid to get out of.

"Baby, it shouldn't be like that," he moved in to seduce me. "With us..." he said, looking through my eyes and into my soul, "it won't be like that. I promise." He held my face in his hands, "You do know how much I care about you, don't you?"

I turned up my palms, eternally insecure, gesturing for him to tell me as many times as he could possibly tolerate. "I care about you more than you know," he said.

Is that code for I really care about you but don't love you?

He must have sensed my need for never ending reassurance. He gripped me tight to his body. "I need you, C.J.," he said. "I want you in my life. I'll take care of you if you let me, and Dani too."

More than anything, I wanted him to take care of me, and Dani too, if the time came for that. I had to get out of my marriage first and I had to do it by myself. He couldn't be involved in that, not any more than he already was.

"I'll never tell you what to do," he said, "and I would never ask you to do anything. I want to be with you, and I'm here for you, for whatever you need. I've waited this long, haven't I?"

"Yes, you have," I said. "But you don't have to wait anymore. I'm yours, my home is with you."

After another blissful kiss, he led me back through the plastic hanging doorway, past the work cars; Spy1, Spy3, and into the foyer outside his office. The light was still on and the door was cracked open.

"Is this your office?" I asked and took a step forward anxious to gather any intel into his tightly guarded private life. "Let me see."

He squeezed my hand and pulled me away from the door, "Don't go in there."

"Why not?" I pushed open the door, and my jaw dropped onto the filthy floor.

Red flag, red flag!

"Oh my God! This is a disaster," I gasped. "It looks like wild monkeys live here. How in the hell do you find anything?" I stood in one place, the only place to stand, and I circled around.

"I don't." He laughed, "It's a problem. Sometimes it takes me twenty minutes to find my car keys."

"Twenty minutes? I'm surprised you find anything at all. You told me you were disorganized, but this isn't disorganized. This is hoarding."

I walked further into the lair of filth—my first peek into his secretive world.

Not so impressed.

Half a dozen coffee mugs peppered what I assumed was a desk, each one sprouting its own furry greenish animal. The carpet looked like the floor of a feed lot, littered with dirt and straw, and stacks of paper overflowed from the desk into the garbage, the garbage onto the floor, and the floor to the ceiling. Heaps of who-knows-what was fanned out in every direction smothering most of the walking space. An out of place Terry Redlin print hung crooked on the wall next to an air conditioner that dangled from a few red wires.

"Come on, let's get out of here, this is embarrassing," he said tugging on my shirt.

"Well it should be," I snarked, "Don't you ever throw things away?"

He walked past me and let out a frustrated groan, then sat down in his office chair and spun in a circle holding his arms out as if to say see...it's not that bad. He was comfortable in his office filth.

"You need help," I said, then stood between his legs. He laid his head to the side as I drew my fingers through his dark, fine hair. I kneaded and squeezed his neck and shoulders while he purred with sounds of pleasure.

He looked up at me with bloodshot eyes and bed head, "That feels so good, I wish you could stay."

"Me too." I said, then kissed his lips and wriggled out of his grip. I reluctantly walked away, every step in the opposite direction of him felt wrong and painful in so many ways. I leaned against the door frame not wanting to leave. "I miss you when I go—I didn't know it could be like this." I shook my head in amazement at what we'd found with each other.

"I guess this is how it feels when two people find true love."

What?

What did he say?

Did he just say he loved me?

I mean, I dreamed he would tell me that, but certainly not this soon, and certainly not until after I'd said it first, or at least until after I was divorced. I was so dumbfounded, I couldn't respond. I just winked, then turned and walked away.

Those words, his words, became emblazoned on my heart forever.

***

Cheating on Levi felt right. It felt guilty, and disrespectful, but it still felt right. After my office rendezvous with Grant, I blasted through my front door overconfident and filled with excitement more than I was consumed with remorse. I wasn't going to take any shit from Levi. He was not going to ruin my secret bliss. Or so I thought.

That night Levi cornered me as soon as I got to the kitchen. He spattered out some nonsensical fragments about how nobody loves him and how he doesn't even exist.

Pity party, table of one.

Nothing was more off-putting to me than an unconfident man, and Levi had become the most un-confident man I knew. Surely I'd contributed to his unraveling, but it wasn't me alone who caused his self-destruction.

Levi would forever be the laid-back, fun guy. I would forever be the sole bearer of decisions at the dentist, the doctor and school conferences; the parent that thinks it's not okay for our kids to do the things we did as teenagers, that it's not okay to smoke pot out of a coke can or drive the back country roads just to have a place to drink. I would forever be the mean mom who says no, after he's already said yes.

No matter the amount of conversations, arguments, or attempts at compromise, Levi and I were never going to see eye-to-eye on the things that mattered the most. We would never have conversations about politics; I would vote one way, and he would vote the other. I tried to save for retirement, learn how to invest, and figure out a plan for the rest of our lives, he just never seemed interested. I wanted to travel, to live, and see the world, he liked staying home.

When I wanted to fix our marriage I came home with books, ideas, and plans for us to find what we'd lost, but he didn't think anything was wrong. I even tried to change enough for the both of us so he wouldn't have to. I ignored my innermost feelings and took my mom's advice instead.

I laid down and took it.

In more ways than one. Even when I didn't want to. *But since it wasn't hurting me, and it made him happy,* mom said, *it was okay to do that. Sacrifice makes a happy marriage.* So I pimped myself out to my husband.

I tried to focus on Levi's good qualities and not his bad. I gave up on living an outgoing, social life and started living like someone I was not with the hope I would settle into it, and save my marriage. But the real me could not be dissolved or stuffed down. Eventually I would always creep back to who I really was.

It had been eleven years since the first night I met Levi, and five since we'd been married. I'd been with him long enough to know that I'd made a colossal mistake.

I had to start distancing myself even more, I would need to tell him soon. He couldn't go on thinking things were fine, oblivious to my detachment and looming disappearance.

"What's wrong with you? Don't you love your family anymore? You're never home," Levi said as I rummaged through the refrigerator for a late night snack.

"Bullshit," I said, hiding behind the condiments, "I'm just not here when you're here." I pulled out a jar of pickles. "I take Dani to school and pick her up, every day and I'm with her every night. How dare you say I'm never home." Glass bottles clanked together as I whacked the door shut with my elbow.

"I never see you anymore." Levi said, his voice pleading.

"Maybe that's because I want it that way. Look at us, all we do is fight." I set the pickles on the island and popped the lid.

"Is there someone else?" Levi said calmly.

Shit, what did he see? Nothing, I've been extra careful, he's just guessing.

"No, there's not someone else," I scoffed, hostile and defensive. "Don't you get it?" I yelled. "How many times do I have to tell you? I'm. Not. Happy!"

"Stop it," he said antagonizing me, "You exaggerate, it's not that bad."

There's nothing like invalidation to make a wife feel lonely and unheard. I hung my head, thoroughly invalidated...once again.

"Come here," Levi said as he extended his arms and took a step toward me. Which inferred that he expected me to go from screaming mad, to spreading my legs. The reality was that his gesture made me go from screaming mad to psychotic anger. My disdain for him oozed from my mouth like a weeping cold sore.

167

"Don't you dare fucking touch me! I'm so sick of this. Sick of you! I don't want to do it anymore. We've tried too many times to get along. Things get better for a few weeks, maybe a month, then we're back like this again." I threw my hands up. "You can't tell me you're happy. How could you be happy when I don't even want to sleep with you! I don't even want to be around you."

"So what are you saying?" he said, like a dumb-fuck who hadn't heard anything.

"So what am I saying? What am I saying? Are you deaf? I'm saying what I have been saying for years, I. Hate. Our. Marriage. I'm miserable. How many times do I have to tell you? I'm not kidding. Not exaggerating. I'm serious. And that you think I'm not serious, makes me fucking enraged! You never listen to me!"

"Well maybe if we had sex more things would be better."

His statement made my insides burn like I was being embalmed alive. "So let me get this straight," I said, "What you're saying is that it's my fault that we don't get along, because I don't want to have sex?"

"Yesss," He drug out the word as if he'd finally gotten through to me.

"You are so fucking ignorant, I don't know why I married you."

"Well why *did* you marry me then?"

"I don't know. But maybe if you had made an effort to spend quality time with me once in and a while, and maybe if you weren't such an invalidating jerk, I'd have wanted to fuck you! But now. No way. It's over. I'm done."

"You won't even come near me!" He yelled, "How could I have spent time with you? You won't sit by me. You won't lay beside me. You won't even kiss me! I repulse you, how do you think that makes me feel?"

"You're right, about all of it," I said callously. "Why do you want a wife who has such an aversion to you anyway?"

I ate pickles, crunching them with my mouth wide open, being as vile as I could and contemplating how to end this argument. I was tired. Tired of him, tired of arguing, I was emotionally exhausted, and it was nearing midnight.

168

I slid a bottle of white wine off the counter then held it up as if it was on display. "If you can pronounce the name of this wine—I'll give you a blow job," I said crunching loud with my mouth open then laughing at myself for even thinking of it. "I'll give you three tries."

Funny how the proposition of a blow job can lift a man from a deep pit of anger to panting like a dog a second flat. I handed the bottle to him. There was no way in hell he was going to get this right, and even if he did, he wouldn't know. And, there was no way in hell I was even going to kiss him, let alone get him off.

He looked at the label, "Guu-were…".

"Nope," I said before he could finish, then hung my body over the cold granite.

"Geez-wore-zat."

"Nope. One more try," I mumbled.

"Goo-werz-traa…"

Before he was done with the last pathetic syllable I said, "Nope," popping the word on my lips just to drive the point home, then walked away and locked myself in the bathroom.

"Well what is it then?" He yelled through the door.

I yelled back exaggerating each syllable, "Guh-Voorts-truh-Mee-nur."

"That's what I said!" He yelled at the door.

I sat on the ledge of the tub.

> *This sucks so bad. :(*
> *I'm having a miserable*
> *night. I wish I were*
> *with u. Text if u can.*
> *I'll be in the bathroom*
> *for 5 mins. Otherwise,*
> *goodnite. :) I'll text u*
> *in the morning. :)*

I didn't wash my face, I sat on the toilet with my knees knocked together, elbows digging into my thighs, and my chin in my hands. I shut

169

my eyes and contemplated sleeping in the bathtub as I waited for the chime.

> *Baby, I'm so sorry.*
> *I promise it will never*
> *be like that with us.*
> *U deserve so much more.*
> *I am always here for u.*
> *Call or come over anytime.*
> *P.S. I meant everything I said*
> *tonight. B sure 2 delete. :)*

I didn't want to delete. I wanted to eat his words, sleep with them, bathe in them. I snuck out of the bathroom, I put in my earbuds, built a great wall of pillows down the center of our king size bed then snuggled under the covers. I tucked my phone under my body and laid on my side. My playlist started with Clair De Lune and I was out by Symphony No. 5.

***

It was Saturday night, Grant was on stage at some bar gig, and it was time to deploy my devious plan to one up his nudie. From in between his sateen sheets I left him a voicemail.

"Hi baby," I said, my hands shaking from what I was about to do, "instead of a naughty picture, I thought I'd leave you this voice mail."

My heart beat fast and my insides quivered, I'd never done something so tawdry before. I wanted to back out, but forced myself to take the risk, to push past my boring beige boundaries.

"I'm in your bed, alone—dreaming about you, wishing you were here so you could touch me. But for now…I'll just do it myself and pretend it's you."

Chapter 26

"LOVE MODERATELY. LONG LOVE DOTH SO.

TOO SWIFT ARRIVES AS TARDY AS TOO SLOW."

—WILLIAM SHAKESPEARE, *ROMEO AND JULIET*, 2.6.14-15

Las·civ·i·ous:

Revealing an overt and often offensive sexual desire.

—Dictionary.com

Oh yes, I was definitely being lascivious.

"I'm sliding my fingers into my pink and black lacy panties, the one's you like, and I'm imagining it's your capable hands touching me, pleasuring me, circling like this, petting me softly...like this."

I paused for dramatic effect, then teased him with a five minute steaming hot erotic tutorial on exactly how to pleasure me.

"I wish you were here to finish the job, I can't wait for you to explore all of me." I threw in a few pleasure filled moans then finished act three.

U! U naughty, naughty
girl. :) U sexy vixen.
Just wait. I will teach U!

I was getting what I had always wanted, *him* wanting me, but getting what you want also comes with a crippling fear of losing it.

"We told him not to," Dylan said. "No one else dared to do it, the log was all mossy and slick. It was so stupid. If he fell there was no way we could've pulled him out. No one was even down river."

"Dylan! Why did you let him do it?" I yelled into the phone.

"We couldn't stop him," Dylan said, "I tried to talk him out of it, I didn't want him to do it. The snow-pack had just melted and the river was raging through the gorge. I couldn't even look at him while he was out there."

"Where was this?" I asked. "Where are you?"

"Devil's Cascade. We're on our way back. Should be home in a few hours."

I had called Dylan to see how the guys only canoeing trip was, that's when he told me about Grant—about his high wire stunt above Devil's Cascade.

I was on the bike path a few blocks from my house when Grant finally called. "It's so good to be back in civilization," he said, "with cell service and you!"

I was instantly put back together, so lonely without him I didn't realize how empty I was until he came back. "It's so good to hear from you. I've missed you. How was your trip?"

"It was interesting…" he trailed off, "no one got killed or lost, so it was good. We're on our way home, we stopped at a gas station so I snuck away to call you. Dylan's in the other car."

"I know, I just talked to him, and he said you have a secret dream to be like Nick Wallenda."

"Oh…he told you about that," he said shamelessly.

"Of course he did. He said it was stupid, and that if you had fallen they wouldn't have been able to save you."

"No, it wasn't like that." He blew it off as nothing, "It was a calculated risk. I knew what I was doing. I wouldn't have fallen. Baby, I wouldn't risk my life, especially not now."

The whole thing didn't mesh well with me. He was a chronic risk taker—aerobatics, sky diving, solo back country hiking, fire walking. Yes, fire walking. And when you find someone that feels as much a part of you as your own beating heart, losing it would be more than catastrophic. Losing him, would be the total annihilation of me.

"Gotta go babe, we're about to leave. When can I see you?" I heard Dylan's voice in the background. He'd freak if he saw my number on Grant's phone.

"How about tomorrow night? I can work late again." Although I hadn't *actually* worked late in months.

"Perfect. Where should we meet?"

Dylan was close, I could hear him. "Hurry up bud, who are you talking to?"

"Your sister," Grant said, and my mouth fell open.

"Yeah right," I heard Dylan say.

"Honey—you're so bad," I said. "Let's meet at your place tonight?"

Silence idled between us as he pondered my bold proposition. Going to his place was dangerous. If we got caught there, what would be our excuse? At least at my work or his work, we could maybe pull off the ol' he's buying a gift certificate for his mom thing, but at his house?

"Do you think that's a good idea?" He said.

"No, but where else is there?"

"Good point. Let's do it. Mwah!" He kissed his lips together, then hung up the phone. Before I even had a chance to tuck my phone away, he'd already sent me a text.

*I hope U outlive me, so
I don't have to know what
life is like without U.*

Really? Is he for real? How could he be so sensitive, and caring, and fun, and adorable, and...real? Men like this don't actually exist, do they?

Sometimes I felt like he might just be an all star player, and that I'd wake up one day to find out I was just another name on his list that I'd been duped like a hundred others before me. I could never quite get past that feeling, I didn't know why but I was always waiting for the other shoe to drop.

***

Sneaking around at his place seemed so deceptive. So much worse than sneaking around at the yoga studio, or his work, or in my car. It took our affair to a whole new level of official. It made our time together that much more thrilling, and that much more terrifying.

I was filled with jittery anticipation and energy. A wave of wooziness washed over me when his text chimed in.

> *Honey, I miss U and can't*
> *wait to sneak tonight.*
> *Hee-hee. :)*

I called him immediately after my last client, "I'm done, but I don't remember where you live. That one night is kinda...foggy."

He gave me directions to his place and instructions on how not to get caught going there. "Make sure no one is following you, circle the block, go down a different block, look behind you. Park in the grocery store parking lot if you think you're being followed. Don't risk pulling in if you're not absolutely sure."

His stone seriousness made my already caffeinated nerves even more jittery.

What if Dylan stopped by his place? Or what if Levi had someone I didn't know follow me? What if Levi started a fight?

The thought of a fight between them terrified me, if it happened it would be a bloody brawl. Levi was a dirty street fighter, brutal, aggressive, and unafraid to get kicked in the head. I didn't know what Grant was capable of. I just knew he had skills, lethal skills. I knew he had a black belt in Karate and that he'd been teaching self-defense. I'd never seen him in action and we'd never really talked about that part of his life.

"Call me right before you get here and I'll open the garage door," Grant said.

I rounded a narrow corner into the alley behind his place and saw a garage door starting to open. I checked the numbers on trim 3410, *Yep.* Then crept my Beetle underneath the door while it was still opening. The moment my tires rolled onto the smooth surface it began to close behind me. I sat unmoving with my shoulders lifted, cringing at the sluggish, creaking door that threatened to reveal our secret.

When the door finally sealed to the concrete, it blackened out the remaining twilight. I could still make out his deadly male form standing in the doorway wearing nothing more than a sultry smile and faded jeans. His torso was bare, his skin free from scars or even a single blotch of ink. Unlike me, his was an unadulterated canvas. Grant was Dylan's age, five years my elder at thirty-four, but he didn't seem to age like a normal man would. He stayed youthful, unchanged through all the years I'd known him.

Water dripped from the tips of his hair onto the mounds of his shoulders as I buried my face into his modest chest. He let out a pleasure filled groan as I drug my fingertips along the ridge of his back. I memorized his unique form, traced his outline, created a mental blueprint of his anatomy never wanting to forget it. He held me to his warm skin, tightening his grip arm over arm, constricting me, and his heartbeat pulsed through his lips as he welcomed me in with an adoring kiss.

We leapt up the stairs two at a time into the security of his two bedroom condo. Then galloped like frisky teenagers into the kitchen where a bottle of Echo Domani merlot was already un-corked and breathing. He'd been waiting for me.

On the cork, written in black Sharpie ink, it read...

G + C

"Aw, that's so sweet!" I covered my heart with both hands.

He picked up the cork, leapt onto the counter and tossed it into a large bowl on top of the cabinets, then jumped down and poured us each a shallow glass.

"To us and the first of many glasses of wine together," he said as we clinked the rims.

Then without warning he picked me up with a single arm around my waist, walked me to the couch and set me on the armrest. The vice of his grip crunched the bones in my back. I hid my grimace with a fake laugh.

"I put toothpaste and a new toothbrush in the bathroom for you." He said as he wiggled between my legs.

I furrowed and pushed him back. "Does my breath stink that bad?"

"Of course not, but you can't leave here with red-wine teeth now, can you?"

"What if I don't want to brush my teeth? What if I want to go home with red-wine-teeth?" I took a sip and sloshed it around, swishing it over my gums. "I like being with you. If I go home with red-wine-teeth, maybe I'll get to come right back."

"Honey, we get to spend the rest of our lives together," he said as he slid himself deeper between my legs. "I still wish we had gotten together sooner or that our lives could be longer." His words were so sweet and surreal I couldn't even respond.

I wrapped my legs around him and pulled him in. The smell of the bold burgundy aroma lingered on his breath, and the scent of his masculine skin made my eyes roll back into their sockets. I melted into him knowing full well that my clothes would pick up his scent.

"How long do we have tonight?" He asked. Every sentence began and ended with an indelible kiss.

"As long as you want me," *kiss, kiss, kiss,* "Or until ten o'clock," *kiss, kiss, kiss.*

"How come your place is so clean?" I looked around and at the pictures of his family in dust-free frames, and the fresh vacuum lines on the carpet.

"See, I'm not a hoarder," he said fanning out his hand to display his organized, clean home.

"Then how come your office is a landfill? Your mom cleans your place for you, doesn't she?" I accused.

He shook his head side-to-side as if to say no, while quietly saying "Yes."

"I knew it! Does she do your laundry too? Your dishes?"

"Sometimes...but mostly she just irons my work shirts."

I shook my head, and made a few clicks with my tongue and cheek.

"I pay her!" He shouted before I could tease him further.

We sat facing each other on the love seat, which I lovingly dubbed The Short Bus. It became our sacred place, the place we spent hours tangled under a warm blanket in meaningful conversation. It was where we learned about each other, where hours passed like minutes, where he became my best friend, and where I fell tragically in love with the man that had always seemed out of reach.

That night marked the beginning of increasingly frequent visits to his place. Each successful rendezvous encouraging another. Levi put Dani to sleep three nights a week while I worked late, and I took the other four. I crammed in all my work during the day so I could rendezvous with Grant at night.

The next time I crept back into his garage I was greeted with his hands around my face, and his eager lips on mine. He kissed me like I was his adoring wife and whispered in my ear, "Hi sexy. I have something for you," then crushed me into him, one hand around my waist, the other holding a yellow drill.

"You're the sexy one." I said then looked down at his mess, "What are you doing?"

"I changed the locks, here's your key," he handed me a sharp edged shiny silver key.

Oh. My. God. He's giving me a key!

I'd never gotten a key before, not even from Levi nor did I ever expect one from Grant. I stared at him in disbelief.

"We don't need any unexpected visitors, now do we," he said, "and this way if you and Dani need to come here, or anytime you want to come here, you can, and you'll be safe. Even if I'm not home." The muscle fibers in his forearms twitched as he finished drilling in the final screws. "I'm not listed, and only a few people know where I live, so we should be extra safe."

"Why aren't you listed?"

"Just a precaution," he set down his drill on a heap of plastic and metal, then pulled me up the stairs.

"Where are you going to keep that key?" he asked.

"On my key chain?"

"Uh...no."

"Ummm, yes. There's a dozen keys on there. I'm not even sure what they all are, he'll never notice one more. If I hide it, and he finds it, that would be worse."

"You're right," he said, "You're so smart baby." Then he picked me up and carried me into the kitchen.

It felt so good when he held me, I couldn't bring myself to tell him how much it actually hurt me too, my back wasn't getting any better.

An open bottle of Blackstone Merlot waited on the counter, and beside it the cork. Written in black Sharpie ink, it read:

MY LOVE,

YOU HOLD

THE KEY TO

MY HEART.

He showed it to me acting all shy-like then tossed it into the secret place beside the other.

"How many other women have had a key?" I asked, eternally insecure about the status of my specialness.

He tilted his head as if to say, aren't we past being insecure about ex's? "Just one," he said, "my mom."

"Yeah right."

"Really. Just her."

I squinted at him, skeptical. "I guess that makes me the luckiest, most special woman on the planet then."

"Yes it does." He squeezed me to him. I winced and held my breath as the crunching sound that only I could hear emanated from my back.

"Aren't you supposed to get me drunk?" I furrowed my brow, holding up my glass and showing my disapproval. "I didn't say anything last time cause I didn't know it was going to be chronic, but this is a pitifully cheap pour. I think I can handle one full glass. I'm a big girl."

"You..." He growled, "gimmie that," then he snapped it away to top it off to the appropriate level. "There, is that better? Cause that's all you get. You can't go back to your house drunk or we'll have trouble."

The pain was bad, I was going to need a bigger drink but I stopped short of asking him for a tumbler.

He pulled a blanket from the dryer and we snuggled under its comforting heat squished against one another on The Short Bus.

A dark blue, evil-looking book titled Effective Interviewing and Interrogation Techniques stared at me from the coffee table. It hid at the bottom of the pile, underneath a monolith of anatomy, chemistry to anthropology textbooks—the kind of textbooks normal people sell back to the college after they're done. The kind that Grant kept because he'd highlighted them and kept them around for light reading at bedtime.

"Did you use interrogation techniques to get your ex-wife to confess?" I pointed to the book.

"Sort of," he shrugged. "I knew she was cheating. But she did confess eventually."

"Do you ever see her anymore?"

"Nope. I filed for divorce right after our wedding and never saw her again." A coldness for her was evident in his voice.

"Really? You've never seen her again, not even once?"

"Not even once."

"Isn't it weird that you and Dylan had your receptions in the same room on the same night—and that you became best friends and both got divorced? And, isn't it weird that now you're sneaking around with your best friend's baby sister who was also there on your wedding night?"

179

"It's very weird," he said, "but it's even weirder that I was at your wedding too."

He said it so nonchalantly that it took a few seconds for me process and respond.

"My wedding? To Levi? You were there? I never saw you." I said.

"I saw you," he insisted, "passed out in your wedding dress!" He burst out laughing, then apologized, "I'm sorry baby," then laughed again.

Memories from my zombie wedding caused a hot flush of embarrassment to sear through me. "I looked for you, but I never saw you."

"Well I was there," he said, "but you weren't around so I went looking for you. That's when I saw you upstairs, passed out." He tried to hide his chuckle.

"Grant," I said, "Seriously, I wasn't passed out, I just put my head down for a little rest."

"Uh huh," he teased.

"Well, maybe I was passed out a little," I said laughing with him now. "Grant, I thought of you on my wedding night." Instantly his jokester demeanor melted into that of a sincere gentlemen, and he smiled at me with sanguine eyes. "Did you really show up that night?" I asked.

"Yes, of course I did."

"Well why didn't you stop me then?" I yelled.

"I wish I would have."

I believed in fate, in destiny, and I believed that he was mine. I leaned in for a kiss.

"Life keeps bringing us together," I said. "Even when I tried to get away from you, I couldn't."

"I knew we were meant to be," he said, "I've just been waiting for you to get free."

"Why didn't you tell me sooner?" I yelled again.

He sent his warm hand up my leg and lovingly caressed my skin. "Honey, I wanted to. So many times. You have no idea how long I've wanted you." I was breathless from his confessions, then bewildered by what he said next. "Baby...we should keep a journal."

"What do you mean? A journal for what?" I asked, perplexed by something I never thought I'd hear from a man.

"You know...a journal." He continued. "So we can write about all of the things we do together—so we never forget." He tangled his legs tighter around me, and I ascended into relationship heaven.

"Honey, I would love to keep a journal, I'll get one for us. I'll get a keepsake box too, something we can put mementos in—like plane tickets and wine corks and post it notes we write to each other."

"That'd be perfect. You'll have to get a really big box," he added, making my heart swoon.

Each time before I left his place, I went through my new dental hygiene routine. I scrubbed the red tint off my teeth and wiped the crimson tinge from my lips. I sloshed with scope and re-hydrated with the Burt's Bee's chapstick he'd left on the counter for me. I sniffed my clothes, I didn't think I smelled like him.

I stepped out of the warm bathroom and prepared for a professional frisking. He looked me over, examined my innocence, and turned me in a circle. He touched and patted whatever he wanted, then swatted my tush and said, "I'd know you were up to something."

His grin was intoxicating, and the few deep lines in his face coupled with a few flecks of silver in his hair reminded me of his maturity, and that he wasn't just a handsome roaming bachelor, he was a mature man looking for true love.

"Be safe, baby, don't let anything happen to you," he always said before I left. Then each time, we stood in the doorway reluctant to be apart.

He never asked about Levi, or if I was filing for divorce, or when I was going to take off my wedding ring. He just loved me for who I was and where we were at in every moment. He waved goodbye and blew a kiss, then bent down as low as he could, until the garage door sealed shut.

I felt lost when he was out of sight, empty and insignificant, like I was leaving my home. I belonged with him and just knowing this life, the life of my wildest dreams really did exist, made the emptiness of not having it, that much more excruciating.

My throat swelled and my mouth went dry, making it difficult to swallow as I approached Levi and I's house. I feared Levi would see through me, see wine on my tongue or smell another home in my hair, or just know my sins by looking at my face. But he never did. He never noticed a single thing. I was actually getting away with it.

Sizzling, uninterrupted nights of repressed passion became our normal routine, and with them came a sexual desire for one another that increased exponentially each time I visited.

It became hard to be around each other and focus on anything else. But he was worth any amount of waiting—waiting for what, I don't know, we were already breaking all the rules. What did it matter if we broke some more, but we agreed to wait.

I suggested we wait until Fiji.

***

*Babe! Uh-oh. Hurricane
heading toward Maui!
Hope it's still there when we go!*

Chapter 27

"HE LOOKED AT HER THE WAY ALL WOMEN WANT TO BE LOOKED AT BY A MAN."

—F. SCOTT. FITZGERALD. *THE GREAT GATSBY*

"I've always wanted to go to Fiji," I said. "We could stay in those over-the-water bungalows and consummate our relationship there."

"That is a great idea," Grant agreed, so until then, we decided to play pretend.

On one sultry summer evening, in the dim evening light of his bedroom, we were nearly naked, and barely able to hold back from ravaging each other and breaking our pact. We played a torturous game of desire vs. willpower.

He started, "Let me tell you what I'm going to do to you the first time we make love." Heat pulsed through my veins at the thought of it. "Imagine that you're standing over a glass floor in the center of our bungalow above the turquoise ocean." He brushed my skin with the tips of his fingers, making me shiver. "The ceiling fan is circulating air over our suntanned bare skin, it's the perfect temperature. Its sunset but you're still wearing that little black bikini, the one I've dreamed about taking off of you."

"Yes, baby, keep going. I love it," I said, standing against the cold wall in his bedroom in nothing but my bra and panties.

"Imagine that I've just taken a shower, I'm in nothing but a white towel," he went on, "I'm holding you in my arms, relishing you…" He acted out the words and I could almost feel the breeze from the palm-leaf fan blowing warm Fijian air over my skin and him adoring me.

"Imagine me kissing you, passionately on your lips then moving down…" He tugged on my hair, pulling my head back gently, exposing my neck. I closed my eyes. "I'll start here, like this…" He grazed his lips across my bare chest, "then I'll move to your breasts, like this…and touch you, like this..." he went on, "I'll kneel down in front of you...like this, and trace my lips everywhere along your beautiful body...like this."

"Yes, baby, more, more," I begged. We both laughed at our devious little game.

"Don't worry," he said, "I won't stop. I'm going to kiss you everywhere." He sensuously did just as he'd explained until I was ready to implode. "I'll slip down your bikini and caress your tiny hips," He went on, then slid one side of my panties down and traced along the contours of my hips with his tongue. "Then I'll move in closer...like this," he looked up at me and grinned. "I'll put my hands all over your body for hours, then I'll stop so you can rest before I start all over again."

He stopped our pretend session, which was only half pretend and let out a frustrated sigh and bowed his head. "This is killing me. I love it, but it's killing me."

I never wanted it to end. I'd longed for this kind of romance. Sensual, confident romance, with a man who's unafraid, with a man who will help me become unafraid. I absorbed every moment of our encounter committing it to my eternal memory.

"We're not stopping," I said when I knew he was reaching a breaking point. "I haven't gotten a turn. Lie down." I demanded, pushing him backward and onto the bed. Then I whispered in his ear, "After you've had your way with me, I'm going to have my way with you. I'll unwrap your towel...like this," I tugged at the elastic on his boxers then slid them down, but only a little, "I'll rub myself all over your naked, gorgeous body...like this." Then I sat him up and straddled his lap. "I'll clench onto you tight...like this," I wrapped my legs and arms around him, he groaned in pleasure. I whispered in his ear, "I've longed for you to be inside me. I've thought about it so many times, how you would feel, how we would move." An agonized groan escaped his frustrated lips, but it only encouraged me to tease him more. "I'd say yes right now if you asked me to," I went on. "I'd beg if you want me to. I'll beg for you to..." He cut me off before I could finish.

"God, Babe!" He yelled into the air. "You're killing me."

"I'm sorry, do you want me to stop?"

"No. Yes. No!" He groveled. I flung myself down on the bed beside him and propped myself up on my elbow. It took every ounce of restraint I had to not tear off my panties and beg for real.

"Say you'll take me to Fiji so we can just do this already," I whined.

"Of course I'll take you to Fiji, I will take you anywhere you want to go, start making a list."

"Will you take me to Jamaica?"

"Yes, of course."

"And Napa?"

"Yes," he said, nodding playfully.

"What about Hawaii?"

"Definitely Hawaii."

"And the moon? Will you take me to the moon?"

"I would love to go to the moon with you. Maybe we'll be able to someday."

"Maybe," I said, "I have one last request."

"Anything."

"Will you take me flying with you?"

"Yes! Baby, I will take you up anytime you want to go."

***

It was time.

I couldn't touch Grant one more time with my wedding ring on—I wouldn't. I made excuses to be away from Levi, excuses for working late, and excuses for being frigid. I needed to find the courage and just do this already.

Prison yard barbed-wire surrounded the broken laundromat parking lot, and bells tied together with twine clinked on the glass door as

185

people toting laundry baskets walked in and out. I sat in my car in the parking lot and made a call to a distant friend, Addy.

"Addy, I need a divorce lawyer."

Addison was a stunning woman in her thirties and smart, but like too many women I knew, she too had married a toad and was now divorced.

"C.J., I'm so sorry."

"It's okay. I'm fine. I just need a quick divorce. I need to get this over with. Who did you use?"

She schooled me for half an hour in the art of war and divorce.

"So, like a shareholder, I would get a fifty-one percent say in what happens to Dani?"

"Yes," she said. "That's custodial custody, that's what you want."

Dani was safe with Levi. It was he and I together that became a collective poison that contaminated her childhood.

"What about child support?" I asked.

"If you get custodial custody, he'll have to pay," she said without emotion, "otherwise you'll have to pay him." She told me not to feel bad about taking the money.

I didn't want his money or the strings attached to it. I just wanted to be free. I wanted him out of my life, and I wanted him to go quietly and not come back.

I sat in my car outside the laundromat as college students and single men went in and out with their clothes baskets. It was a reminder of what single life was like and how I wanted nothing to do with it. My greatest fear was that I'd end up divorced from my husband, dumped by the boyfriend I left my husband for and folding my clothes in a laundromat watching soap operas.

I looked up the lawyer's phone number. "Quick Cheap Divorce," the advertisement said.

A day later I found myself sitting at a cardboard table, in the basement of an apartment building with a divorce lawyer that seemed more like he was about to cut out one of my kidneys than give me than legal advice.

Mr. Quick & Cheap got straight to the point without judgment, personal comments, or a box of tissues.

"So..." He set his elbows on the wobbly table. "What do you want?" He asked, and my statement went something like this.

"I don't want anything except custodial custody of my daughter and my dog, he can have the rest. I can take care of myself."

He advised against it, in fact, he wouldn't even write it down. I was forced to reconsider.

"Okay how about this," I said, "I want the house, the dog, the bed, the upstairs furniture, my piano, part of the kitchen dishes and custodial custody of Dani. I will keep my own bills and any debt, he will keep his. I will pay for the mortgage and waive my rights to child support. He will have to find somewhere else to live and leave me alone."

Simple. Done.

Deeming me incompetent, Quickie took over.

"You can't negotiate the financial wellbeing of the child," he said. "One of you will have to pay. So here's what we're going to do. I'll create a first draft, and we'll go through it together. You can revise anything you like at that time." He slumped back and crossed his arms. "If he signs the papers, we're done. If he doesn't and we have to make another draft, that'll cost extra."

"Who delivers the papers?" I assumed he had a delivery guy who would show up while Levi was filling gas or something, stuff an envelope in his hand and say *you've been served.*

"You deliver the papers," he said.

Shit.

"I'll call you in a week, you can come back and revise anything you want then."

Quickie shook his head as he slid my documents into a manila folder. He hadn't even written anything down. He'd seen it before, women needing to get out for one reason or another, willing to forfeit their entire lives just to get away from a broken marriage. I stared at a cigarette burn in the carpet and knew I was in the right place. It was as broken and burned as I was. Which was comforting actually, anything more put together than me would have made me feel even worse.

I needed the only thing that could make me feel better.

***

What time r u done tonight, baby? I'm skipping trivia. Need 2 give u some lovin'. ;)

Chapter 28

"I HAVE SINCE AN EARLY AGE ABJURED THE USE OF MEAT,

AND THE TIME WILL COME WHEN MEN SUCH AS I WILL LOOK UPON

THE MURDER OF ANIMALS AS THEY NOW LOOK UPON THE MURDER OF MEN."

—LEONARDO DA VINCI

God—I know it's been a while—and I'm really sorry but I wasn't sure if you were real or not and I didn't want to insult you by praying only when I needed something. But really, what'd you expect, since you're invisible. And don't give me that faith lecture, I need proof!

Why the hell am I doing this?

God, I'm sorry, I don't mean to doubt you and all but you really haven't given me much to go on here. If you are who you say you are and you're so forgiving and powerful and all that, then I need your help.

I know I've been bad—really bad, but this hangover will not go away and it's been five days. I feel like I might die, something's wrong, I feel my life's energy draining out of me.

If you let me live I promise to never, ever eat meat again. I'll stay healthy, and take care of myself, and devote my life to a good cause. Please let me live, and I'll keep my promise okay?

Love—C.J. from Minnesota.

And that—is how I became a vegetarian.

Turns out it wasn't a five day hangover but some rare pneumonia. I lived anyways, and never ate meat again.

Surely my genius boyfriend would see the folly in eating animals.

"I made us dinner!" Grant yelled as I walked through the door of his place.

I was mortified at his proud declaration, but aroused when I saw him shirtless in the kitchen standing over a plastic cutting board slicing vegetables.

"Baby, that's so sweet," I rubbed up behind him, wrapped my arms around his warm skin, and stood on my tiptoes to kiss his stubbly neck.

I peeked over his shoulder and watched him cut red onions and avocados, but all I could think about was bovine spongiform encephalopathy. How it might be living in-between the plastic grooves of the cutting board since it was likely that he'd used that same cutting board for raw hamburger. To me, eating farm animals was the equivalent of eating the family pet. I could not, would not, eat it. Ever again. Nor would I buy it or prepare it, for anyone. On this, I could not budge.

"Looks great, what are we having?" I said.

"My favorite sandwich."

Yeah right...an all vegetable sandwich is your favorite? How sweet of him to lie for me, aww...

I pressed my lips to his. "Looks like just my style. You're not going to try to slip some meat in there are you?" I said as I strutted away, wine glass in hand.

"Baby, I'd never do that to you," he said, "the only meat I'm going to slip you is..." But he didn't finish his sentence. He peeked around the corner and flashed me a devilish grin.

"Well stop teasing me already and just do it then," I said from the couch as I sipped on a delectable glass of Cabernet while he prepared a vegan dinner.

"I actually eat this sandwich often," He boasted, "see, I can do vegetarian. I like vegetarian food."

He said it like a meat-eater would. With the assumption that there's some other grocery store that vegetarians shop in. A funky smelling place filled with weird and unrecognizable health food.

He handed me a large dinner plate with a whole grain veggie sandwich overstuffed with avocado, hummus, red onion and alfalfa sprouts.

Impressed.

The guys I knew and grew up with would never have deviated from a summer sausage and cheese with mayo on white bread sandwich. This veggie masterpiece was impressive. We sat cross-legged on the floor because the kitchen table was occupied with half-dry laundry, wads of crumpled receipts, and half a dozen old phone books. From my dinner seat on the floor I noticed his laundry closet, overflowing with clothes that had matriculated onto the floor and now crept down the hallway. And on my way in, was the first time I'd noticed the canoe. It sat resting in the unused stall of his double garage. A virgin, fire engine red, tag-still-on, brand-new canoe. Except this canoe would never see the waters of the ten-thousand lakes we called home. No, this full-size, just off the factory floor canoe, was filled-to-the-brim, hoarders-style, with unopened mail. A few *years'* worth of unopened mail.

"How did you stay single all this time?" I nodded toward the overflowing heap of clothes, easing him into my next question, about the canoe. He stopped my gutty humor with a marvelous response.

"Because I compared all of them to you."

"You did not..." I said, hiding my awestruck expression, hoping I could coax him into saying it a few more times.

"Yes. I did," he said, "and none of them came close. You wrecked dating for me." He smiled, "why do you think I rarely brought girls down to the lake? Because I couldn't face you. I didn't want to compare them next to you. I knew how I would feel."

"Honey," I said with a lump of happiness in my throat. "You don't know how good it feels to hear you say that. I can't believe it's really you." I crawled into the space between us, then leaned over his dinner plate, he pulled back.

"*Me...I can't believe it's you!*"

I heard it, I rationalized it, I even believed it, but I was still unable to fully absorb the gift he was offering. I was too damaged. Un-loveable. I'd read about my condition in a book called *Receiving Love.* It said that if I didn't figure out how to accept and feel the love he was offering, if I kept rejecting it, I'd lose him. My chest filled with anxiety.

"I'm scared you might change your mind about me. Since—you know—I'm married, and I cheated on my husband, and you were a husband who got cheated on."

"I'm not going anywhere baby, I knew what I was getting into," he said, "I know who you are, and I know where your heart is."

He was so secure, he acted like we'd been together for a thousand years—and somehow it felt like we had. I twirled my broken vow around my finger, yearning to take it off.

"I saw a lawyer today," I said, "he started the paperwork. I want to get it done as quickly as possible, so I found an apartment too. Just in case he contests me staying in the house, which I think he will." I took a large gulp of wine. "Levi has always said there's no way in fucking hell he'd let me keep the house." I shrugged, "I figure I'll need to compromise so I need to prepare to move."

"Is this what you want to do?" I was delighted to hear the smile behind his voice.

"I want you, so, yes."

"Aww, baby," he said in a way I thought only girls were allowed to say. "Come here," he held out his arms and scooted toward me. "I'm here for you. Always. If there is anything you need just ask."

"Thank you, but I'll be fine. I need to do this myself." He couldn't help me move or figure out where to live or give me money. I had to do this on my own.

The ultimate irony in all of this was that when I went home to my husband, somehow that had become the affair. It was time to tell Levi, time for me to take off my ring and get out. It couldn't wait any longer.

I have to do it tonight.

***

"I am not happy!" I yelled as I whisked plates from the island and threw them in the dishwasher, cleaning up a kitchen mess I didn't make.

"I haven't been happy for a long time. What it is going to take for you to listen to me, to hear me!" I turned to face him. "I can't do this anymore."

Then I stopped, I couldn't finish, it would crush him. As much as I loathed him, I'd loved him once too, and I didn't want to hurt him.

His programmed response rolled out like ticker tape. "You exaggerate," he said with a lazy drawl, "everything's fine. Just knock it off." Then he'd reach out his arms for the usual peacekeeping hug laced with silent undertones of wanting makeup sex.

"No. Don't touch me," I stepped back, beginning to boil.

"Oh God not this again," he threw his hands up, annoyed at my continued unhappiness. Then dropped his arms letting them slap against his body. He turned to walk away.

"See! This is why we don't get along. You don't listen to me, you don't hear me, we don't communicate, at all!" I needed him to hear me this time. "I. Can't. Do this anymore!"

"Do what?" He scoffed.

"Do what?" I said calmly, but his insolence enraged me and I bellowed it a second time so loud I startled myself. "Do what? I fucking hate you. That's what. I don't want anything to do with you. I hate living with you. I hate sleeping with you. I hate you. I'm done I'm done I'm so fucking done with you." My body shook from rage. "Why would you want me anyway? Why would you want a wife who treats you like this?" I slid down the dishwasher and thunked to the floor. "I can't change how I feel. I've tried. I don't want to do this anymore. I can't. It's killing me."

I had no tears now, no feeling...I was numb and unresponsive.

There was a long silence between us. I examined the vinyl floor, he examined me, leering at me, disgusted by me.

"Well," he said, "what do you want to do then?" He assumed I had a plan, like I had every time before. Something to help our marriage get better when things got lousy. A romantic trip, a night at a fancy hotel, or a massage in the bedroom. My plan did include all of those things, just not with him.

"I don't want to be with you anymore. I can't live like this, and I won't let Dani live like this." I stood up, wiggled off my wedding ring and set it on the island. The tinging sound it made when it hit the black granite echoed in the silence.

"So what are you saying? You want a divorce?"

"Yes."

"No. No way. We're in this together, remember? We're not giving up, I'm not leaving."

"In what together?" My voice strained, "we don't even have a marriage, we don't even like each other, there's nothing to give up. It's already gone."

"Dani!" He roared. "We are not going to do this to Dani."

"You think us staying together is good for her? Are you blind? Look at us! I don't want to show her that this is what marriage is."

"I'm not leaving," he said, his demeanor smug, hiding the hurt. "You can leave." He threw up his hands at me, "*You* go. Get the fuck out of here if that's what you want."

His face was that of a husband scorned, twisted and wrought with anger and pain. I brought out the worst in him, and he brought out the worst in me. I hated who I'd become with Levi and I hated who he became with me.

"Don't even think about taking Dani or Bodi, they belong here, with me," he yelled. "If you want out, then you leave. In fact, why don't you leave right now, I really don't want you here anyway. This is *my* house!" His angry eyes scoured my soul.

"This is her home and Bodi belongs here too. I'll take care of the house, all the bills, I don't want anything from you. They belong here, and I belong with them. Please..." I begged, "Let me keep them in the house, please. You can take whatever you want, just leave."

He leered at me with vicious eyes, "I will never. Ever. Give you this fucking house. Bodi is mine. Dani is staying with me. You want out, then you leave."

I slept on the floor in Dani's room that night and listened to what sounded like a hurricane picking up speed and blasting its fury through our house. He slammed doors, threw books, and yowled one word profanities.

Bodi's coarse fur was my only comfort that night as I lay on the scratchy carpet next to Dani's bed. Then even he trotted away, annoyed with my neediness. It was well after midnight when I sent Grant a text. The blurry white letters were a strain for my exhausted eyes.

Sorry so late. Rough
night. I'm okay for now.
I'll call u in the morning as soon as
I can. Goodnite. :) Don't txt back.

***

I anticipated Levi wanting to reconcile, but I didn't expect the depth of commitment he offered. He confided in his mom, telling her everything he knew, asking for help. I ignored her call. He consulted his friends, my friends, called Dylan to see what it would take to change my mind. I ignored their calls. He genuinely wanted to make us work. It was an effort deserving of respect—noble, but years too late.

***

Dani and I would be the first tenants in a new apartment complex a few blocks away from Levi's house. It was modern, with white trim, sprawling oak floors and a large white fireplace. It was within walking distance to Dani's school and available in two weeks.

Without divulging my plan to anyone, I lined everything up. Movers to help with the furniture and my piano, advance payment of my rent and a deposit, forwarding address, I paid off Quickie, then had exactly eight hundred dollars cushion in my checking account. Most of which I'd gotten a month prior by confiscating our joint tax refund before he knew it had even come in because as I expected he would, he withdrew every last cent from our joint accounts. The only money I had left was tied up in my personal retirement accounts which thankfully he had no access to.

Divorce mistake number one: *I asked for a divorce before I moved out.*

Week one slogged along painstakingly slow. I created an invisible, yet highly detectable, stay-the-fuck-away-from-me shield. But even my transparent and seldom presence was enough to churn up a vile anger between us. Living in that house, with Levi, became like riding a roller coaster through the bowels of marriage hell. Up, down, over and around the same moot points.

Grant and I agreed to lay low until I moved out. If Levi suspected something, now would be the time he'd follow me or have me followed. By Thursday of that first week, we were unable to swear off each other.

Thursday

He knew I was coming over, right? It was Thursday. We planned for Thursday.

Grant wasn't answering his phone. After work I decided to go to his place anyway. I let myself in like he said I could, but he was gone. I expected to find him hiding, filming me in some elaborate prank like he had so many times before. I expected the doorknobs to be greased with KY, trip wire to be strung low on the wall in the hallway and a condom wrapped around the shower head. But instead there was nothing, only silence.

I walked into his bedroom.

That's when I saw it.

I clutched my chest, holding in my heart, preparing for the worst.

I knew it, I knew it was too good to be true, I knew it!

Chapter 29

"HE'S MORE MYSELF THAN I AM.

WHATEVER OUR SOULS ARE MADE OF,

HIS AND MINE ARE THE SAME."

—EMILY BRONTË, *WUTHERING HEIGHTS*

A long white rectangular envelope was propped against the pillows on his bed. On the front he'd written my name—Charmaine, with a wavy underline.

He never calls me Charmaine, I'm "baby", or "honey", or "sweetheart". I'm "C.J."

That my actual name was written or spoken meant that whatever this was, it was serious. I clonked down on the edge of the bed with the envelope in my hand. The evening light shone through the window and made a long gray shadow of my silhouette on the floor; a fitting self-portrait, an accurate portrayal of the gloom that had just crept over me.

I never really expected him to stay with me anyway.

Inside the envelope was a card with wispy hues of lavender, and a single white whimsical feather floating down. A long Hallmark sentiment was written in gentle cursive across the front. And before I even read it, I postulated what it said, he was about to *let me down easy*. It would say something like, *even though you're one of the most amazing people I've ever met, I think we'd be better off as friends*. Gutted by fear, I slumped over the envelope horrified that I was about to lose the greatest love of my life.

To my awe and amazement, what I got instead, was nothing short of a glorious beginning to the rest of my life. The love poem on the front was filed with promises of forever, true love and meant-to-be's sentiments. The inside was covered with two wondrous pages of Grant's unique handwriting.

Baby,

This card was the most perfect card I could find. You are the greatest thing that has happened in my life, ever. You really have proved to me that people can truly be happy. When I'm around you, I feel so wanted, so liked, so adored, you are like nothing I have Ever! Experienced, and it honestly feels so great that I can hardly contain myself!

What we have is so special, you know it too. I have fallen so hard for you C.J....When we're together, each time brings me closer to you, and is even more amazing than the last. You're not only the last person I want to be with; I swear you are the last person I'll ever be with. The thought of anyone else is not even there. And if anything ever happened to you, I don't know what I would do.

I know things have happened fast, but I've always tried to convince myself that when you find the right person, you know right away. Things have happened at the perfect pace for us, so I will never care what anyone thinks. I know your heart was out of your marriage a long time ago, and it's just been hanging there, in the balance, waiting for the right person and the right time, and my goal is to spend every day convincing you that giving it to me, was the right thing to do...

Love, Grant

I sat at the edge of the bed—read it twice, slower the second time to make sure I'd read it correctly. My eyesight was blurry from a deluge of tears, I could barely see the words, I could barely breathe.

When the door opened I sprung to my feet, ran to him and wrapped myself around him. With the card still in my hand I said, "You are the most wonderful man in the entire world!" I clung to him as he walked with me back into his bedroom.

"Honey," he said, emotion seeping from his eyes, "I'm so crazy about you—I love you."

"Baby, I would die without you. I love you." He laid me down, underneath him. "I wish we could have been together sooner. I want ten-thousand more days with you."

He looked at me and we smiled, yearning for one another in a way only we could ever understand.

"I could only *hope* to have ten-thousand days with you. Baby, let's make the most of every day, I mean it. Let's never take each other for granted, let's travel around the world, let's have babies." He embraced me tenderly into his firm body, "I love you so much. Now I know why Tom Cruise jumped on Oprah's couch."

We laughed with a wild abandon, we understood reckless love-sick behavior.

I believe we were given a gift—an otherworldly love, a rare love. A love that stretches beyond humankind into the ether where it endures, a love where no amount of time, or space, or circumstance can stop it from fulfilling its destiny.

The dictionary defines "paragon" as "a person viewed as a model of excellence."

If anyone could be that, it was him, and he was mine. My paragon.

Grant lingered over me, staring at me, as if it was the first time, or the last, "I'm finally getting what I've always wanted," he said. "I guess dreams really *do* come true."

"I guess they do."

He caressed my lips with his thumb then kissed me softly, touched me with his capable hands across my ribs and down my sensitive sides. He explored the contours and grooves of my body then gripped the top of my yoga pants, waiting for permission. I could feel his primal desire to have all of me.

Without warning he stepped out of his jeans and slipped off his shirt. His flawless skin hugged taught against his supple musculature as he stood magnificent before me. Seducing me with his translucent eyes and predatory grin, he watched as my unspoken desire for him grew. He slipped his fingers underneath the elastic of my yoga pants, then tugged them down slowly from side to side, then off.

My not-so-beige, barley-there lingerie received approval with a chorus of seductive hums. He paid full attention to my every twinge, every hitch in my breath, taking notes, examining my subtle reactions to his touch.

I ached for him to lose control, to shatter his disciplined demeanor and unleash an untamed man. He was a beast, wild and hungry, but he was also a beast-master; calculated and patient, able to withhold his desire, to forego primal pleasure for something more connected and deep.

Curiously, as his restraint lessened—mine got stronger, but our pact to wait until Fiji was still no more fool-proof than a teenage boy intending to use a condom. My torso curled and breath whooshed from my body when he forced my panties to one side, exposing me. He didn't touch me. He left me nude and defenseless, begging for him not to stop.

I tugged on the elastic of his boxers and whispered, "Take them off."

He moaned in agony, ready to accept defeat then he pressed his lips to my ear, "You naughty, naughty girl, I know what you're doing."

"Take them off." I complained then forced my way on top. My hips were surrounded under the wide sprawl of his hands, and he moved me into place. "Maybe we should just...put it in? I mean, just one time, you know, to see if it fits?"

I spoke casually as if unaffected my own preposterous suggestion, but my heart beat wild in my chest at the thought. A devious laugh of pleasure and torment echoed through the room as absorbed what I was saying.

"What a great idea," he said, "Yes, let's just see if it fits."

Slowly, I lowered myself down an inch at a time. Squeezing and wriggling side to side almost imperceptibly. "What if I just sat down, and didn't move. Just once, like this. That wouldn't count...right?"

I bit my lip, refusing to break character, thrilled to be punishing him with such a brilliant enticing offer. I rocked my hips almost undetectably on top of his lap.

"No...of course this doesn't count," he said, his voice thick with testosterone as he lay still, immersed in sensation. A moan of pleasure slipped through his euphoric grin. I stopped.

"Now, you're sure this doesn't count...right?" He grabbed me hard, frustrated but refrained from moving—he loved the tease, the test of his will.

"You're killing me." He yelped, shaking my hips under his hulk tight grip. "You naughty girl, I love it. I love you."

We played our naughty little game of pleasure and agony. Shamelessly exploring each other in a way that may, or may not have violated our pact.

I sat still because a movement would make it count. "Don't move," I said, panting with desire. He turned his head, stuffed it into the pillow and released a disgruntled groan.

"Shh..." I teased on his lips before I finally broke. "I changed my mind," I said, "I have to move..."

We interlaced our fingers and he dug his elbows into the bed to hold up my weight. I'd waited a lifetime for him, and I couldn't wait any longer to have all of him. After a few delves, I stopped.

"Oops—my bad, did that count?" I said with my fingers lightly touching my lips.

"I think maybe that did count." He nodded, "I guess we can keep going then?"

"Um...I guess we can."

He threw me onto my back like I weighed only a few pounds, readjusted my wedged panties pushing them farther away from the center, then hovered his long thick torso over me securing my hands above my head. He was intimidating, yet I'd never in my life felt so taken care of, so safe.

Careful not to crush me under his weight, he made love to me.

He stopped for no apparent reason, collected me in his arms then pulled me onto his lap as he knelt on the bed. He stared past my eyes into somewhere deeper. "I know I've said it before but I can't believe it's you," he said. "You were the only thing missing from my life, it feels so great now that you are here. Everything has changed, nothing else matters." He tucked my hair behind one ear and gazed at me adoringly.

I stretched my arms out over his shoulders, "I feel the same way, baby. But before this goes any farther I have to tell you something. Grant, I'm not on the pill."

"Shit. I was just thinking about that. Do you have any condoms?"

"Do I have any condoms? No. Do you have any condoms?"

I secretly hoped he would say no. Because saying yes would mean he'd slept with someone fairly recently, most likely in that bed, or that he had condoms just in case something came up. The thought of him wanting someone else, sleeping with someone else, touching someone else the way he touches me, caused a painful ache in my chest.

"I don't have any," he said.

Yes! Thank God.

Then my phone rang.

"I have to check it," I said as I cringed, not wanting to leave his lap. "In case it's Dani...I'm sorry." I slid off of him and jogged to my cell phone with both hands covering my butt.

"That was Dani, she was crying, she's at a friend's house and needs to be picked up. Grant, I have to go. Like now..." I added, then crinkled my face not knowing what else to say other than, "Do you want to finish quick?"

He slumped his head and we shared a chuckle at our not-so-desirable circumstances. "Of course not baby. We don't have condoms anyway so maybe this is a good thing."

"Honey, I'm so sorry. I will make it up to you," I scrambled around the room gathering my things, not forgetting to take my card so I could read it again sixteen more times that night.

"Don't be sorry, and you don't have to make anything up to me if you don't want to," he added with an adorable smile.

I pulled on my clothes and fixed my bed head. "So I guess this really doesn't count?"

He pulled up his jeans and tucked his unsatisfied parts into the now crowded space.

"I guess not, which means...we just get to do it again. But next time, we'll be prepared."

***

Don't ever let anything
happen 2 u! Wear ur seat
belt, stay healthy, minimize
all risks! :)I know u do those things.

Chapter 30

"OB·LIT·ER·A·TION: TOTAL DESTRUCTION.

—DICTIONARY.COM

Stress seemed to catalyze the debilitating effects that were happening deep within my spine. I was deteriorating rapidly and if I didn't get real help, real soon, the end result would be nothing short of cataclysmic. The pain was life-taking pain and nothing that I'd done or tried was working. I was running out of time and money for remedies that proved useless.

I stuffed ice packs into the fold of my yoga pants each time before I left my house, but throbbing and stabbing pain followed me relentlessly. My daily walks had dwindled to fifteen minutes of circling the same block, going up one side and coming down the other. I couldn't walk too far from home in case I'd have to crawl back.

My unusual behavior at the mall sent a shock wave of panic through passing patrons when a sneeze threatened to blow up my insides. I preempted the implosion by dropping to the floor, tucking my head into my knees, and squeezing myself into the tightest, smallest globule I could. It was the only position that could contain the massive internal pressure of a sneeze without shattering my spine. When I dropped, a few people around me felt the need to follow.

I hoped that once I got away from Levi, my condition would improve. I was convinced that the stress of our marriage was a major contributing factor in my physical demise and once I plucked myself from that environment, I could begin to heal.

The final divorce papers were ready.

Quickie tossed down an inch thick manila envelope that hit the table with a thunk. In it, was the manuscript that detailed how I was to divide my life and belongings. I asked for custodial custody of Dani, the king size bed, the washer and dryer and the upstairs furniture. He could keep the downstairs furniture, the big screen T.V., half the kitchen items, the house, and the dog. If at some point he decided to sell the house, I would be entitled to half. It seemed fair, except for having to give up Bodi, which was unthinkable and analogous to abandoning a small child.

Divorce mistake number two: *I gave up the dog.*

Getting over the hurdle of him having to pay child support was going to be a gargantuan fight, for which I was ready. I needed everything to be agreeable—I just wanted out. In cheap blue ball point pen with zero emotion I scribbled my signature on the last page.

The last evening I spent in our house was the first time I would tell Dani and Levi what was about to happen. He knew I wanted a divorce but refused to have a conversation about it or talk with Dani together, so I had no choice. I had to follow through by myself or not at all.

Before Levi came home from work I sat Dani down on the floor in her bedroom. She had just turned nine. "Honey, I need to tell you something." She crisscrossed her legs and plopped down in the center of her pink room. I put my hands on her knees and gulped air. "We are getting an apartment, it's really nice, you will love it." I spoke slow, assessing her reaction and judging how much she could take. "You will have your own room and your very own bathroom. You'll still have your room here, that won't change. Bodi and Daddy will be here too."

I gagged at having to tell her, I didn't know the right way to break a little girl's heart. And I couldn't bring myself to say the D word. "Mommy can't stay here anymore," I continued as sporadic sniffles puffed up her tiny chest and tears rolled down her chin. "You'll get to stay at both places. Honey, Daddy and I love you very much. This has nothing to do with you; you are a great daughter. It's just, you know sometimes how you hear Daddy and me arguing?" She stared at the carpet, each breath now came with a full body flinch. "I can't argue with Daddy anymore, it's hurting me, it's hurting Daddy, and we don't want to hurt you."

A loud, angry voice bellowed from her little lungs, "You and Daddy are getting divorced?" She yelled. She'd figured it out before I even had the guts to say the word.

"Not quite yet, but in the future—yes."

She hated me for what I was doing, I knew she would, but someday...she would forgive me—right? Eventually the hurt would lessen and a new perspective would emerge—right? Not all kids of divorced parents are fucked up—right?

She wailed in her room for half an hour as I sat on the floor and cried with her, watching her convulse with a despair she didn't create or deserve. She asked questions, like who will get the T.V., where would Bodi stay and how will she get home from school, then she asked if she could play with her dolls.

I intercepted Levi the moment he walked in the door, asking him to come into our bedroom, before he could see Dani.

"Since you won't leave. I'm going to," I said, "and Dani is coming with me. I've already told her."

"Told her what?" his voice was hostile, "that you're abandoning her? That you're abandoning this family?"

"I'm not abandoning her, she's coming with me. I have a place for us, and we're moving out."

I didn't tell him when, or any other specifics. I was direct and cold and regurgitated the same statement over and over, *there is nothing you can do to change my mind. I'm moving out.*

Throughout that night, Levi alternated between crying and yelling. Then at six am he left for work without saying a word. He was clueless that today was the day, and that he'd be coming home to an empty house with no bed and no wife.

There was no other way. There was no sitting down like adults and talking about how to divide our things; no having a reasonable conversation about what's best for Dani. There was only hatred and contempt that made a mature and rational conversation absolutely impossible.

On the morning I left, I took out a piece of yellow legal paper and wrote him a letter.

Levi,

I didn't know how to tell you I was leaving today, I'm sorry I couldn't tell you sooner, but I didn't want to fight anymore. I never meant to hurt you and I hope that someday you'll understand and agree that this was the best thing for both of us and Dani.

All of the paperwork is done; you just need to sign on the last page. I tried to divide our stuff evenly and I won't take the child support. I've already opened an account that it will go into and it will get routed right back to you, all of it, I won't touch it, I promise. I don't want money. I just want you to let me go without fighting about it anymore. Don't try to talk me out of this, it's already done.

I'll have Dani call you later, she's with me.

C.J.

I set the yellow letter on the kitchen island next to the divorce manuscript then hurried to pack and move all of my things within the hours of his work day. I hauled a dozen boxes in and out, up and down, wincing with each step, pushing myself to the brink of collapse. When Ibuprofen didn't cut it, I added Celebrex, Flexeril, and a fresh ice pack every thirty minutes—just enough for me to stay upright until the job was done.

I had no one that I could ask for help when moving day came. I'd kept everyone I knew at arm's length to avoid disapproval and I couldn't ask Grant, it would be suspicious. More so I needed to do this without him. This was a life I created without him, and needed to get out of, regardless of him.

Dylan disapproved, mom and dad disapproved, *it was too fast* they said, *I needed to think this through.* I kept Lissy in the dark about my plans along with everyone else I had ever known, in fear of them finding out my secret or lecturing me on how I was breaking the sacred vows of marriage. I would move myself even if it killed me. I didn't want the help of anyone who was not fully supportive of my decision. So I had no one.

Not only did I not ask anyone to help me, I hadn't even told anyone I'd filed for divorce or that I was moving out. I'd only mentioned to a few people that I wanted a divorce and that I was serious. No one seemed to understand or support my decision and thus I couldn't tell them the whole truth until it was done.

I had enough money to hire two men for two hours to move my big items. The rest I muscled on my own at the expense of permanently damaging my already broken back. On the last trip out of Levi and I's house I sat beside Bodi with a handful of treats. He was my respite after Nanook died, and having to lose him too, was unbearable. I didn't see how I had another choice. He belonged in the house, in the yard, not in an apartment, and there wasn't a place in Dani's school district that would take pets. I secretly hoped and thought that Levi would default on the mortgage payments and be forced to move out, then I could move back in and keep my dog.

I gave him a treat in exchange for a kiss then sobbed into his fur. My involuntary whimper made him tilt his head and lick my tears.

"Goodbye buddy," I said from the bottom of the stairs. "I love you, I'm so sorry, I'll come back and visit, okay? Take care of Dani when she's here with you."

I fell to my knees when he trotted over begging to go out for our daily walk. I squeezed him and wailed through another goodbye, "be a good dog, don't bite anyone." I held his head to look in his eyes and felt sharp stab of pain in my chest.

"I love you buddy." He wagged his single coil tail fast like a metronome. I stood up, wiped my face off on my shirt and walked away. The tears I cried for having to leave him behind kept coming for hours, then days, then months.

I picked Dani up from school later that day and brought her to our new apartment. She cried and asked to go home. I cried and wanted to go home.

Levi signed the papers a few weeks later with no contest. I heard that our divorce was final when it was publicized in the local paper later that fall, hung out on the gallows for our entire town to see.

**

Gonna get the plane
gassed up. Love you!

Chapter 31

"AND THOUGH SHE BE BUT LITTLE, SHE IS FIERCE."

—SHAKESPEARE, A MIDSUMMER NIGHT'S DREAM, 3.2.355

Divorce mistake number three: *I should have gotten out sooner. Much, much sooner.*

My hair was falling out.

In the single stall shower of my lonely apartment, clumps of dark hair collected in the drain. It wasn't until my stylist asked, "Honey, why are you losing all your hair?" that I realized how bad it really was.

In the months after I'd moved out, depression, in its most destructive form showed up at my door and refused to leave. By day I was a broken, single mom, with a fake smile and by night I was with Grant, leaping and dancing and planning how to satisfy our wanderlust. I couldn't have been living any more of a polarized existence.

The physical pain came and went with little correlation to anything I did and there were still no clear answers as to what was wrong with me. Not only was I not improving, I was blacking out from the pain. It began with a deafening ring in my ears then tunnel vision before everything went black. The first time it happened I was by myself. I knelt down so I didn't fall, it only lasted a few seconds before I came back. The second time I wasn't quite so lucky.

I'd just pulled up to a red light when I felt myself fading. I yanked the emergency break to keep my car from rolling back, then slumped over the steering wheel. When I came to, cars and trucks were honking and drivers were staring as they pulled around me.

Thanks for the help assholes, I thought as I quickly put it in gear and drove away semi-coherent and crying. That was the second incident in two weeks.

I'd exhausted every resource I had trying to figure out what was wrong with me. I'd went to a dozen different specialists and racked up thousands of dollars in bills to no avail. Desperate for relief, I was sucked into buying one useless remedy after another; herbs, acupuncture, acupressure, energy healing, raindrop therapy, Rolfing, and of course, I'd seen many, many chiropractors. Each convinced that if *I just kept coming back*, they could fix me. All of that was *after* I'd been through the traditional route; x-rays, physical therapy, anti-inflammatories, muscle relaxants, pain patches, second opinions and psychiatric care. A diagnosis was out of reach.

I was incapacitated from simple movements like sitting, or getting out of bed. Each caused a relentless stabbing followed by an endless deep ache. I concealed my torment, I tried to live normally. But I fooled no one. My clients, Dylan, and even strangers were starting to notice. Some guy at the grocery store offered to carry my bags when he saw me struggling to walk with a few plastic sacks and Dani held my hand, leading me gently as I limped up and down the stairs to our apartment. Everyone saw that something was wrong but no one knew what it was. I didn't know what it was.

Grant saw my guarded movements, erratic spasms and muted wincing and asked what was wrong, but I didn't tell him the full extent of what it was. Because *I* didn't even know what it was. He deserved a woman who could have babies, and live a normal, long life. And if I couldn't figure out how to get better, I wouldn't be able to give him that. The fear of losing him to this, whatever it was, was more excruciating than the pain itself.

***

My new apartment was aesthetically beautiful yes, but it was emotionally empty and Dani felt it too. She never wanted to be there. She stayed with Levi three nights a week and the other four I almost had to force her to stay with me. I tried to make it a home for her, for us, but everything I did was futile. We dyed Easter eggs, carved pumpkins, hung lights on the house plant and balcony at Christmas and stapled stockings to the fireplace. But still, our new place never became a home.

We had one T.V., and no cable and spent most of our at the apartment watching our favorite chick flicks over and over while I laid on her bedroom floor strapped to hard piece of thick black plastic.

It was called a traction table but it was more like a medieval torture device that pulled my ribs away from my hips with sixty pounds of pressure. It was like being sawed in half, it separated my upper body from my lower body and I laid in it every day, sometimes twice a day. It worked at first, offering me partial relief in the hours after. Then a few weeks, the relief lessened, and after a few months the pain and depression only deepened.

On a lonely Saturday afternoon when Dani was with Levi, I clutched the shiny black bench in front of my piano and lowered myself down, then placed my fingers on the ivory keys. It was the first time I'd played music in the hollow rectangle that was now my home. Lonely sounds echoed through the rooms as I played every dark and somber tune I knew. The only music that seemed fitting within lonesome walls.

My somber playlist ended when my phone vibrated on top of the polished ebony. It was Grant.

"Hi, baby. Meet me at the hangar in an hour."

"The where?"

"The airplane hangar," he said.

"Oh. Okay! Where do I go?" He gave me directions and instructions on where to go and what to wear. I stuffed an ice pack down the back of the only jeans I owned and pushed a small white pill into my pocket. As I walked out, my hiking boots clunked across the thin floor loud enough to wake the people in the apartment below. I locked the dead bolt behind me, leaving misery, my alter identity trapped inside.

***

"Come on, get in." Dylan said, coaxing me into a hammock that was tethered between two totally inadequate trees overlooking the lake. I wasn't more than ten years old the day he prodded me into that rickety, cream colored, fish net hammock mom picked up from a flea market. It was something to keep us occupied outside and out of her hair.

"Get in, I'll give you a nice push." Dylan said.

This, from the brother who would fart in his hand and then cup it around my nose. I knew it wasn't going to be a *nice push*.

"Get in," He whined. "I'll push you slow, come on. I won't do anything, I promise."

I fanned out the cream netting, straddled the wobbly cradle then sat down in choppy thunks as the ropes slipped down the bark of the trees.

"Wrap yourself up," he said, helping me into the cocoon that encased me in its maw.

He pushed gently at first, then faster, ignoring my pleas.

"Come on, I'll flip you all the way around," he said. "It'll be fun, just hang on."

As if I had a choice. I was already on a trajectory to do a full loop when the ramshackle netting spit me out and flung me to the ground.

This, I imagined, was how my private flight with Grant was going to go.

***

I had on my only pair of jeans, a long sleeve shirt and sunglasses like he'd asked. All I was missing was a compass, in case I survived the crash, and a set of dog tags for identification, in case I didn't.

Just before the gravel road, I slid back the little white pill with a sip of warm water from a slightly stinky Aquafina bottle rolling around in the back seat.

"Hi, baby!" Grant yelled, peeking out from behind an open panel on the side of the plane.

It looked like one of those old-fashioned World War II planes with an open cock pit. Except this one was modern, with a paint job that morphed it into a carnivorous animal with a gaping blood-red mouth filled with jagged teeth. It sat in the spotlight of the sun, next to a private grass air strip that had been carved from cutting down a swath of cornfield.

Grant trotted over to me and wrapped me in a hug that lifted my boots from the ground.

"I'm so happy you came, I can't wait to take you up. Honey, just think...we'll get to do this anytime we want—watch the sunset, fly over the lakes, sightsee in October—your favorite month." He set me down smooched my lips with and audible *Mwah!* Then slapped my tush. "I don't think I've ever seen you in jeans. Mmm...you look so good, baby, I can't wait to re-create the other night." He said with a salacious, hungry expression as he scanned my curves.

"You'll have to fly me to Fiji for that." I said then smiled the same hungry grin.

"I can do that." He said.

He was donned in aviation gear from head to toe, looking pistol hot; I didn't need to go to Fiji, I would have gotten naked and let him do me over the plane right then. I was completely willing to make love to my hero on the wings of a plane and have Aerosmith playing in the background. I was sure he would indulge me in that fantasy someday.

He pulled me into the hangar and fitted me with eighteen pounds of flight gear. "Honey, how safe is this?" I asked. "I have a child you know." He tugged and cinched a ridiculous amount of straps and buckles.

"Don't worry, it's completely safe, it's more likely that you'd die in a car accident on the way out here. Honey, I'd never do anything to lose you or take you away from Dani."

"But what about John F. Kennedy Jr? And all the other small planes that crash each year, I bet those pilots said the same thing."

"I'm sure they did, but I don't take risks. Only calculated ones anyway."

"You do take risks though I've seen you."

"I don't anymore," he caught my attention with the most sincere expression "I want to live forever now that I have you. I promise I will always take extra precautions."

The extra-large parachute he'd strapped to my tiny frame was so bulky and heavy I felt like a deep sea diver stranded in an Iowa cornfield.

He finished tightening all one hundred buckles then double backed the straps yanking so hard both of my feet floated across the ground.

"Why don't you just put your foot on my stomach and cinch them tighter?" I complained.

"Does it hurt? It's supposed to be tight."

Had I not taken OxyContin I would have probably passed out, but I couldn't miss this date, I'd do whatever it takes to go flying with him.

"It's fine," I said. "Why are we wearing parachutes anyway? I don't know how to skydive."

He reached into the tote and pulled out a second parachute for himself. "We're not going to skydive, not today," he said as he hurled the large green pack over his shoulders, "we're not going to take any chances. These are for an emergency abort."

"Can you actually sky dive from this plane?" I asked.

"It's not designed for that, but I did do it once. Well...*I* didn't do it, I was the pilot, she, *just a friend*, jumped out," he said. "We videotaped it; you should watch it on YouTube sometime. I flipped the plane upside down; she unbuckled and slid right out."

"I don't want to have to do that," I said. "Aborting then parachuting from a flaming bottle rocket is not on my bucket list."

He laughed. "You're in good hands baby."

"Oh, I know and I wish your hands were all over me right now."

"You got it. Tonight?"

"Yes. Tonight."

"You ready?" he asked.

"For you or the plane ride?"

"Both."

"I've never been more ready," I said.

I'd Googled *aerobatics* after seeing the magazine on his coffee table so I *sort of* knew what I'd signed up for. I suspected that this flight was a test—to see if I could hang. Literally hang, upside down, sideways or any other way he could flip, roll or spin us.

He slid on his sunglasses and gave me a kiss. Our every interaction was combined with a kiss. Look at each other—kiss, smile at each other—kiss, give a compliment—kiss, say a smart ass remark—kiss kiss.

"Whatever you do, don't throw up. If you throw up it will land right in my face." He said with fear in his voice. "You don't think you'll throw up do you?"

"I hope not," I shrugged.

He took a deep breath, disliking my answer. Then we stood facing each other in our paratrooper outfits and he kissed my lips again with a wet, swirly kiss.

I hobbled to the plane unsure of how I'd be able to maneuver all the gear strapped to my skeleton *out* of the plane if I needed to escape a burning inferno. He helped me into the front seat of the cockpit then forced a hideous leather helmet fitted with a microphone onto my head—mushing my hair to my forehead and ears.

"Why does it say experimental?" I asked, looking up at the large red letters across the top of the plane.

"Don't worry," he said, then began the flight procedures tutorial. "In case we need to get out. I'll say 'get out, get out, get out' three times. Then you abort."

"Hold on. Do you mean you'll yell 'get out, get out, get out' three times for a total of nine? Or just the first three?"

"I will say it three times then you abort," he said. "How do I abort?"

"I'm getting to that. Be patient. If you need to abort, unbuckle yourself like this," He buckled me into the co-pilot's seat with a harness that looked just like the one in Dani's car seat when she was two. "Turn this dial clockwise," he said.

"Which way is clockwise? As if I am looking at it from your perspective or mine?"

"From my perspective," he showed me again. "Make sure to get clear of the plane before you deploy your chute." He grabbed a metal handle that was tucked inside a pocket on my chest. "If you need to deploy the chute, pull this straight forward, hard, with both hands. Remember," he said sternly, "pull it straight out, away from your body…*hard,* only after you clear the plane. I wouldn't want anything to happen to you, baby, then I'd have to die too."

"I feel the same. Do you think maybe we can die together like the old couple on *The Notebook?*"

"Never seen it."

"You've never seen *The Notebook?*"

"Is it good?" He asked.

"Yes, it's good. Anyway, can we die together? Maybe we can just go up for a joyride when we're really old and never come back."

"Yes," he said. "Let's do that. After our grandkids are old. I never want to know what life is like without you." Kiss, kiss, kiss. "This gage will tell you how many 'G's' were pulling." He pushed a reset button and the needle dropped to zero.

"What are G's?"

"You'll see. Put your feet up there on that metal bar. Don't touch any of these cords and keep your legs away from the joystick." Then he leapt into the pilot's seat behind me.

"Hey, can you do sky writing in this plane?"

"Yes," he said. Then yelled, "Clear!" Loud into the air.

Except for the farm cats, there was no one around for miles.

***

U can have me
always & forever. :)

Chapter 32

"ONLY FROM THE HEART,

CAN YOU TOUCH THE SKY."

—RUMI

What if he dies in a plane wreck? No one would ever know I was the love of his life, and that he was the loss I could not bear.

The propeller stuttered and skipped before the white bird roared to life. He revved the engine like a teenager with shiny new Mustang, then we rolled onto a narrow strip of well-manicured grass hidden within a tasseling corn field.

It sounded like we were talking through walkie-talkies, with a scratch at the beginning and the end. "Baby, are you ready?"

"Yes!" I tried not to sound scared but I was terrified.

We catapulted forward, whizzing past a golden blur of corn, heading toward a shelter belt of thick pine trees. The plane shook so violently I was surprised when it actually lifted off of the ground. I felt the crushing G force against my chest as we careened into the air just above the bristly trees.

The native tall grass prairie had long since been replaced by flaxen fields of rolling wheat and dense green quadrants of soybeans. The landscape was a patchwork quilt of crops all the way to the horizon. A river cut through the valley, meandered through groves of trees and around heirloom farms where rusty metal silos stood tall in the front yards.

His voice came scratching over the radio, "I love you baby!" He yelled, thrilled that I was hearty enough to go flying with him.

"I love you!" I yelled back against the roaring wind.

"Think you're ready for some action?" He asked.

I forced fearlessness, "Bring it on!"

"Okay, hold on!"

With a sharp dig, he veered the nose straight up. The G force crushed my insides and sucked my face tight to my skull like I'd had an overdose of Botox. But I was far from looking beautiful while being whipped with gale force winds, I felt more like a Saint Bernard with my lips and gums flapping, peering out the window of an SUV at two hundred miles an hour.

The gazillion straps and buckles that guarded my life and kept me inside the experimental aircraft had tightened around my every bulge, squishing my breasts and pressing the air out of my lungs.

"Hang on!" He yelled through the head set.

I white knuckled the abort handle above me as we looped up and over, making a full backward somersault. I looked at the G meter—4. Adrenaline and lack of oxygen made my head feel goofy, but surprisingly, I was still fine.

Not so bad, I can do this.

"You good?" He asked.

"I'm great! Let's do it again!"

He angled the nose upward, the tail plummeted and immense pressure crushed my chest and ears as we began another upside down loop. The ratchety hum of the plane went silent as it dug deep into its guts fighting against the gravitational forces it was being asked to overcome. I was sucked back into my seat and my seat was sucked back into me as we jettisoned up and over.

The G meter held its position, moving only if the G forces exceeded the previous meter's reading. I checked the gauge—5.

"You still good?"

"Yep!" I think I wasn't sick because my senses were so assaulted they'd slipped into a coma and stopped reporting their findings.

His encouragement sputtered over the radio. "Honey, you're the best woman ever! Everything is so much better with you!"

Worth it—so worth it.

"I'll do one more loop, then we'll do something else, okay? Can you take one more?"

"I think so!" I yelled into my headset and gave him a thumbs-up.

He darted to a higher elevation, the temperature dropped ten degrees and the atmosphere became eerily calm. We dug in one last time, the tail dropped; air pressed out of my lungs and my blood was forced downward into my boots. When we came out of the loop, my head bobbled in slow motion, woozy from the pressure and I was being strangled by the very straps meant to save my life. I looked at the G meter—6. I didn't know if that was a lot or a little, but it was enough for me and he sensed it.

"No more G's, I promise." He said just before he rolled us horizontally through the sky in a candy-cane pattern, then pitched us straight up into a vertical climb.

I'd heard a story about how Grant had taken one of our friends flying then pulled a maneuver where he flew straight upward allowing the plane to stall. Then when the plane plunged downward he could test his skills on how to get it to fly properly again. It scared the eyeballs out of our friend. Just when I thought I heard that white bird start to cough and choke, he planned it out and spared me from the crash test landing.

"No more tricks okay?" I yelled over the headset, my voice constricted and dry.

The air went smooth—from stomach clenching stunts to an eagle's eye view. I was now looking at the skyline, a panoramic vista that was breathtaking; a thousand shades of tie dyed lavender and blue, and wispy, cotton balls of fluff surrounded us. We flew like we were suspended in the thin atmosphere. It seemed like we were barely moving.

I had never thought about touching a cloud, not for real. It wasn't something I ever imagined I could do. But now, we were sprinting straight toward it. It got shivering cold and my eyes refused to blink as we entered the semi-transparent plume. For a few brief moments we were engulfed in a hazy heaven. I reached out to touch it but the wind nearly dismembered my arm. Grant laughed loud at my idiocy; I could hear him howling over the roar of the wind. We were inside the marshmallow cavern for a few fleeting seconds before it spit us out, back into the familiar atmosphere of the pale blue dot, but a few seconds was enough to give me a glimpse of what heaven, if there is a heaven, might look like.

"Baby, look!" He yelled. "Straight ahead, low on the horizon, do you see the brightest star?"

"Yes!"

"That's Jupiter," he said.

I became fixated on the shimmering speck, the wonder of its presence and how its existence had escaped me all these years. It lived right above me as I lived oblivious below, mistaking it for just another ordinary star. He was showing me a world of new and wondrous things and was helping me see them through new eyes.

It was just before sunset when we landed smooth on the runway in the middle of the corn field. We taxied to the hangar, he helped me out then helped me take off my aviation gear. With both arms tight around my torso, he lifted me off both feet for a celebration hug.

"I'm so glad we survived," I said, teasing. "Just kidding, Grant that was spectacular. You're spectacular."

"You make me that way. And, you make me want to be even better. Meet me at my place?" He said.

"Yes," I nodded, "cant wait."

"Bye, love. I'll be right behind you," he said, as he finished putting away our gear and securing the plane. "Open the wine and get cozy." He blew me a kiss as I walked away.

When I rounded the corner and was concealed behind by the steel building I released my breath, abandoned my smile, and fell to my knees.

The gravel stamped pock-marks into my palms and tears raced toward my chin. I closed my eyes, bit my lip and winced as I forced myself to stand. I was lame. Once a thoroughbred with shiny chestnut hair, promising victory to her supporters, she was now injured, downed in her stall, unable to run and waiting for the bullet.

I slid one leg into my car, then flopped down uncontrollably into my seat. I pulled in my other leg and drove away sobbing. It wasn't getting better, I was getting exponentially worse.

I lay on the carpet in his living room waiting to go numb. Red wine and another little white pill were starting to kick in, and soon, at least for a little while, it would be as if there had been no pain at all. My phone lit up.

On my way 2 u, baby, and
u r not going 2 believe
what I'm going 2 do 2 u.
After a brief rest, I'll
slowly turn u over and
back 2 me. I'll pull u up
on ur knees and slowly
put myself gently inside
u, deeper and deeper.

I loved our scandalous sext messages, I'd never done anything so saucy. I was impressed by his continued commitment to shock me as another one chimed in.

I'll reach down and
touch u just the way u
like it, just the way u
showed me, and then
I'll show u how I like
it, things you've never
known, things we've
never done...until u...

By the time he walked through the door, my pain was anesthetized, but my skin still tingled under his touch. I tilted my head back in delight, allowing him full access to kiss me the way I needed to be kissed. I laid on the floor dazed by romance, wine and pain killers.

"Our life together will be so great, baby," he said, "it already is. But it's about to get better." His sly grin tipped me off that he'd been planning something.

He dropped in another cork, Blackstone Syrah, it read:

G+C
1st Flight

He filled my glass with a generous pour and ordered me onto the floor.

"Sit here," he pointed to a nest of blankets and I obeyed. He slipped my tank over my head and skimmed his lips across my exposed back, humming a delicious *mmm...*

The lacy straps of my bra slid easily down my shoulders and he settled in behind me. Grant's warm hands kneaded my constricted muscles melting them into pliable taffy.

"Baby, you deserve to have this every night," he said.

"I do?" I said, groggy and bobbling from side to side. "This is heaven. I haven't been *that* good of a girl."

His low voice rumbled, "Oh yes you have, and I have a surprise for you—several, actually." A sneaky grin hid behind his voice. I undulated under his touch as he pressed his hands deeper into my tiny musculature. "I bought us some massage oil, candles, and...you know. I hope that's okay, only if you want." He swung his head to the side to catch my expression.

"Of course that's okay, that's perfect. So I guess we're not waiting until Fiji?"

"I think we already blew that," he said, "but we'll still go there someday, you know we will."

But I didn't know *we will*. This was all way too good to be true, and although he hadn't faltered on any promise *yet*. I'd never been in a relationship that hadn't let me down. In fact—I'd never even seen a relationship where the woman wasn't let down. *Nothing is this perfect.*

"Stay here." He kissed my lips with his signature loud smack, "Mwah!" then catapulted over the back of the couch disappearing long enough for me to finish my wine and lose any last inhibitions.

When he sauntered back, he was beaming with the aura of a man about to make love to his woman. He held out his hand, pulled me into him, and escorted me to his bedroom. With his hands gripping tight around my hips, he lead me into the scent of sensual jasmine, and into the dim-flickering light of candles. It was just enough to make out each other's silhouette without revealing any embarrassing details.

And the sound...ah, the sound.

I had no idea what it meant at the time, but I knew it was exotic, authentic, and from a world I didn't know. Sultry foreign sounds reverberated off the walls intensifying each touch.

The smell, the music, the way we swayed, it was perfect and planned, calculated down to the placement of the pillows on a bed of fresh linens. In the center of his warm room, we stood, woven into each other, flaming with sexual desire from nothing more than fingertips on skin. He traced the contours of my back touching low where the skin was sensitive and normally would have made me cringe. But tonight, I realized...I had no pain.

"I love the music," I said as we swayed.

"I picked it for you—for us." He pulled me tight against him moving our hips as one.

"Who's is this?"

"The Buena Vista Social Club." He dipped me, "they're from Cuba. Baby, let's go to Cuba someday."

"Cuba?"

Not my first pick.

"I was thinking more like...Palu—but I'll go anywhere with you. Can we even go to Cuba?"

"Someday we'll be able to. We can go to Palu too."

I turned away from him, keeping with the syncopated Cuban beat, practically begging for more of him to touch more of me. "When are you going to teach me to dance?" I asked.

"You already know how to dance," he said in a sexy, deep voice and I felt him press hard into me.

"I mean real dancing, not just moving to music. I want to ballroom dance, with you."

"We will. I will teach you everything. There's a Tuesday night swing club we can go to for practice." He spun me around. "Do you want to learn the tango?" He asked.

"Well that's an easy answer," I said, "yes."

He held our arms in the signature tango pose, "How about..." then swept me into a tango lunge with one leg reaching way back. "I'll teach you the tango on our next date. Tonight is Cuban night."

A jealous thought of all the women who'd gotten to dance with him flashed in my mind. His dancing partner, women in classes he taught, private lessons, surely they had been swooned by him when he put them into the tango position. Then I reminded myself, *he's with me, not them, he's about to make love to me, not them.*

He unbuttoned my jeans, then followed them to the floor guiding me out. His lips navigated the length of my body from my ankles all the way back up to my wanting eyes. He grasped my shoulders and turned me away from him, "Lay down," he said, "on your stomach."

I could have died, every moment agony and ecstasy in equal measure, and nothing had even happened yet. He pulled back the down comforter and instructed me where to lie. The sateen sheets were cool against my skin, making his warm hands even more titillating. He stood over me with sensual vanilla jasmine massage oil in his palms. My hips moved to the Cuban beat, unrestrained, uninhibited, a show he enjoyed.

"Baby, you're so hot," he said it like he was about to devour me whole. His slippery hands made long strokes from my shoulders to my waist, his fingertips fanned out and covered the entire wingspan of my back. Each time, he slipped a little further into my panties, and with each sensual stroke, I sighed in ecstasy.

"Thank you for the massage, you're so wonderful," I muttered.

"You don't have to thank me, I love touching you."

I sighed again, even more aroused from his words than his touch. He teased me until I nearly begged him to take my panties off, then finally he slid them down to my ankles letting them fall to the floor. Then he teased me more.

It was an unbearable agony he forced me to endure, long pauses of him stepping away to watch me thrash and suffer after naughty strokes over my most sensitive areas.

"I *will* get you back," I declared.

"I can't wait," he said, flipping me over. His ice blue eyes stared at me and his voice was drowning in testosterone, "I've waited so long for this...for you, all of you."

The mood changed from deliberate mischievous teasing, to unrestrained primal desire. He radiated through me, filling my every cell with a fantastic and wild love. Pinned underneath him, with my arms pressing against the wall, he took his rightful place of over me, guarding me, making love to me.

He set his lips on my ear, "I love you so much, I can't believe it's really you."

We lay side by side under the thin sheets, exhausted and exhilarated—our oily bodies touching in as many places as possible. Shadows flickered on the wall and *The Buena Vista Social Club* was still playing on repeat. He searched through the sheets for my hand then interlaced his fingers in mine.

"I knew it would be good, but I didn't think it would be *that* good," I said and we laughed.

"Me neither, we fit so well together," he said. "Stay here." Then he shimmied off the bed, turned off the music, and left the room.

When he came back, he was wearing clean boxers and his guitar. He sat at the edge of the bed, one leg dangling down, closed his eyes and started to strum. I pushed up onto my elbows, laid draped under his cool sheets and couldn't believe what I was hearing. I recognized the song, I loved the song, I'd suggested he learn this song. He did, he learned it for me.

"Time After Time."

I closed my eyes and swayed along to his masculine voice singing those romantic words. I felt his love for me.

Then we sang every song we could think of, sometimes just him, sometimes just me, and sometimes we sang together. I fumbled through lyrics singing only a chorus or often only a single line, but I still sang, something I hadn't done with anyone in a long time. I sang until I couldn't sing any more.

It became our after sex tradition for him to sing late into the night, any song I requested "Wicked Game," "Cry To Me," and "She Will Be

225

Loved." were among my favorites. If he didn't know my request he would slip his guitar pick between his teeth, pick up his phone, Google the lyrics and cords and play it anyway; any song, any genre, any hour of the night. Even if he sang it completely wrong, if I requested it, he tried to sing it.

It was there at the edge of his bed with his guitar and our nearly naked bodies where we fell madly and unequivocally in love.

The next morning I woke up paralyzed.

Chapter 33

Daylight peeked through the crack of the blinds, and his overwhelmingly male body was still pressed against mine. He lay contented and untroubled as I lay hopeless and incurable. I reached my arms above my head and clamped on to the corner of the mattress. I tried to pull my limp body closer to the edge so I could roll off then crawl to the bathroom.

His voice was sincere, I sobbed the instant he spoke. "Baby, what's wrong?" He hovered over me radiating concern. "What can I do? What is it? Is it your back?"

"Yes," I wept.

"Honey, what do you need, how can I help?" He sat up, ready to act.

"I don't know…" I turned my face away as tears pooled on the pillow beneath me. "I just need some time; it'll get better as the day goes on. It's always the worst in the mornings. There's a bottle of ibuprofen in my bag, will you get me 800mg?"

"Of course," he mobilized immediately.

"Do you have an ice pack too?" I asked.

"No, but I can get one." He slid on yesterday's jeans and buttoned them around his trim waist. "Here you go," Grant held out his hand, offering me four small rusty colored pills and a glass of water. "Take these, I'll be right back with an ice pack, ten minutes. Can I get you anything else?" I shook my head embarrassed by my helpless condition. He kissed my wet cheek. "Baby, I'm so sorry; tell me how to help you."

"You're doing it." I said through a forced smile.

When I heard the garage door close, I rolled onto the floor then inched my way into the bathroom to get my overnight bag. Crawling brought sensation back into my legs but made the stabbing pains in my lower back worse. Every move contracted a muscle that pulled on a bone that caused more crunching and grinding. I took another little white pill—not because I wanted to—because I had to.

Grant came back with a five pound bag of ice, the kind you get from an aluminum cooler outside of a gas station. He stuffed a plastic grocery bag full, laid blankets on the couch, propped up pillows, and helped me into position.

We were sitting at opposite ends of the couch, each with a generous mug of coffee when he asked, "Honey, what's going on, why does your back hurt? Was it the flight?"

"No. It's been like this for a while, I don't know exactly how it happened. I just know it's getting worse."

"Why didn't you tell me how bad it is? I want to know these things." He set down his coffee and kneaded the muscles in my legs and feet with both hands—his strained expression revealed a deep, honest concern. "What do you *think* it is, baby?"

I looked down into my coffee, searching for an answer I didn't have. *How can I not know what's wrong with me and why can't anybody help me?*

"Honestly I don't know what it is—I could speculate but I can't be sure. I've been to a dozen different specialists and gotten a dozen conflicting opinions." I shifted, uncomfortable in any one position for too long. "No one seems to know exactly where the pain is coming from, but everyone seems to have plenty of expensive and useless advice. I've just been trying to deal with it Learn how to live with it."

"There has to be help for you. Where have you gone?"

I told him everything, everywhere I'd been, traditional and non-traditional, and everything I'd taken. "I was told I wasn't a candidate for surgery, that people with lower back pain without nerve pain don't have good results."

"Did you get a second opinion?"

"Yes."

"Did you go to Minneapolis? Or to the Mayo Clinic?"

"No."

"Then that's where we need to go."

An ill feeling crept over me, he'd expect me to keep looking for a solution, expect me to get better, and I'd keep letting him down.

"Don't worry about the money," he said, preempting my complaint.

But I did worry about the money. Rather a lack of the money I would need to go to Mayo, and I wasn't going to ask him or anyone else for money. I was twenty nine, made a moderate income, I needed to take care of myself.

"You need to find real help. Medical help, don't go anywhere else. You need to go to someone at the top. I know an orthopedic surgeon in Colorado; I'll call him and ask where we should go. Do you have x-rays or medical records from past doctor visits?"

"Of course."

"We will find a solution okay?"

But he didn't understand, "I did see an orthopedic surgeon," I said, "he said I wasn't a candidate for surgery. He gave me Vicodin and Oxy and sent me home. I take it when I need to, more than I want to."

"If you need pain killers take them. We will find you help. I will help you," Grant said.

"There is one thing that takes the pain away," I said raising an eyebrow.

"What's that?"

"Sex."

***

Our journal was wrapped in a light green silky fabric scattered with sparkling silver flecks. We kept it under his bed and said that we'd write down the things we didn't want to forget. We made a pact that we wouldn't read the other person's entry until a year from the date they were written.

It was so hard not to read the things he wrote—I kept my promise for at least a month before I read his first entry. This is what it said.

After trivia night with the guys, I expediently made my way back home in great anticipation to see my honey :)

We, as always, had great conversation as we sat on the short bus together, while drinking five-day old wine that seemed to give us both a headache. C.J. brilliantly suggested that sex may be the perfect remedy for our malady. Thankfully, she did not pull the all too common "I have a headache, therefore, no sex!" Heh-heh!

We retreated to my bedroom with her favorite massage oil, and I proceeded to strip away any stresses that may have contributed to C.J.'s headache. In a very passionate love making episode, we telegraphed everything that was unsaid, and everything that was about to happen...ah!

We woke up this morning to our busy, busy lives once again, but what better way to start the day, than to wake up next to the girl of your dreams!

-Grant

Chapter 34

"IN DREAMS AND IN LOVE... THERE ARE NO IMPOSSIBILITIES."

—JANOS ARNAY

"The summer of 2009—the summer we fall in love." Those words, his words, as they slipped past his lips, became tattooed on my heart. It was a summer of adrenaline and uncertainty, new love and letting go.

Sneaking around became the one thing we shared exclusively—a blood secret. We wore disguises; baseball caps, sunglasses and oversized flannel jackets to the movie theater. I snuck into his cabin and he snuck into my apartment.

At the lake, I went for long morning walks and met him at our secret spot where he would pick me up in a borrowed green minivan, we'd drive somewhere off the grid, sip coffee, talk about everything important and nothing at all.

In the glaring midday sun, when everyone was cooling off in the water, he whistled for me from behind the trunk of a huge maple tree. He trapped me between his arms and kissed me feverishly while the clamor of laughter and conversation were just feet away.

We found ways to be together, away from spying eyes. We hid in the grotto, I loved the grotto. Our secret place where a small stream of fresh water wide enough only for a paddle boat flowed lazily between the lakes. Surrounded by eight-foot-tall reeds, we floated for hours, drifting among the swamp life and gazing up at the vast ocean of blue sky. In was in the grotto where calm water turned into bubbles before a big brown beaver poked his head out and took a curious look at us. We never saw our buck-tooth friend again, but we never forgot him.

No one knew our secret and we'd have to keep it that way, at least for a while. Like family and friends do, they were already liberal with unwelcome advice, *wait a year to start dating again, a relationship too soon after divorce will never work*, they would say. Probably sound counsel, part of me was scared they were right, but it just wasn't an option to wait. They didn't know that what Grant and I had existed in a realm that transcended their conventional advice.

We spent evenings around the bonfire with friends and family, singing songs and stealing glances. Then disappeared strategically twenty minutes apart to avoid speculation. I walked along the twinkling shoreline underneath the light of a million stars, then as soon as I saw headlights on the road I ran through the yards and after his car until the brake lights lit up.

He drove to our secret spot, plowing down a swath of five-foot tall marsh grass that rebounded behind us and concealed our crime. There, behind an old storage garage, next to the sounds of a midnight swamp, we made love in the passenger seat of his car. A tricky feat, we maneuvered in ways that only a contortionist could appreciate. On several occasions our secret spot rendezvous didn't end in the intended way, but always ended with rolling laughter.

Under the cover of a starry midnight sky we would scurry through the yards and out to the end of a vacant dock where we spread out a thick quilted blanket and pillows. Over the water and underneath the North Star, we drifted into a blissful sleep. Sometimes we made love, other times we contemplated whether or not to freeze our brains when we die. Every time, he encircled me in his arms and we shared our thoughts on how lucky we were to have found such an extraordinary love.

On a Tuesday, for no particular reason, he left me another card.

To the love of my life,

I am soooo lucky to have you, if you weren't in my life it would feel so empty.

We will have many more years together, that is certain, let's live every day as if we were spending the last day of our lives together. Imagine what the world would be like if everyone lived that way—the way that you and I do.

Here's to you, honey, and here's to us making the most of every remaining day of our lives.

I love you, baby!

Love, Me!

One rainy July weekend we hid-out at Grant's place instead of going to the lake. We made love and sushi and I gave him his first Thai massage.

"Will I be able to do it?" He asked.

"Weren't you listening?" I said. "You don't have to do anything. It's lazy man's yoga. It's perfect for you. Now, get down there."

"Isn't Thai Massage a euphemism for some type of kinky sex?" He asked as he slithered into the center of my plush, chocolate-colored Thai mat.

"It's not kinky sex, we can do that anytime."

I walked to the window and closed the blinds, leaving them open a sliver, letting the dim glow of the sunset flicker through the narrow slots.

"I'm so inflexible," he groaned from the floor.

"All the more reason you should be doing this. Now just shut-up and relax."

The unmistakable sound of ocean whales whirled around us, emanating from the dust covered CD player that sat on the floor of his vacant spare bedroom.

"When I taught Karate I was really flexible," he whined again.

"I don't care. Just relax."

As insignificant as it was, being flexible was the only thing I was better at than him. The pressure of being good enough next to someone so perfect was something I had never anticipated. Everyone I knew and total strangers too, didn't talk about me the way they talked about Grant. Next to someone so talented and likable, I often felt inadequate and small.

He lifted his head, "Honey, don't hurt your back. Maybe you shouldn't do this."

"Lie back down and don't worry, tonight is about you, and if you try to help me move your limbs, it will only make it harder. So just lay there like a flaccid penis," I said with a Botox expression, which instantly turned into gut-busting laughter.

I began at his feet, kneading and squeezing and pressing reflex points. Then I circled his ankles, cracked his toes and manipulated his entire body through a traditional Thai Massage. I plucked, pinched, and stretched every limb, metatarsal, and phalange. I acknowledged every minuscule muscle fiber and joint.

I alternated walking on my heels and toes across his hamstrings and back, massaged his scalp, squeezed his head, tugged his earlobes and pulled his hair. I sat on him, stepped on him, and stopped the flow of blood in several major arteries until he fell into a nirvana he never knew existed.

The muscles in his arms were a chiseled landscape as they cradled his head. I stood over him, done with the Thai sequence but not done with him. I slipped off everything but my bra and panties, then slid his silky black Adidas sweats to his ankles and off. I finished with a specialty service not available on the menu elsewhere—a service that didn't end with a simple palms-together "Namaste." I acted as if it was standard protocol, just part of the sequence. Then proceeded without permission to touch everything that had not yet been touched.

He returned the massage favor, lavished my every curve with techniques of his own, techniques I'd never experienced before, techniques not taught in Thai massage school. Then we made love on the floor without saying a word. And once again, for a brief time I was in a place where it didn't hurt. Being with him, making love to him, at so many levels erased all of my pain.

His eyes were inches from mine as I lay contented and euphoric.

"Let's go to Bodega," he said.

"Is that a good idea?"

"It's late, I doubt anyone will know us there, and if we get caught, we can say we happened to run into each other. You're newly single, so it's not so unlikely you'd go to a wine bar." His eyes followed his wandering hands. "Except you're not single—you're mine." He wiggled an arm underneath me and over me, then laid his head on my chest so could run my hands through his hair. He loved it when I ran my hands through his hair.

The sidewalk was wet and the air warm as we strolled to the wine bar, bowing our heads as cars passed. Burgundy and silver neon glowed from an oversized wine glass on top of the roof above the doors. Grant ordered us a bottle of wine, some type of Reserve Cabernet, a delicious ending to Thai and sex. We sat illegally close to one another, flirting and drinking and learning how to make zucchini lasagna from the food network on the television above the bar.

Across the room I noticed a lone couple snuggled on the couch next to a crackling summer fireplace. "I can't wait until we can do that," I whispered in his direction, bumping him. He leaned in to me and the bartender glanced up, spying our secret exchange.

"Soon, baby...soon."

"Grant, would you play a song for us tonight?" The bartender asked as he stuffed a cloth into a wine glass, meticulously drying it to a spot-free shine.

"You should, everyone loves it when you sing."

"I can do that," he said.

His warm hand lifted from my thigh, he winked and kissed the air beside me, then walked to the small crescent stage and picked up a guitar.

Silence swept through like a cold front, and the room went still as he started to strum. Porous red brick walls held the rich sounds of his guitar, and his eyes looked through me from the first word to the last as he sang his love song.

He was casually draped over the guitar, his body pulsing with vibration, holding back, waiting for all the right moments to use his gusto. When he was done, the couple on the couch clapped and looked at me not him, she flashed me a warm smile. She was curious, happy for me. I wanted to make her my surrogate friend and tell her everything—how much I loved him and what I had gone through to be with him, and tell her that tonight was the first time we'd been in public together without disguises.

"That was the best acoustic song ever, baby, you're amazing." I wanted to leap onto him and kiss him for the gift he had just given me, holding back was difficult and my stomach was tight with emotion.

"Oh quit it, I love singing for you," he whispered in my ear.

A white coat flashed in my side vision, the couple by the fireplace was walking toward us.

"That was great, thank you so much, what a treat." The woman said, reaching her hand out to him and cupping his forearm. She looked at me with a knowing smile, then back to Grant.

"We loved the way you were singing to her."

***

Hi Darling:)

Before I go to bed, I wanted to write you a little email that you can wake up to:)

So here we go...Honey, you are the absolute greatest thing in my life, and I know I say that, or something like that a lot, but it's the absolute truth. I don't know what life is like anymore without you; you've asked me what I would be doing right now if you were not around, and I don't know, and can't really remember what I did to occupy my time before you (B.C.— Before Charmaine:).

I can't even fathom a life without you now. We're on such a great adventure together, that words truly cannot describe it (or if they can, I just don't know what those words are...maybe paragon and veneration get close, but not quite.

Thank you so much for wanting to be a part of my life, and letting me be a part of yours; there isn't anyone else I would want to spend it with, and I have a feeling you feel the same, and that feels so awesome! I miss you very much right now, and every moment that goes by is occupied by thoughts of you, of us, the future, and the here and now...

I will see you tomorrow! (It's Tuesday already!)

Love, me...

P.S.—Imagine...you and I, warm bodies close, perfect fit, my steamy exhalation on your neck, your tiny hairs stand up, goose bumps spread across your body, my lips touch yours and we kiss, with tongue, softly...I go lower, it's perfect; you want me, and I want you. I make my way back, across your stomach, between your breasts, barely touching your skin with my lips...

Chapter 35

Fruit and Wine, Twister night

We started the evening with a healthy dinner then broke out Twister while listening to Kenny Wane Shepherd. I won. Okay, that's not true, but it was close. We then proceeded to drink some red wine, Renfold's Merlot to be specific, along w/wine soaked black berries, raspberries and strawberries I had prepared for C.J. in advance. Some of the fruit was eaten directly off of "Sushi Girl".

We then retreated to my bedroom, where we lay in bed, naked bodies next to one another, embracing...

The next morning, we woke up at 6:30am, only hitting the snooze button a couple of times. Then, of course, our addiction—Coffee! We fueled up on a couple of cups to start off the day. What better start than to wake up next to the girl of my dreams, touch her soft, beautiful skin, pretty hair, then share in conversation of a cup or two of Caribou...

-Grant

Chapter 36

You are a babe, you know! Can't wait to see you, love sneaking with you, even though I would rather not sneak! But if I had to, you would be the one to sneak with :)

I love you so much, honey...I'm really, really looking forward to our getaway...let's have fun (there's no way we couldn't :)

Soon...

-Grant

Chapter 37

Fantastic adventures, surreal landscapes and the promise of a future with him lacing us through all of it was unbelievable. The more amazing our life together became the more I feared it was teetering on the brink of extinction. I couldn't shake the feeling that something was about to puncture this fantasy and I would fall thousands of feet back to a bleak reality, without him. I didn't know whether it was his initial hot and cold spells that made those feelings linger, or if I sensed something else looming. I didn't have any actual evidence that such a travesty would occur, but I couldn't eradicate the notion.

Ob·ses·sion:

The uncontrollable persistence
of an idea in the mind, sometimes
associated with psychiatric disorder.

—Dictionary.com

Yep. I was obsessed.

With him, with losing him, with us and I was withering away. I'd officially begun *The Divorce Diet* or was it the *New Love Diet*? I guess it was both.

Did this state of euphoria exist to make me skinny and thus more attractive to my suitor? I wondered.

I lingered in the space between obsessive psychosis and new love euphoria; the place where all other beings in the universe ceased to exist except for me and the object of my desire. Some type of biological gene had turned on causing me to lose all interest in food and hobbies and anything other than the tasks that moved me closer to my goal: permanent procurement of my new mate.

We drove a few hours away from our hometown and into the towering pine and hardwood forests of Northern Minnesota for what I hoped would be an unforgettable birthday weekend. Along the Lake Country Byway we meandered through miles of protected wetlands and nature preserves that sprawled out between quaint antiquing towns— each one equipped with its own gourmet chocolate shop and vanilla bean coffee bistro.

The forest trees were a blurry Picasso out my window as we drove holding hands and getting high on gourmet fudge and exquisite coffee. We dreamed out loud about all the places we'd visit in our lifetime. Places like *The Museum of The Rockies* and the campus at Cal Tec, Kilauea and Krakatoa, Bettie's Pie's and Longboards on Kaanapali. We'd visit his high school friend in Japan and indulge in Thai Massage in Chang Mi. At the time, I didn't actually believe any of it would happen; it was really only just a glorious dream I didn't mind dreaming.

When we arrived at the ancient moss covered forest, it captivated my senses and entranced me with its organic beauty. A million pine needles concealed the dirt floor and crunched beneath our feet; a thick canopy towered above, shading the sun, creating the perfect environment for lichens and moss to thrive on the goliath trees around us.

Chippewa National Forest. Check.

Grant wrapped his warm thick hand around my wrist and led me through a small opening in the trees. We followed a game trail, ducked under branches and stepped the over rotting trees. Narrow rays of light illuminated the millions of sea foam green and blaze orange lichens covering large swaths of the trees and boulders.

Where the pine forest morphed into a grove of white birch, moss bogs blanketed the ground making a lush, springy carpet. The forest had opened up into an enchanting meadow—a silent alcove, hidden from even the sun. A place where unicorns reveal themselves from behind hidden forest doors. We traversed across a complex network of fallen trees to the center of the wild atrium. It was a mossy meadow preserved in a time, hidden from loggers, and hikers, and real-estate developers.

"This is amazing!" I said. "You are amazing. You've kept your promise."

"What do you mean?" He leapt confidently from one floating bridge to the next.

"You said we would see the world and here we are."

"Of course we'll see the world. This is only the beginning."

"We should sleep outside here sometime," I said. "It'll be our secret alcove. We can use the same sleeping bag and make love in this enchanted forest."

"Yes baby, let's do that. I'll save coordinates."

"Save the coordinates?"

"I brought my GPS so we can start saving the coordinates of all the places we go," he said, "so we can write them in our journal then come back and visit them someday."

We explored the mystical forest, saved the coordinates of our secret alcove and of where we would come back and harvest our first Christmas tree. Every moment was dreamlike and romantic beyond my wildest expectations. Just before the trail lead us out, we knelt down near a weathered gray bench that looked over a vast wilderness of tall trees. He pulled me close and warmed my shoulders in his embrace as he positioned us for a panoramic shot overlooking the valley.

"Don't fall, baby, I would die if I lost you," Grant said.

***

The directions said: look for an unmarked gravel road a few miles south of Moose Mountain.

I threw my arm across his chest and pointed, "This is it! Turn here!"

Dust filled the air behind us creating a reddish evening glow as he veered left onto an unmarked dirt road. "Honey, this is great. I can't wait to see where you're taking us," he said.

"She'd assured me that we wouldn't be found—that this place was off the grid."

It was his birthday surprise. Dozens of private acres overlooking Moose Mountain Lake—and it was all ours for the weekend. The land was owned by a client of mine whom I'd asked a favor of.

We pulled up next to an idyllic log cottage. It was small, but with vaulted ceilings, one bedroom, no windows, and a field stone fireplace you could see from outside. Nestled in the trees overlooking a mostly uninhabited lake, the only view to the inside of the cottage was through a patio door facing the woods. A steep trail lead to a bonfire pit, then to the secluded lake. It was the epitome of lake-country living; the epicenter of the north woods and we were the only humans around for miles.

The evening air was brisk, the wind calm, and the lake eerily still. Vibrant gold, green and blue colors of the woods reflected a mirror image of the trees and sky making a blurred line where reality stopped and the illusion began.

"How did you find this place? It's amazing! Honey, you are the most wonderful woman in the world. This is the best birthday ever." He kissed my proud cheek.

"I thought that one birthday of yours that we spent together was the best," I said.

"That one was good, but I have a feeling this will be better."

"One of my clients owns the property, I asked her for a favor."

Grant reached for my hand as we walked down the steep slope to the platter shaped lake to watch the remaining sunset. We walked past the reedy shore where the amphibians were emerging from the cool mud and beginning to croak their happy croaks. At the end of the dock he squished me into him and we swayed in silence taking in another wondrous setting sun.

"How many sunsets do you think we'll watch together in our lifetime?" I asked.

"Thousands." He said.

"Wow, that's a lot. How many time do you think we'll sleep under the stars?"

"Hundreds," he said. "We should write them all down in our journal."

"We should also write down how many countries we think we'll visit, and how many jobs we'll have and how many different houses we'll live in." I said, "Someday we can look back and see if we guessed right."

"That's a great idea," Grant said. "Let's also write down how many kids we think we'll have and grandkids too."

"You think we'll have kids and grandkids?" I asked with my heart wide open and needing to hear it again to believe it.

"Of course we will. Hopefully we'll have lots and lots. Only if you want though. You do want more kids, right?" He said with sincere smile.

"With you? Yes. I would love to have babies with you."
"You ready to go practice?" He said nudging me and kissing my neck.

Once we were inside Grant knelt in front of the fireplace crumpling old newspaper as I unpacked my secret bag of goodies, lining them up on the kitchen counter. A bottle of Two Vines Merlot, a corkscrew and plastic cups, a book of matches, a massage oil candle, a pre-packaged brownie and one birthday candle. Then I flashed him a quick glimpse of a small red tube with "Kama Sutra" on the label.

***

*Just imagine me slipping
ever so slowly inside u as I kiss ur
neck and love u the way
u deserve 2 b loved.*

Chapter 38

I unwrapped the single fudge brownie and lone birthday candle, then gave a forceful cough to cover the flick of the lighter.

"Happy birthday, baby," I said as I strode toward him with his birthday brownie.

He didn't want the brownie; he was hungry for a different kind of dessert. He clasped my hands and pulled me behind him into the bedroom. In the tiny space of the bottom bunk, with only enough width for one body, our two bodies became entangled.

"I bought a candle that melts into massage oil," I said. "It's called Into the Woods. I thought it was fitting. And...I bought this..."

I wobbled the little red tube from side to side.

I stopped him from grabbing it, "One thing at a time, we have all weekend to use the trinkets I bought for us. Now put your hands behind your head," I demanded, and he gladly assumed the position. "Keep your hands there, don't move," I commanded—wanting him to touch me so badly—but wanting even more for him to explode with desire.

"My sexy little vixen," he said with his eyes fixed on my every move.

I made love to every inch of him with every inch of me.

We barely fit in the scanty space of the single stall shower. I pressed close against his slippery body and laid my head on his round shoulder, absorbing his affection. Our bodies pulsed as one as we stood unmoving until the last drop of hot water ran cold.

"Wine?" He asked, self-assured and unashamed as he towel dried his naked lithe body.

"Do you have to ask?"

I tried to maneuver my towel in such a way that it hid my maternal breasts but also looked like I was drying myself confidently. I had yet to reveal my breasts or let them come out to play. They stayed held up by my hands or by my very supportive and sexy underwire bra, and I had no intentions of letting them come out and fall down tonight. He'd probably never seen the breasts of a woman who had breast fed a child, and I wasn't about to horrify him with my national geographic style droopy, grumpy breasts.

Droplets of water pooled on his stubbly upper lip and transferred to mine as he kissed me. "I'll grab a blanket and the wine. Meet me by the fireplace," he said then squeezed past me and out of the bathroom.

I wiped the dripping mirror with my towel and looked at my reflection through the streaks. My hair was shorter than it had ever been, cut into an edgy, choppy sort of style that stopped blunt just below my chin. My nails were painted glossy black and my eyes were smudged with a smoky charcoal tinge all the way around.

The harder I stared, the more my reflection seemed to retreat into the mirror, and the more I felt like I didn't know who I was looking at. Nothing felt real, I didn't feel real and I didn't recognize the person staring back at me.

So much had changed. I was single and in disbelief at how fast it had happened, it had only been a few months since that first night I stayed at Grants. Now I was divorced, living on my own for the first time since I was seventeen, overjoyed by the greatest love I'd ever known. Yet simultaneously lashed with pain.

As I stood in front of the mirror I was naked in every way a person could be naked. I'd demolished the only relationship I'd known for the last twelve years, left my home, left my dog, and tore Dani's heart into pieces in the process. I'd drained my bank account and could barely work to rebuild what I'd spent because my back was broken or something worse. I was lying to everyone about everything, stripped bare to the innermost layer of who I was, everything I knew and almost everything I had was gone, and now, with no one and nothing that could do it for me, I'd have to rebuild. I'd have to create a new life and a new me.

Twenty-four hours after our erotic holiday we surfaced hazy and depleted like creatures from the underworld. I grabbed the wine cork from the counter and stuffed it into my bag, he'd written on it:

G+C

"The Cottage"

I left a thank you card on the arm of the sofa just before we walked out.

"What did it say?" Grant asked.

"It said thank you for letting us fuck our brains out on your bunk bed, be sure to have the maid change the sheets."

I looked at him and we laughed like crazy.

***

I didn't know what it was at the time, but looking back on it now, I am certain it was an out-of-body experience. The news in the letter was devastating...

Chapter 39

"WHAT THIS POWER IS, I CANNOT SAY... ALL I KNOW IS THAT IT EXISTS."

—ALEXANDER GRAHAM BELL

Whether some part of my weightless consciousness actually separated and drifted away from my weighty earthly body...I can't say. But the perspective that my mind experienced was exactly that. Exactly what others have described as being out-of-body.

I was a teenager when the first happened. I never told anyone, frightened they'd think I was practicing some sort of satanic ritual and commit me to an asylum. My mind seemed to sink into itself, retreating inward to the center of my brain where my consciousness lives. Then, condensed into its smallest molecule, the weightless form broke free from its earthly body.

Each time it happened, I drifted upward into a corner of the room and my vision became acute tunnel vision that only allowed me to see straight forward. The periphery of the room was shrouded, inaccessible in that moment, and looking to the right or left would cease the episode and snap me back into my body. It took a tremendous amount of focus to stay in that elevated perspective, like looking into a black and white pattern encrypted with a three dimensional image. If I could hold my focus long enough, I would stay afloat, but as soon as I broke my concentration, I was snapped back into my body.

These out-of-body-episodes stopped happening when I was in my early twenties. After they stopped, I realized that each one of them had coincided with a traumatic event. I guess it was my mind's way of getting out, if only for a little while I was able to escape my body and whatever it was that was causing the pain. It had been ten years since the last episode; I'd almost forgotten that they'd even occurred at all. Until *Master* showed up. The pain had gotten so bad I'd given it a name, *Master*. He would summon me and I would lay at his feet. I would cry and beg for mercy but the grip of his bone crunching fingers was inescapable. I was nothing more than a fragile human puppet at the mercy of my Master. He moved the strings and I did what he said, if I disobeyed, the punishment was severe.

I laid my head in my hands and wept before I'd even opened it. I knew it would be bad. We'd gone to see a spine Doctor in Minneapolis, the best of the best and the results from an MRI and new series of tests had come in.

Dear Ms. Summers,

It is conceivable that it may require more than one surgery to relieve your pain. Our findings indicate the following...

The list was long and insurmountable, and written in a vernacular only an orthoneurospinal surgeon would be able to decipher with words like "thecal sac" and "cauda equina."

There were a few things I did understand though, like rupture and compression, degeneration and narrowing, arthritis and stenosis, words that belonged on a letter to an eighty-five-year-old man who'd worked construction all his life. Not on a letter to a five foot four, hundred and ten pound, thirty-year-old vegetarian fitness instructor.

I felt my essence, all that remained of me, starting to leave. I didn't want that body anymore, I wanted to leave it behind and find a new one. That's when my unconscious mind granted my wish. Me and the letter drifted upward and into the corner of the room where I could see myself below, sitting beside my bed in my lonely apartment, weeping. I don't remember why or when I snapped back but when I did, I called Grant.

A boulder had rolled down my throat and lodged itself, preventing the formation of clear words. I read Grant the letter with a wounded whimper.

"Baby, we will get through it," he said, listening patiently while I choked on my tears.

A few minutes later, he was knocking at my door.

Chapter 40

Yesterday, C.J. had the first of two procedures that will help to reduce her back pain. Based on the results of the previously done nerve blocks, this most recent, more permanent procedure looks very promising. But either way, we will solve this back problem, as I, along with her are making it a mission. And there is no mission failure here!

-Grant

Chapter 41

Dylan took the news about Grant and I being together surprisingly well.

"I already know," Dylan said when I confessed I'd been discretely dating Grant since *after* my divorce.

"What?" I wrinkled my face, "how do you know?"

Dylan gave a slim detective's smile, "It wasn't hard to figure out. You two always disappear together."

Good work, Detective, good work.

I shouldn't have been surprised, there'd been signs that our family and friends were suspect of our sneaking. There were even signs that some of them were hoping we'd get together.

Grant's sister, known for her matchmaking efforts had asked him, "What about Dylan's sister? She'd be a good pick."

"Yeah, maybe. But I think she's married." Grant said.

Over dinner one evening Dani suggested, "Mom, maybe you should date Grant."

My mouth dropped open and food fell out. "Maybe I will," I said.

One of my clients, who happened to be Grant's cousin, offered to set me up with him. "You'd be perfect together," she said.

To which I blushed and replied, "Maybe someday, I don't think I'm ready to start dating yet."

When Grant's mom found spinach and soymilk in his refrigerator she accused him of dating someone in secret. "I drink soy milk and eat spinach!" He said, but she was keen to his lies and since she cleaned his place, surely she found makeup residue in the bathroom sink or long brown hairs on the floor when she cleaned.

It was endearing that people closest to us reaffirmed what we had without knowing we had anything at all.

"Does Levi know?" Dylan asked.

"No. I don't think so." I said. "Why?"

"Because he's going to kill you when he finds out. He already suspects you're with somebody."

"How do you know?" I asked.

"He called me."

"Levi called you? Why'd you answer?" I crossed my arms and shook my head. "I don't talk to your ex-girlfriends. I don't want you to tell him anything about me," I spit as I said it, "and don't be the one to tell him about Grant."

"I won't." Dylan said.

I didn't believe him. If Levi asked about Grant, Dylan might tell him the truth. He didn't cover for me when I got thrown in juvenile detention for drinking and driving, and he wouldn't cover for me now. He felt sorry for Levi and didn't like what I had done to him, didn't like how quickly I left. Dylan said Levi was devastated by the divorce and depressed. That made me feel terrible so I asked him not to tell me or talk to me about Levi again, that I needed to move on like he'd moved on.

Dylan had found the love of his life in a girl named Nikki. She was standing next to him when I divulged my secret relationship, but she already knew. She'd pieced it together over the summer and asked me what was up between me and Grant. I was tired of lying, I needed to tell someone about the wondrous love I'd found. So I confessed my indiscretions to my future sister-in-law. The girl with the most rad tattoos I'd ever seen. Tattoos unlike my own mistakes, which I was now covering

252

with Band-Aids and Dermablend. No, she'd made good choices, bad-ass, hot girl tats that looked so right for her body they seemed to take on a life of their own. Nikki had long straight hair and a rock star way about her, she was the perfect female match for my death-metal-meets-country-music brother.

I didn't confess everything to her of course, just enough to satisfy the part of my soul that wanted to scream it from the top of the boat tower over the whole lake. I'd asked her to keep it from Dylan until I was ready to tell him.

"Does Dani know?" Dylan asked.

"No, and she won't know until there's a ring on my finger."

"Does Grant know that?" Dylan said in the most unsupportive way. "You think it'll come to that? He's just so picky."

"Yes, he knows that. And thank you for reminding me of how picky Grant is."

"C.J., Grants had a lot of girlfriends. That chick from the Hamptons, the one he flew across the country for, and the blonde who went to Australia, I think she still stays with him sometimes, he's been with some hot women and he's dumped all of them. Even Molly, he even dumped Molly. Don't get me wrong, Grant's a great guy, the best, but he'll never settle. That's all I'm saying."

I stared at the floor and watched a single tear fall from my chin. "I know, he's too good to be true," I said.

I was crushed at the thought of Grant with other woman. Dylan's discouraging words made me feel insignificant and foolish for ever thinking Grant would choose me. I instantly doubted everything about what we had.

How could I have been so naive?

This is going to end in disaster. I guess that's how affairs are supposed to end. I guess I'll get what I deserve for cheating.

More tears dropped as I regressed back to the girl who knew that everything about Grant was a farce. That he was just leading me on, lying to me. That he was only staying around because he made a mistake and didn't want to dump his best friend's sister, or felt guilty that I'd gotten divorced

"I just don't want to see you hurt," Dylan said. "It would be great if it was real, my best friend and my sister, we'd take amazing vacations and travel the world together, it'd be perfect. But, C.J., Grant's never been able to pull the trigger."

Dylan was right. There was so much I didn't know, so much I'd overlooked; so much of Grant's past that he hadn't shared. Things you'd normally disclose to the person you love, thing's Dylan knew that I didn't.

I wept as I left Dylan's house that day and lived on an emotional teeter totter each day after. Up, down, *he loves me, he loves me not.* I didn't know what to believe. I only knew that the one thing capable of dispelling all of my doubts, would be a ring.

***

Four Months Later

The first blizzard of the season revealed its fury in the dark night. An icy wind whirled around our feet as we wedged our luggage into the trunk of a taxi glowing neon yellow in the four am darkness. Our flight was leaving in less than two hours. Dylan sat in front, Grant, Nikki and I squished into the back. Grant and Dylan had forgone their yearly guy's trip to Jamaica and instead, it was just the four of us.

We'd tried to be good travelers and go to bed at ten, but anxiety and excitement over the coming trip fluttered through the air keeping everyone awake, and falling asleep in the same house with Dylan was risky. It significantly increased the probability of waking up with Sharpie on your face or a dick in your ear.

So instead of resting for the long flight, we walked through a winter white-out to Bodega. On the plush couches next to a sizzling fireplace, we drank Red Rock Merlot, ate stinky cheese and salty olives. Dylan and I exchanged awkward glances. It was the first time he'd seen Grant and I together as a couple. The first time he saw how we looked at each other, how Grant looked at me, how he kept his hands on me. Dylan was able to confirm with his own eyes that his best friend really was sleeping with his little sister, and that just maybe, it was love.

Because Dani was staying behind with Levi, I had a conundrum.

Do I tell him exactly who I'm going with before he finds out on his own?

Since who I was going with really was of no concern to him, when we discussed the arrangements for Dani, I simply told him I was going to Jamaica with Dylan and a few friends. He was suspicious, I could tell by the long pause of silence. But he didn't ask any questions.

A deal is a deal and ours was that I would give him every dollar of child support back, which I did, in exchange for total autonomy. In every way that didn't deal with Dani, we were over and I had no obligation to him whatsoever. I knew that after we got back from Jamaica he would find out somehow, pictures and gossip would circulate, someone would tell him the group of friends really was two couples and all his suspicions from years prior would be confirmed.

Once arrangements for Dani were taken care of I couldn't have been more thrilled to be leaving town, except that I couldn't sit, walk or stand without Vicodin. Not *one* of the inhumane treatments had worked. Not one. There was no relief without straight up pain killers, alcohol, and sex, together.

I'd been in and out of the hospital for months trying things, each time with Grant by my side, each time with hope in my heart, and each time failure soon followed. I agreed to one last treatment before Jamaica, a final round of nerve burns. A barbaric ritual in which a long instrument is inserted into your back and buttocks in all the places it hurts the most in an attempt to locate the exact nerves sending pain signals to the brain. Once located, they would be burned or cut, damaged so badly they're rendered unconscious and can no longer send out their distress calls. It was a procedure they keep you awake for, but ask you not to move. A procedure so intolerable they send you home with flowers after each visit.

I'd acquired a multi-varietal rose bouquet. I estimated each long stem cost about six hundred dollars. They stood elegant and tall in a clear vase on the kitchen counter top of my hollow apartment. Each beautiful petal reached toward the window, begging for sunlight, yearning to escape its unnatural, claustrophobic environment. I watched them wilt, dying to be outside but there was nothing I could do, I couldn't uncut their stems and return them to a green field. So I just accepted their death and watched them die, one by one, adding new ones to the graveyard of the dead.

I couldn't throw them out. They were a symbol of what I'd been through and how many times I'd been through it. They tallied up my pain, quantified it, and somehow they seemed to die for me when I couldn't. But long after they were gone, I was still the same; alive and crippled with pain.

I had nothing more to lose, I was drugging myself heavily just to be able to walk. There were no procedures left for me to try, no other countries or research facilities for me to call, no more Guinea pig experiments to belly up for. I was out of money and out of hope. It was surgery or suicide.

The surgery that I once was told didn't work for people who only had back pain and no nerve pain had suddenly become an option. No one knew what to do with me or how to help, or if surgery would even work. I couldn't even twist around to wipe my own ass, so they could've suggested amputation and I would have consented. I scheduled the surgery, but had to wait five long months.

Jamaica was a welcome reprieve from the gloomy reality I'd have to face once I returned. So I was off to the same island with the boyfriend I obsessed over on my honeymoon with my former husband.

***

*Honey, I'm so sorry about
what u endured today.
:(That sucks, so I'm
already thinking of the
many ways 2 make it better. :)
Where should we go next?*

Chapter 42

"LOVE IS MY RELIGION"

—JOHN KEATS

"I'll take care of you," Grant said. "Jamaica will be good for you, for us. It'll get your mind off things. We'll get some sun, drink a few red-stripes. You can relax and don't have to do anything, maybe you're back will feel better."

I spent my days in Jamaica hopped up on pain pills, Heineken, and sex. The pain came and went in varying degrees of intolerable. While Dylan, Nikki and Grant strolled down the beach with an unappreciated ease, I walked behind, keeping pace with the one-legged man walking with a wooden crutch and guitar slung on his back.

"C.J., you should try some ganja," Dylan said from the sofa of our apartment on the beach. "It'll help with the pain."

"Dylan, I hate pot, it makes me paranoid and fat. You do it. I'll video tape."

Dylan sunk backward into the damp sofa, "Okay," he agreed, then plunged his two fat fingers into a can of neon pink flarp (putty in a can that farts) that he'd brought with from the mainland, "so we could enjoy farting sounds anytime we want," he'd said.

Grant was right, ten days in Jamaica, laughing, drinking, and having drunken sex did more to remedy my broken back than three previous years of medical and alternative interventions.

We explored the island on island time, we snorkeled the shores, drank Blue Mountain coffee, and ate papaya jam. In the evenings we sang songs and played guitar around the beach fire. The locals gathered to sing their reggae tunes and listen to our foreign songs. In the hot tub, under a million stars we drank lime margaritas until the bartender cut off the drinks and the electricity.

And we had sex. Lascivious sex. In the shower when no one was around. Grant was keeping his promise; our life together really was transforming into what I'd dreamed it could be, into what he said it would be—happy.

When we got back from Jamaica, anyone who didn't know before, knew now—Grant and I were an item. A hot item surrounded in scandalous speculation without a drop of proof. My parents were thrilled, his parents were thrilled, and Dylan seemed to have come around full circle to supporting us; although I think he was still crossing his fingers. I finally told Lissy why I'd been so distant and she immediately forgave me, but as I did with everyone else, I withheld any information pre-dating my divorce.

As far as I knew, no one knew we had an affair. Anything they thought they knew was only speculation.

I was more confident than ever that what Grant and I had was not going away. He'd dropped hints, told me we should be finished having all our babies by the time I was thirty-five , asked me if I wanted a small or large wedding, sized up my finger next to his own. He was feeling me out, and I was impatiently thrilled.

A proposal seemed imminent. It was all I could think about. Grant took marriage seriously, so if he proposed, I'd know with definite certainty that this life, our life was for real. I'd finally be at ease knowing my heart wouldn't be broken tomorrow.

It hadn't even been a year since I was divorced, but I was ready to be married again, to Grant. No amount of time could have made me more or less certain, he simply was the one. So why should we wait? But all those hints he'd whispered, all of our midnight talks about forever, apparently for him, didn't come with the same urgency to tie the knot that I felt. The months dragged on for me and still, there was no proposal in sight.

He'd had plenty of opportunities, after Jamaica we hopped a flight to Arizona where I met the rest of his family and spent a romantic Valentine's Day. He swept me away from place to place, from the desert to the mountains. He had the next trip planned before the first one had even begun. And at each new place, I was more and more anxious for him to propose. Everywhere we went seemed a perfect landscape to seal the deal, but at every departure my left hand was still a little too light.

It was almost June fifth, the day Dani would turn ten and the day I would go in for surgery. Since Grant hadn't proposed on one of our whirlwind winter adventures, I became pre-occupied with speculating when and where it might happen. Was he waiting for the summer so he could sky write it? Was he planning a trip I didn't know about? But we didn't have any big trips planned because of my surgery. Would he propose the night before I would risk death? Or in the morning just before I went into the operating room?

That's what I would have done—proclaim my love the moment before my soulmate gets wheeled into the operating room. So he'd know just how much I needed him in my life, and that he needed to fight to stay alive.

Yes, I decided.

That's the moment he's been waiting for.

***

We have the same desire, 2 live 4 the other person, being selfless. It's been working so far. :) Love being in love with u, babe.

Chapter 43

"DIS·SOCI·A·TION: THE SPLITTING OFF OF A GROUP OF MENTAL PROCESSES FROM THE MAIN BODY OF CONSCIOUSNESS, AS IN AMNESIA OR CERTAIN FORMS OF HYSTERIA"

—DICTIONARY.COM

Dr. G thought Grant was my husband and referred to him that way at our visits. We looked at each other and smiled, neither of us corrected him.

The wall in front of us was lit up and covered in x-rays. Dr. G explained the gravity of my condition, I numbed the bad news by making jokes. Jokes about what looked like shrapnel lodged in my abdominal cavity. I thought it was some sort of mistake on the x-ray, something stuck to the board behind me when they took the picture. It wasn't. But there it was, the size of a paper clip, shiny and glaring at us from inside my body. No one knew what it was or how it got there—we just knew it was there.

"I guess my dream about being abducted by aliens was true," I said. "I knew they cut me open and put in a tracking device. Doc, since you're going in there," I said with a straight face, "could you remove it so they stop following me?"

The out of place object seemed to be tucked under my left rib cage but it had obviously migrated from somewhere else. There was a trail of scar tissue leading up to it. Dr. G was surprised I didn't know what it was and said he couldn't remove it. But he did say that it looked like a surgical clip. You know, like a medical device left behind from a previous surgery.

After my persistent complaints, a personal investigation of my medical records and a formal hospital investigation, turns out, that's exactly what it was. Some sort of surgical clip, "although the exact type and original location couldn't be determined." They said. But I had more questions: *shouldn't it be in my medical records if something was left in there? Wouldn't it have a serial number or something? Will it puncture a lung? What if it migrates to my brain?*

The answers I got were vague and always ended in the same sentence. "At the time of your surgery, it was standard practice to leave those things in."

I had my spleen taken out in the 90's not in 1802. I dropped the issue, too mentally exhausted to fight Goliath. Dr. G. wasn't concerned with my surgical clip so neither was I. I just wanted to know what would give me the best possible outcome for *this* surgery.

To which he replied, "It's not good, and it won't be easy...but I think the best course of action is..." He spoke quickly as he inspected the gallery of images on the wall. There were cross-sections of my vertebrate, magnified vestiges of what once were intervertebral disks. He zoomed the MRI images in and out as he analyzed my innards.

One of his thick thighs bounced with energy as he spoke. I heard...Blah, blah, blah...bone graft, blah, blah...pedicle screws, blah...hardware. Emotional trauma had a way of causing me to dissociate and if severe enough, float out of my body. This was not quite an out-of-body experience but an odd muting of my hearing and tactile senses. As Dr. G laid out the reality of my injury, I turned into a cosmonaut.

"Is that my best option?" I asked.

He said yes.

"Then do it."

***

Naked and perched on the edge of a slippery white tub in a stale smelling apartment, I sat shivering. I was two hundred miles from home and shaking with fear. I cradled my breasts in my hands and rocked myself. I was beyond petrified.

"You ready, babe?" Grant asked sweetly.

But no words formed on my lips. My mind had left, escaped from the trauma of the present moment, molted its shell and left only a skin suit behind.

I leaned forward and hugged my knees, sorrow seeped from my eyes and water drizzled down my naked body as Grant lathered my back. Rusty colored suds from the betadine soap flowed in to the tub as he cleansed my skin.

"I'm sorry, honey," he said realizing my strife, "I just want to be thorough." He kissed my wet head. "I love you. Don't worry, okay. You'll be fine; I'll take care of you—always. Is there anything I can do for you?"

Propose?

Of course I didn't say that out loud, I wanted to. I wanted to know that if I woke up tomorrow and never walked again. If I emerged from the operating room wheelchair bound, the victim of a rare statistic from an accidental nick in my spinal cord, would he still stay with me? In my heart I knew the answer but in real time I wasn't convinced. A deep ache holed up inside me, a permanent glug in my throat, an inexplicable lonesomeness. I didn't want to be single, I wanted to be married. To him. Before I went in for surgery.

That night I laid underneath him, hiding. *Maybe it's not too late to back out of this insane agreement.* I contemplated faking illness and re-considering surgery. I couldn't sleep. I needed him to make love to me, and he did. He held me like it was the last time, or the first time, or every time—he was consistent in his promise to live each day to the fullest, not taking our time together for granted. That night our bodies undulated, gripping one another tightly with undertones of tension and loss.

At five am we drove to the hospital, I was the first surgery of the day. I'd heard that being first in line was the best place to be since later in the day doctors get tired, procedures get rushed, spinal cords get nicked. I contemplated that maybe the opposite was true, what if my doc is hung-over from the night before, stayed up late with his mistress having sex and gray goose in some fancy hotel room?

I tried getting a whiff of Dr. G's breath when he sat down beside me—I didn't smell any booze or see any lingering passion in his eyes, my concerns quickly dissipated. He was unusually alert, knees still bouncing and overly enthusiastic about operating at six am. He was a true marvel-driven and intelligent beyond normal human capacity.

"You ready?" He asked, and what was I supposed to say?

Yes I'm ready, just be careful when you stuff my guts back in—I'd like to be able to take a shit again someday. Oh, and please make sure everything that goes in comes back out, you know...surgical clips, sponges, junior mints. And try not to paralyze me okay? I like my life, and could you do me a favor and tell my boyfriend to propose already?

"Just don't leave anything behind," I joked. His face lit up with laughter and he patted my shoulder with a reassuring hand.

"I won't leave anything behind that's not supposed to be." His smile was comforting and in that moment I trusted him. Then I counted the number of bodies that would be seeing me passed out and naked:

(1) Dr. A, who would be cutting me open in the front.

(2) Dr. B. who would be assisting with the second incision in the back.

(3-5) A team of hazmat suits came in, Doctors C, D and E. They marched through the heavy cream curtain and formed a circle around me. Each were assigned to monitor a set of bodily functions while Doctors B and G gutted me and stuffed their pudgy fingers into my abdomen and back.

(6) Dr. F gave me a sedative so I would sign the consent forms.

(7) Then Dr. G explained the procedure one last time— drill...screws...graft...blah...blah...blah...flip...repeat,   repeat, repeat.

Grant held my hand until he wasn't allowed any further. He kissed me goodbye and told me he loved me without a tear in his eye or a black velvet box in his pocket. There was no proclamation of his greatest desire to marry me or reassurance that he would stay with me if my legs came out attached where my arms were supposed to be.

The last thing I remember thinking was, *I wonder which one is doing the catheter and will see my Brazilian waxed pooter.*

***

June 5th

C.J. has been in surgery for five hours now. She looked good this morning when they took her away, I am sure she will be just fine. The nurse came out several times and said she's doing great. My sweet honey, I would have taken the pain for her if I could have.

I ran in to my cousin John, a cardiologist here. I told him about her surgery, he said she's in good hands—the best. No more injections and sickening procedures in that fucking low back place. Ugh, I can't imagine what she went through in there.

Well, back to waiting, she should be getting done soon. I can't wait to see my honey! I would die if I lost her now. I'll keep you posted...

-Grant

It's been seven hours since C.J. went in for multi-level, anterior-posterior spinal fusion. It's taking longer than they expected, but they said she is still doing fine. I wonder what they found in there? Maybe another alien implant? Hehehe...

I am getting anxious and want to see my honey and take her home. I can't wait for this all to be over. It's been a long day waiting and wondering.

-Grant

Dr G. was just here and informed me that C.J.'s doing great. She's in recovery now. It seems they encountered a few unexpected problems and had to do a procedure that took a few extra hours. Dr. G. said she had an 85% collapse in her spine and they had a hard time getting their instruments in-between her vertebrae. He said she had arthritis everywhere, like we suspected, which they shaved off, my poor sweetheart:(They obliterated those facet joints that seemed to be causing her so much pain (it's amazing what modern medicine can do!)

She is strong and I know she will recover as fully as she can and I will do whatever it takes to help her!

Well...at least she'll be an inch taller when she wakes up! Going to catch a glimpse of my honey now, I'm exhausted, stand by...

-Grant

Chapter 44

Day One: Vegetarian Ice Chips

"I feel great! It doesn't even hurt. I can't believe it doesn't hurt," my words came out in a slurry, the product of a seven hour Propofol cocktail.

"I have no pain!" I proclaimed, certain it was a miracle and eager to report my surprisingly comfortable status to anyone who might be listening.

Then a nurse with toothpick arms opened her beak and pecked away my optimism. "Dr. G injected pain killers directly into the site," she said sadistically as she looked at her watch. "They'll wear off in about...four hours. Then you'll have pain."

To my gratefulness and dismay over the next few hours Toothpick-Arms never left my side. She was occupied by bleeps and swooshes, monitors and bags of dripping liquids. She tolerated my inebriated babble.

When the four hours came and went, she seemed just a little too happy she was right. If I remember correctly, she even sneered a diabolical "told you so," after my first scream. I don't remember leaving the recovery room, I only remember waking up in a private room on a cold canvas tarp with tubes flowing in and out of every orifice. I was paralyzed, again.

Not permanently, thank God, if there is a God. But moving even the tiniest muscle in my pinkie finger or wiggling my toes induced a ferocious pain. A sneeze, cough or an itch was unthinkable. And being moved became a ruthless act of senseless violence that teetered on inhumane treatment.

Just being awake was cruel. Like I'd been the victim of a violent crime, every inch of my body was wounded as I lay beyond helpless. Aside from breathing, the nursing staff had control of my every bodily function.

How foolish I was to think I'd want Grant, my mom, my dad, and Dylan by my side. Oh the folly in my reasoning, after blinking my eyes open from the coma of anesthesia, all I wanted was to writhe in agony alone. Taking a large enough breath to utter a single word sent waves of violent pain from my back outward to my extremities.

Each hour a team of assigned nurses barged into my room like hirelings and tortured me with their procedures. I tried to make them stop but they were contracted robots and could not be reasoned with. They stood towering over me as I begged and screamed and pleaded for them not to touch me.

"No, no! Don't fucking touch me. I'm sorry...just please don't move me, it's too soon, it's too soon!"

The hired trio of scrubs each had a post. One shimmed a pillow between my knees, one held the tarp on the right and one on the left. They pulled me and the tarp to one side of the bed, squeezed me inside like I was the meat in a taco, then flipped me over. Each flip was felonious. They had hardened hands and empty almond shaped voids where eyes should have been, they ignored my wails.

"I'm deaf in my left ear so I won't be able to hear you if you flip me over. Please, please don't touch me," I screamed.

It wasn't true of course and they seemed to laugh at my pitiful little lie. A foaming disdain oozed from my mouth when anyone came into the room to help me. I'd become possessed like the girl in the exorcist and spoke in vulgar tongues to protect myself. But it wasn't really me, doing those things, it was hungry, drugged me.

For years I'd practiced meditation, taught myself to eliminate distractions and develop laser-like focus when necessary. Out of sheer amusement, I'd also practiced how not to scratch an itch. What I found from this silly endeavor was that no amount of willing an itch to go away would work. The itch would inevitably become a major distraction then

266

multiply itself until my entire body itched uncontrollably and I had to scratch everywhere.

I didn't know it until that day, but morphine made me itch. Not the kind of itch that feels like a loose hair dangling across your shoulder. This itch made me want to scratch out my eyeballs and tear off my skin. I didn't beg for pain killers, I didn't beg for Vicodin, I begged for Benadryl, but I could only have it every four hours and it only worked for one hour. I could get a dose of morphine on demand but had to wait four hours for more Benadryl.

"Not yet, you have another three hours," They said.

It wasn't like I was asking for Ketamine, I just wanted that little pink harmless pill!

"Grant, please go get me a box of Benadryl, please."

"Honey, I can't. I wish I could, but I can't."

"It won't hurt me. It's harmless. Please, I can't take it!"

I pleaded with him as I painfully maneuvered my arm to scratch my neck, chest, chin, scalp, knee, hip, shoulder, ankle, other arm, neck, chest Ugh! All movements that caused searing pain throughout my insides. I groaned out loud, frustrated by my inability to even pound my fists into the bed. I was a wounded whale, beached on a tarp, going insane from the itch.

Day Two- Vegetarian Ice Chips

"Good morning, baby. How you doing?" Grant said so sweetly, but not even his voice or his presence made it better.

I was defeated and had stopped fighting the staff for Benadryl and the right to refuse the flip—now I was just begging them to put me into a coma.

"Honey, I don't think they can do that," Grant said. "I'm so sorry you're hurting, I wish I could do something."

You could propose.

I thought it, I didn't actually blurt it out.

The nurses warned me that surgery might bring on my period, but they should have issued a flood warning for what showed up on the second day. I laid in the wetness not caring—because helping me, cleaning me, would require moving my legs, opening my knees, changing the sheets——during all of which I would have to incur being moved and touched and talked to. It was absolute misery and I'd named all the nurses Annie.

I stared at the white board that hung on the wall at the end of my bed and each time a new Annie came on duty he or she would write their name on that board so I would know what to hate them by. Below their name in red dry erase marker was what I was allowed to eat. At the end of day two it read Vegetarian Ice Chips. Not clear liquids, popsicles, apple juice or sprite. Only chipped ice. Vegetarian chipped ice.

Day Three: Vegetarian Ice Chips

The Annie's expected me to get up and shower on day three. They'd removed some of the tubes and were planning their attack to bathe me.

"Mom, please don't let them touch me, will you help me?" I begged. My mom would be gentle; she would sympathize with my misery.

Mom was clumsy and fumbled with the tangle of tubes that had to go with me into the shower. Incapacitated by pain and humiliation, I cried, I couldn't answer her questions. I barely knew she was speaking until she cried with me as she gently took off my gown and saw the incisions underneath. I sat on the white stool under the running water.

Shooting pain jabbed my entire torso merely from the act of sitting. The weight of my body on top of the newly bored holes in my vertebrate caused pain beyond comprehension. Mom pulled the nurse's cord as I slumped over dangling on the edge of consciousness.

When I was pronounced still alive, my mom pulled her shirt over her head and stood before me in an old white sports bra that was now gray. The elastic was gone and two boobs became one underneath its thin Lycra shelf. It was the sports bra I'd tried to get rid of that my frugal mom deemed still usable and re-purposed as her own.

She took off her shoes, rolled up her jeans, and stood beside me in the shower gently dousing me with water. She washed and conditioned my smelly hospital hair, and soaped my body avoiding the incisions now covered in wet tape. I sat lifeless, naked and hungry.

Day Four- Clear Liquids

I fantasized about Annie walking in with 7-Up or ginger ale, or a lemon-lime popsicle. I salivated at the thought. So when she strolled in with in chicken broth in a brown plastic bowl, "Chicken broth? I'm not eating fucking chicken broth. I'm a vegetarian." I said. "Remember, vegetarian ice chips?" I jutted out my chin and pointed to the wall in disgust.

"This is what the doctor ordered for you," she said. "You can't have solid foods."

She set down the bowl of steaming, stinking liquid chicken on the tray in front of me then opened a straw and dropped it in. I nearly kicked it across the room.

"I know I can't have solids. I don't want solids, I want liquids. Clear, vegetarian liquids."

"Well that's not what's written in your chart," she walked toward the door to retrieve a clip board.

"It's been written up there for the last three days," I said. "Can I please just have some apple juice or 7-Up. Something not animal?"

"I'll double check," she said in the most annoying nasally voice then walked out leaving the boiled animal juice in front of me as if she might come back and make me drink it.

I stared at it, disgruntled and hungry and wondered how many days without food I would need to go before chicken broth looked appetizing. At least twenty-one I'd figured. I'd done a fourteen day fast on liquids before and I knew I could do at least another week.

Fortunately I didn't have to, Annie came back with two small foil covered containers of apple juice and a new straw.

"Here you go," she said peeling back the lid on one of the containers, inserting the straw then bending down to put it in my mouth. Before she left, she went to the white board and wrote "Vegetarian Clear Liquids" under my name.

Over the next few days they made me walk in small increments with a walker, despite my protests—after they dosed me with pain killers other than morphine, which I now knew I had an allergy to. Grant held my elbow as I walked and made jokes about my bare butt. When no one was looking, and I couldn't do anything about it, he stood behind me, opened my gown, gave a few dry humps to the air between us and said something like, "Baby, you look so good," followed by diabolical laughter and an apology. I wanted to laugh, but it hurt.

After what seemed like a year in the hospital, Grant drove us the four torturous hours from Minneapolis back to our home.

Chapter 45

Today is C.J.'s first day out of the hospital following her spine surgery. By all indicators the posterior/anterior fusion went very well. The Doc explained that 10mm of spacing was needed between L4-L5 and 12mm Between L5-S1! This means that C.J. is nearly 1.0 inches taller than before the surgery!

It's has been a very trying few days in the hospital, but we are home now snug and sound, and are beginning the anticipated long recovery (which was expected)

Tonight we photographed the strange protruding alien from C.J.'s front incision. I must admit, it looks very curious, as if she is Sigourney Weaver in the movie 'Alien'!

More to come...

-Grant

Chapter 46

"ALOHA `OE."

—"FAREWELL TO YOU"

7 Months Post Surgery

I blinked my eyes open somewhere over the Pacific Ocean but I didn't see blue. The white clouds below formed a false land that resembled the familiar snow covered tundra of home. To my left was an empty seat.

My mouth was dry from the oxygen-deprived stale-air stink that had been blowing on my face while I was trying to sleep. I reached up and twisted the gray knob to shut the vent, then dug out my phone so I could check the time.

4 hours left. Ugh, my back hurts.

My brain throbbed inside my head and my body was permanently contorted around the old blue vinyl seat to which I was strapped. It'd been seven months since the surgery and I was doing remarkably well. On track to make an extraordinary recovery, better than anyone expected—miraculous even. But seven months was still a third of the time it would take to heal.

Sitting was the worst, and sitting through hours of flying made me act out in ways only a food-chicken in a battery cage could understand. I bounced my knees, knocked my head against the window, let out deep annoying sighs, and made jerky frustrated movements. Pangs of anxiety over what this trip was really about stretched my already bulging patience. The moment the wheels touched down I checked my messages.

4 new text messages.

Honey, I miss u. :(Will
send a pic. u send me 1,
2! Don't get caught!

Honey, ask for some
blankies. :) u'll be able
to sprawl out! Strap urself
in the middle seat, and
lie down after takeoff!
:) I'm there with u, love. :)

Ah, good morning, love:)
Slept okay, I think. I had
a dream about babies.
I thought only women had
those dreams! :)

Looks like ur delayed about
12mins. I'm for watching
u! More like watching over u:)

I was looking out the window at the tropical landscape as the plane taxied to the gate when my phone vibrated in my pocket.

Grant's voice rumbled with desire, "I'm so glad you're here baby, I've missed you so much." The moment I heard his voice, the same grip of love that commandeered me a decade ago still held me hopelessly captive. "Honey, it's so beautiful here," he continued, "I can't wait to show you everything." Then he lowered his voice like he was about to tell me a secret, "We should start looking for a place here, somewhere we can spend a few months each year." Before I could even comprehend what he'd just suggested. "Come out the main doors you'll see me right in front. I'm in a silver Malibu. Mwah!"

A place here? Maybe you should ask me to marry you first.

I slowly stood up and whimpered a little as I shimmied into the aisle and reached for my carry-on overhead. I stepped off the plane and into the humid air, tied my hoodie around my black pants and exposed my white skin to the warm weather paradise. I closed my eyes and breathed in the moment.

So this is Maui...I love it already.

He better propose.

The silver Malibu was parked on the curb in the pick-up zone and Grant was standing by the driver's side door looking over the hood in dark tinted sunglasses. I giggled as he walked toward me with his arms open, proudly wearing a Tommy Bahama button up shirt clad with palm trees and sunsets. He lunged for me and gave me a pick-me-up-hug, I winced but welcomed his eager embrace. I was so lonely without him and feeling his love wrapped around me was an overwhelming relief. Being without him, even for a few days illuminated just how much I needed him in my life forever, and how scared I was that at any moment it might all go away.

"Hi, baby. I missed you. How was your flight? I tried to get you on the shortest route here but it's pretty much the same from the coast." He kissed my lips before I could answer.

"That plane ride sucked." I stepped back and looked up at endless balmy sky and squinted my eyes, "But it's so beautiful here! It's worth the hours of sticky seats and stinky arm pits."

He laughed, "Yes. Yes, it is. Let's go, baby! What should we do?" He threw my carry-on bag in the backseat, helped me slide into the passenger seat, and then shuffled around to the driver's side.

"I need to get changed and clean up, it'll only take me ten minutes, then maybe we can..." I winked and he instantly knew.

He looked at me with a surprised, devious smile. "That's a great idea."

I was in disbelief that I was there, with him, that it really had come to this, that I think...this is where he would propose. It was time. I had compromised on the one thing, the only thing I said I would not compromise on. We'd moved in together. He'd sold his place and bought us a brand-new home on nearly an acre of land.

I desired more than anything to spend every night with him, to start our family and live under the same roof, how could I resist? But I didn't think it was too much to ask to be engaged before we moved in together, especially since I had a daughter who was moving in with us. It was my only request, the only thing I said I would not budge on.

I budged. I moved Dani and I in. When I would remind him of my precarious situation, how important it was to me that I don't move my daughter in with "mom's boyfriend," his response was bleak.

"I just can't see how right now. I just put money down on our house. I'll need to wait, and save a bit longer." He would say and I would drop it.

I guess I believed him. Although I had a horrible sinking feeling that maybe, just maybe, Dylan was right—that he would never have the guts to marry again. That it was entirely possible his delay had nothing to do with money and had everything to do with a serious fear of marriage. Especially marriage to a woman who cheated on her last husband.

He had helped me with my rent, monthly expenses and paid a few thousand dollars of my medical bills while I was vomiting in his bathroom and seizing on his kitchen floor after surgery. I felt obligated to cut him some slack after how much he'd supported me. I was grateful and didn't want to seem any other way. I tried to put it out of my mind and enjoy our lives together, unconditionally.

Our hotel was situated right on the beach, a picture perfect holiday resort with hibiscus lined sidewalks and white plumeria flowers scattered across the grounds.

When we got to our room I took a shower, rinsed out the stale-air stink from my hair then lathered myself in coconut-lime-verbena, the complimentary scent. I did a quick once over with water proof mascara and tinted sun screen, even for a quickie, I always wanted to look and smell delicious. I tied my hair back and put on a lacy bra.

"Did you bring the lube?" I hollered to him from the bathroom sink.

"No...did you?"

I imagined him around the corner with the lube in his hand, laying naked in bed, under the clean white sheets, tan and warm, hard and waiting.

"No I couldn't find it at home. I figured you brought it." I said.

"Nope. I guess we can pick some up at the Safeway later." He said, sounding disappointed.

He was as I expected him to be, hands behind his head, naked body flimsily covered in a white sheet. The bed sunk down as I sat on the edge. I kicked off my flip flops, dropped my shower towel and hurried under, sliding my cold toes up and down his warm legs and snuggling close.

His skin was as flawless as I remembered it. I ran my hands up and down his torso, then down passed his hips. He slid his not-so-sneaky hand underneath my pillow and pulled out a bottle of purple and black personal lubricant.

"You did bring it!" I yelled.

"Of course I brought it!"

I swiped it from his hand and inspected the shimmering plastic bottle then snapped open the lid.

"Honey," he pulled my hips in close and pressed hard against me. "I'm so glad you're here, I missed you. I love you so much." He watched his fingers as they slid though my hair, then looked into my eyes, lingering, as if he might say something more.

"I love you, too, baby. Thank you so much for bringing me here," I said as he traced his eyes and finger tips down my flank then over my hips and hills. "But did you really have to make me come alone?" I pushed out my lip and pouted.

"C.J., I told you why I came here first," he sat up and tilted his head, surprised by my complaint. "You said you were up for an adventure."

"Traveling alone isn't an adventure, it's boring and lonely."

"I just wanted to be ready for you. Remember, I told you I had diving trips planned that I wanted to get out of the way so we could be together." He said it in earnest.

Ready for me? Maybe he has an entire wedding planned!

An eager, one track-minded girl *would* make that leap. I imagined that our families were on the island. Dylan and Nikki would surely make the trip in secret, and Grant's sister, she must be there too. *So that's why he sent me alone.*

"I forgive you for making me fly here alone. You're still a very good boyfriend," I said even thought I hated referring to him as my boyfriend and he hated it too. So I did it as often as possible to annoy him into action.

I seduced the sensitive area around his inner thighs and he let out a little pleasure filled moan, "Honey, after sex, and dinner, I have a surprise for you."

I pushed up to my elbows, "what is it, tell me now."

"I can't tell you," he said, "it's a surprise," then he guided me to lie down on my back and slithered his sun kissed body on top of mine.

***

I'll pick up some wine on the
Way home. Let's celebrate, right?

Chapter 47

"Wiki-wiki"

— "Hurry up"

"Humahumanukanukaapuaa. Of course I know how to say it," I shrugged my shoulders and crinkled my face as if to say *why would you even ask me that one*, "everyone knows that one, your turn." I pointed to the next painting that hung on the wall in the narrow hotel hallway. It was a neon yellow fish with a black and white clown face.

"Kīkākapu." He said without stuttering a syllable.

"Whatever," I slapped his arm and furrowed at his quick response, "you don't know." Then latched my arm in his and tugged him along putting an end to our annunciation game. A game that inevitably he'd win since he knew how to pronounce words like "indubitably."

It was an idyllic Hawaiian night. We rolled down the car windows and let the salty air blow across our skin as we drove along the Maui shoreline, rolling blue ocean to the right, and lush volcanic peaks to the left. It was a mid-western girl's paradise. A place I hoped to visit someday but never imagined I'd be sharing it with him, the man that was always so out of reach.

I looked out in awe over the water, watching the locals paddle their long boards into the sunset and parents with kids enjoying one last splash in the shallows. Every cove was teeming with laid back souls, absorbing every last speck of daylight out of the sun-drenched day.

We drove for half an hour listening to Hawaiian radio before Grant pulled onto a narrow, reddish earthen road leading to a most spectacular lookout.

A mammoth cliff had risen out of the water a million years ago now we were standing on its plateau looking over the water to the farthest point on the horizon. There were other tourists there too, they marveled at the seascape and pointed off into the distance. Amateur photographers set up their tripods and peered through the long black barrels hoping to catch an award winning shot.

This is a spectacular place to propose!

I scanned the lookout to see if my family was hiding behind some large boulder. Nope.

"Look! Over there!" Grant pointed out into the ocean.

I'd missed it, but caught a glimpse of the deluge after. Then I realized exactly why we were there. *Whales.* I'd forgotten about the whales. I'd never see whales in the wild and I didn't know you could see whales from the shore. I thought you had to pay, then take a boat tour to see them. Had I known I was going to Hawaii, I would have researched these things, but the trip was such a surprise, I barely had time to pack, or lose five pounds, or get a new swimsuit.

The night before Grant left was the first time I found out about the trip. He started acting strange after work, smiling non-stop, playing island music, dancing, and drinking on a weeknight. And he stared at me continually with a *fuck-me* grin. He played romantic island music in the bathroom, poured bubble bath into the Jacuzzi tub and stripped me nude to the sounds of the mandolin. After a foot rub, sensual kissing all over my body, and a surprise *me-only* orgasm under a mountain of fizzing suds, he finally spilled the secret he'd been hiding for months.

He'd arranged everything and was taking us on a Hawaiian getaway. The catch? He was leaving in a few hours, I'd be leaving in a few days. *So he could get his diving trips out of the way before I came,* he said. Why on earth he thought I couldn't handle myself alone in Hawaii for a few days while he plugged his nose and dove underwater I don't know, but he was leaving, and I was staying.

None of that mattered as we stood near the edge of the cliff looking out over the water. Grant stood behind me, arms around my chest, holding me so I didn't stumble and fall. I was humbled to be a guest observing the whales, we watched as the humpbacks displayed their gigantic, majestic forms. Sometimes in small peeks, and sometimes in large entertaining splashes.

"Isn't it great to watch them in their natural home?" Grant said. Then he whispered, "Fucking whalers..."

"I know, fucking losers," I agreed.

He stood behind me warming me as the breeze turned cool and we watched until last speck of color faded to black and the stars began to speckle the night sky.

Although it was surreal and spectacular and romantic and all that, I still had a one track mind.

When is he going to do it already, ugh...

***

Baby, I'm so in love
with u. :) Soon...

Chapter 48

"PILI OLUA E, MOKU KA PAWA O KE AO."

—"YOU TWO ARE NOW ONE, THE DARKNESS IS PAST"

Three days! I'd been there three and a half days and still no proposal! He'd better do it in the bamboo.

I wedged my foot against the base of the bamboo tree and hugged it with every muscle fiber in my upper body so I wouldn't tumble off the side of an unknown mountain.

"I don't think this is right."

"Let's keep going. Ten more minutes," Grant said. "Let's get to that edge and get our bearings. I think that's the stream we're supposed to follow."

I followed him through the thatched forest of towering bamboo where whole families of hollow trees lived like mangroves. Often they were so interwoven that my narrow frame couldn't fit between them and I'd have to find a different route through. We bobbed and weaved, and gradually descended into what I thought might be the East Maui Irrigation, the EMI. The run-off ditch travel guides warn tourists about; the ditch where flash floods wash away unsuspecting hikers, like us.

"Honey, it's really amazing here and all, and we can keep hiking, you know how much I love hiking with you," *if you consider this hiking, there was no trail, there was barely even ground*, "but I think those directions I found on the Internet were wrong, this isn't it."

"Just a little bit farther," he said as he continued to explore the curious stream-like water basin that we hoped would produce a golden trail to a magical waterfall. "It's a ten foot climb to get over the wall of this ditch, I know I can make it, honey, do you think you can?"

I scoffed, "No, but you go ahead. I don't want to risk falling, I'll just wait here and get gored by a wild boar or attacked by a feral dog."

"I forgot. Honey, I'm sorry," he said then climbed out of the rocky drainage ditch that definitely was not a babbling stream en-route to an elusive waterfall.

"Maybe it's this way?" He pointed into the bamboo, not in the direction we came.

Why is he so adamant about going further? This must be the time. He's trying to get to the perfect spot.

I followed him, eager to reach a secluded gushing waterfall in the middle of a tropical rain-forest where he would pull out a little black box from the cargo pocket of his shorts and proclaim his love and desire to be married to me for all eternity.

Yes! Yes! I would say. *It's about frickin time.*

But the longer we hiked the more clear it became that he had absolutely no idea where we were, nor did I. The trail wasn't really a trail at all. It was a newly blazed path made from two delusional hikers too proud to admit they'd failed to read the directions properly.

The not-a-trail turned into bushes and bramble that clung to a steep volcanic cliff that plunged hundreds, maybe thousands of feet into the swelling ocean below. Burgundy and brown branches protected themselves with razor sharp barbs that slashed clean red lines into our arms and legs as we ascended the cliff.

"Should we head back?" He finally asked as he examined the fresh wounds on his forearms then looked at mine too.

"No waterfall?" I whined.

"I'm sorry, I wanted to take you to a waterfall but it's really all your fault since you couldn't climb that little wall." I raised an eyebrow and slumped. "Babe, I'm just kidding." He said, then snatched me up and wrapped himself around my glistening body. "I love you, even if you can't climb anymore," he teased, then pinned my arms behind my back and kissed my neck, "I don't care that you ruined our waterfall hike." He pinned me tighter to him and let out a devilish laugh into the air. I loved his child-like spirit and our ability to play, the way he challenged me and didn't take any of my shit, and I loved that we shared the same sense of humor.

"You're so fun," I said as he let me go.

"Quit it," he blushed, "you're the fun one."

"No. I'm not, I can't even climb anymore."

"It's no big deal, I was just kidding. We can find lots of other things to do together."

I lead the way back as he videotaped our lost hike and made a dozen comments about my butt. We traversed back into civilization and still, no proposal. I couldn't help but think that if we would have just found that damn waterfall he would have proposed.

When we got in the car I guzzled more than fifty percent of our shared Gatorade, not stopping until he yanked it from me.

"You..." he groveled and grinned that gorgeous I'll-get-you-back grin.

"Now where?" I asked.

"Where ever you want. How about *The Road To Hana?*"

"Sure!"

Are you going to propose there?

Halfway to Hana, after twenty-five miles of switchbacks and hairpin turns, I hung my head out the window and heaved blue Gatorade.

"That's what you get for hogging the Gatorade," he said, just before he pulled over at the nearest lookout.

I stepped out and onto a lush Mountainside forest that overlooked magnificent blue and white waves crashing like thunder on the beach below. I was instantly cured of my sickness.

"Look! There's a trail over there!" Grant was pointing to a small opening between two gargantuan trees that were latched like lattice with climbing vines, "up for another hike?"

Maybe he'll do it on this hike.

"Always," I said.

He wrapped his hands around me and softly ran his fingertips along the scars of my back, then pressed our lips together with a playful smack. "Mwah! You're the best."

"I know. I just vomited from those lips though," I said as I followed him into Jurassic Park.

A mile into our hike, our surroundings became the perfect exotic venue for a proposal. Leaves the size of my Volkswagen climbed a hundred feet to the canopy above, there wasn't even a whiff of another tourist for a dozen miles, and the slow trickle of water was ever present, setting the mood for an unforgettable romantic moment. If there ever was a right time, that was it.

I hugged him, pressed my head to his chest and closed my eyes. He was my embassy. His love for me golden and warm, real no doubt, so why wasn't he proposing!? We'd been in Hawaii for three and a half days!

He stepped back and looked at me. "You hungry?"

No, I just want a ring.

"Yes, starving."

"Let's go back to that pineapple stand we saw on the way in."

We drove along the North Shore of Maui as we indulged in the juicy golden fruit.

"Can I have another bite?" He asked as juice dripped from my mouth down my forearm.

As I fed him another bite of pineapple he sucked my fingers into his mouth wetting them all the way to my knuckles. It was an annoying affectation and he'd done it to me a dozen times before. He thought it was *so* funny. My eyes narrowed and I jerked my hand back, and the pineapple with it.

"Okay! I'm sorry," he pleaded, "I won't do it again!"

"Yes, you will. So you don't get anymore." I turned my whole body toward the window, hid the plastic baggie of sweet fruit near my body then stuffed my face full with large chunks, hoarding every last bite until juice flowed from my chin.

"Mmm, this is so good," I muttered.

"Honey, please..." he begged, "I said I was sorry."

"I'm sorry, I can't help you," I said, my mouth so full a piece dropped out and we burst out in laughter, "there isn't anymore. Unless you want that one. "I pointed to the bite now covered in sand by my feet.

Grant stopped at the next Maui Gold Pineapple stand and bought two more bags of fresh cut fruit. While I sat in the car fat and sticky, I watched him through the windshield eat one full baggie before he would even get back in the car with the other one.

We drove aimlessly along the North Shore's jagged cliffs stopping to watch the extreme surfers and count the number of seconds they were underwater before their heads resurfaced in the suds. We ate our way back to Kaanapali beach, stopping again for papaya and avocados and sushi.

I showered then jumped between the cool sheets. Grant leapt onto the bed and sprawled out beside me exposing as much of his skin to the cool air as he could before we engaged each other in a Greco-Roman style foreplay.

Tomorrow would be my last day on the island.

***

Babe, u are so the 1. :)
Thinking of u always.

Chapter 49

"LOLO WAHINE."

—"CRAZY WOMAN"

It was my last full day.

For reasons I don't fully understand, on occasion, alcohol has the exact opposite effect on my behavior than it normally does. Instead of its usual pleasure conjuring, laughter inducing, witty comment blurting effects, a single drink has the ability to morph me into Medusa. On my last day in Maui when Grant had been planning something wondrous and unforgettable, Medusa made a childish and violent appearance and ruined his plans.

Since it was my last full day, I was convinced that if he hadn't proposed yet, he wasn't going to. He'd had plenty of dazzling chances and private encounters to pick from, he had the money to bring us here so he had money for a ring, there could be no other explanation for his engagement impotence other than he really couldn't commit.

Why would he wait until the last day to propose, who does that? No one. That's who. It's not going to happen. I'd been duped.

Earlier that afternoon we lined his backpack with plastic garbage bags, filled it with ice, stuffed it with a six pack of island brewed long boards and headed to the beach. A hot fury of anger hit me as we walked past a perfectly manicured patch of lawn. It was roped off with a white chain that had an old wooden sign hanging down from the center. It proudly stated its intent:

Weddings Only

Ugh!

It was a green semicircle patch of bliss surrounded by waxy rubber plants and hibiscus flowers. It was perfect. As we strolled past

286

matrimonial Eden, I was acutely aware that there were no white plumerias in my hair, no Dylan and Nikki waiting to stand up for us, no white chairs with our closest family and friends in breezy beach linens, no trellis lined with flowers, and no ring!

The assault to my female ego continued when we stepped onto the beach and heard a roaring crowd in the distance. They were cheering on a bride and groom who were in full garb about to jump from a cliff into the ocean below. Tux, dress, veil and all, the happy couple held hands and teased the crowd. We stopped walking and watched the iconic black and white figures until they lept from the tallest cliff and literally took the plunge. The beach roared with spectator applause hoots and hollers.

I turned and walked away. I didn't care about them, I couldn't be happy for them. I was hurting so badly from wanting what they had. I laid on my beach towel, chugged down an ice cold brew and wallowed in all the things I didn't have, and all the things I couldn't do.

Pity party, table of one.

I knew how to be grateful for the things I *did* have, and most of the time I genuinely was. I knew how to focus on the positive and not the negative, and mostly I did that. Sometimes I just couldn't talk myself out of a bad mood and this was one of those times.

"Come out here, baby! You won't get hurt, I promise," Grant yelled from the rolling waves.

I looked away.

He ran up from the ocean, refreshed and smiling. His happiness agitating. "What's wrong?" He asked.

"Nothing," I snapped with a fierce edge.

I was ashamed of how I was acting but unable to snap out of it. I hid behind the goggle size Coach sunglasses I'd picked off of the ocean floor a day ago, I couldn't even look at him.

"I'll be right back, baby. I'm going to go wash off," he said then trotted away.

I obsessively and uncontrollably ranted to myself as I laid there alone. My temper and my skin felt like they were boiling under the intense sun.

He really isn't going to propose…I can't fucking believe this.

I'm done. When I get back, I'm moving out. I knew this was too good to be true. He'll string me along forever. No wonder he was single all those years, he can't commit—Dylan was right. I can't believe I moved me and Dani in with him. What am I going to tell everyone? What am I going to tell Dani? I knew better. I fucking knew better, how did I let it come to this?

Water dripped from his body as he lay down on the towel beside me. It hurt to be near him. Tears rolled out the bottom of my sunglasses and down my cheeks. I'd talked myself into distrusting everything he'd ever said. All those conversations about our life together and having babies—lies. I was sure he loved me, and I was sure he didn't want to lose me, but I was sure he couldn't make the final commitment. And I wasn't interested in anything but that final commitment.

In my hormonal, slightly inebriated state, I'd convinced myself that he enjoyed the chase but couldn't kill the beast, now that I was officially off the menu. My name was not on our mortgage, or the deed to our home, or anything that could bind us financially together. Our lives were completely dis-entangled, a split would be easy; he would be free, able to go immediately back to his single life. He'd invite women into the home we'd built, they'd sleep in my bed, cook at my island, fuck in my Jacuzzi then be dumped like the rest of us.

"I'm hungry," he said, interrupting my daytime nightmare. "Do you want to come with me to get some food?"

I popped my lips, *"Nope."*

"Do you want me to bring you back anything?"

Yeah, a fucking commitment you asshole.

"Nope."

"Do you want me to bring you a pina-colada?"

"I have a beer."

"Can I open another for you?" He asked so sweetly, he was tip-toeing around my bad behavior and we both knew it.

"I can do it myself."

"Okay, babe, enjoy. I'll be right back." He kissed the side of my head as if nothing was wrong, then trotted away through the sand.

I stared into the ocean. Not even the whales thrusting their enormous bodies into the blue sky could distract me from falling apart. Just being near him felt like pure rejection, and my wounded ego nudged me to disappear, to get away from the pain. I knew it was wrong, but I was too hurt to care how much I might be hurting him. So I stuffed my sand-filled towel into my tote, stood up and decided to leave. I drew an arrow in the sand with my foot in the direction I went walking so he'd know I wasn't abducted, but I wouldn't be there when he got back.

I strolled along the edge of the water for half an hour until the beach turned into a rocky outcropping of boulders that jutted out into the ocean. I hiked across the jagged rocks to a deserted stretch of shoreline, then shimmied up a tangle of exposed tree roots. I sat with my legs dangling over a sharp ledge of rusty colored dirt and closed my eyes.

Inhale and smile...Exhale and relax.

Fuck that! That's not going to work.

I stayed on that cliff and tried to empty my cup over and over, but it kept filling with anger and hurt and all the things unsaid. I had fallen into a pit of irrational despair, lapsed into a female psycho trance and I just couldn't snap out of it. Then out of nowhere a mantra flashed through my irrational mind and imprinted itself onto me:

Just because he hasn't proposed, doesn't mean he doesn't love you.

It was a moment of clarity, the epiphany I needed. It was a single phrase that summed up everything and somehow made me feel better. I repeated my mantra over and over until it pulled me from the bowels of crazy female hormonal hell back into the present moment.

What have I done? He doesn't deserve this. What are the facts here? How self-centered and disrespectful of me to walk away, to disappear without telling him. He would never have done that to me.

I was drowning in desperation, I missed him, I was so sorry I'd been such a crazy bitch and I needed to get back to him fast. I panicked.

What if I didn't find him? What if he wouldn't take me back after my bad behavior? What if he got murdered in our hotel room and the last thing I said to him was terrible and rude!

I jumped from my perch, wobbled across the field of boulders then started running. I hate running. But for him I would run across the universe. I rounded the corner to the straight stretch of beach that lead back to our hotel and saw him in the distance, walking toward me with his shoes in his hand and a back pack slung over his back. He waved his arm high in the air and a smile grew on his face.

My heart exploded in my chest, but not from the running, from love, or from anger at myself for how destructive I could be, or maybe it was from running. Relief gushed through me when he wrapped me in his arms.

"Honey, I found the arrow, you went for a walk, that's great," he said, as if nothing had happened.

"I knew you'd see it. I'm so sorry for being cranky today, and I'm sorry for just disappearing." I hugged him tighter and tears filled my eyes, again.

"You don't need to apologize, you weren't cranky."

"Yes, I was. But I'm better now, I just needed to move my body a bit."

Lie.

"Come on," he said, holding my hand, "let's go to that little restaurant we saw in Lahaina, you probably need to eat."

I wasn't hungry, being overly emotional numbed my appetite, and not eating dropped my blood sugar further exacerbating my moodiness. Since I wasn't hungry, I ordered another drink. The most regrettable drink of my life; a drink that sent me so far back into the throws of madness I wrecked what would have been the best moment of my life. From there on, I wish I could take it all back.

"Have you ever thought about...you know...us, getting married here?" I said while I watched him eat dinner. It was the question that triggered the spiral of out-of-control madness.

"Not really, you?" He said nonchalantly, not making eye contact.

I swallowed the large lump of hurt that was lodged in my throat. "I thought that maybe...we might have gotten married here this week."

"Really?" He raised his eyebrows and his face turned a shade of pale green. "Without our family?"

"People do it all the time, then celebrate with their families back home."

He stayed silent, looked out over the streets of Lahaina and the banyan tree park, "I guess I assumed you'd want your family there."

I shook my head frustrated, then revved the engine of the crazy train.

"You're scared," I accused. "I don't think we'll ever get married."

"What? Why do you say that?"

"Because. We're in *Hawaii*. I'm going home *tomorrow*. We're obviously not getting *married* or *engaged*, and I don't want to seem ungrateful because I love that we're here together, but you told me we weren't getting engaged yet because you didn't have enough money for a ring. Well this trip definitely disproves that. So I can only assume the holdup is that you're scared."

"I'm not scared," he said very matter of fact.

"Grant, I've told you many times that the most important thing to me was that I wanted us to be committed...engaged, before we moved in together. That I didn't want to move Dani in with her mom's boyfriend. You told me not to worry, and I trusted you and now, we're still just boyfriend and girlfriend with my daughter living with us. What do you expect me to think? Because I'm really starting to doubt all of the things you've told me."

The tension between us was thickening and I could see him retreating from our conversation.

"Well I'm not scared," was all he could say, without offering any other insight.

He paid our tab without saying word, then set his hand on my lower back as we walked out of the restaurant. His touch hurt my skin, it felt like empty promises. I walked faster to break the contact I couldn't bare to feel any longer.

As we drove back to the hotel, silent tears dripped down my stoic face. He grazed his hand over my thigh as we drove, the way he always did, loving me. But this time I didn't love it. I moved my thighs closer to the window and away from him.

I blew past our hotel room door and locked myself in the cold bathroom. For half an hour I sat on the toilet with my face in my hands and sobbed. He didn't try to comfort me. I didn't blame him, I'd been incorrigible bitch. I would have thought he'd left the room had it not been for the dull laughter of the television coming through the pocket door that separated us. I washed the make-up off my face, stripped down to my bra and panties, dropped in some Visine, and worked up the strength to walk out.

He immediately intercepted me with kind eyes and an open heart, "Baby, what's wrong? Please talk to me."

I wiggled loose from his grip, crawled into bed and flipped vacantly through the TV channels.

"Are you tired?" He said in the kindest voice. But I couldn't speak.

He laid beside me, snuggling his warm sun drenched body next to mine and reached to hold my hand. He was trying to love me the way he always did, it reminded me of how perfect, how patient he was, and how erratic and impossible I could be. How I could go from life changing mantra to evil self-absorbed bitch in two seconds flat and not be able to come out of it. I hated myself for being so uncontrollably moody.

"Baby, don't cry, I love you so much." He pulled my limp body toward him, kissed my wet face, my hair, my neck, and wiped my tears. "Please don't cry, tell me what's wrong."

I had lost the ability to speak. I could only cry and I cried for the next hour as he held me, not knowing why or what to do. The harder I cried, the tighter he squeezed.

He pleaded with me a dozen times before I found the strength to talk. I propped myself up on a mountain of pillows and looked his gorgeous face that was now twisted into a painful grimace of worry and confusion. I was pushing him away with my silence, punishing him, hurting him, and it showed on his face. I didn't want to be that way, I was just hurting so badly I couldn't be any other way.

I stuttered as I spoke, "I...I just...I thought we were coming here to get married..." He looked away and let out a deep disgruntled breath.

"I'm sorry," I said, "I guess I read the signs all wrong. I actually thought we might get...I mean I'm crying because I'm disappointed."

"Honey, I never said we were going to get married here," he spoke like he was desperate for me to understand.

"I know. I know you never said that, I just thought...maybe it would be a surprise. I thought that's why you came here early, was to plan something."

"But I told you I was coming here early to go scuba diving, to get it out of the way so that when you got here we could be together."

"I know, I know you told me that," I said feeling so stupid. "Never-mind, I don't want to talk about it anymore, I'm sorry for ruining our day and being so stupid. Please forgive me, I don't know what's wrong with me, I feel so off sometimes. I promise I'll work on it and try to get better."

"Honey, nothing is wrong with you and you don't have to apologize. I want you to tell me how you feel. I guess we just had different thoughts about what this trip was going to be. I'm sorry if I led you to think it was something it's not. Baby, I love you and hate to see you cry."

Just because he hasn't proposed doesn't mean he doesn't love you. He does love you, he does love you, remember to receive it, accept it or you will drive him away.

But I couldn't stop a deluge of salty tears from pooling between my cheek and his chest.

He'd finally had enough. He scooted away from me, stood up, ran his fingers through his hair like he was being driven nuts, and walked into the bathroom. I was instantly empty inside, mortified at what it felt like to be without him. I'd been so fucking nuts I drove him away. The pain of losing him was unbearable. I wanted to run after him and beg his forgiveness and apologize again for being so crazy, but I had to pull myself together. I had to get right, get whole and emotionally stable again, he deserved that and I knew I could be that for him I just had to find it again.

When he came out of the bathroom his face was distraught with stress. He stood at the side of the bed and looked down at me with intense blue eyes glossed over with a reddish tinge. I deserved whatever was coming. Something like, *I've never seen you like this, I don't deserve this, I'm not sure this is going to work...or I didn't think you were crazy like all the rest but I guess you're the worst of them all, when we get home I think you should move out.*

"This is not worth you being so upset," he said with anguish in his voice. I started to cry even harder the moment he spoke. "I've never seen you like this, honey. I hate seeing you like this, it doesn't need to be this way."

He walked over to the television and reached his arm way up inside the heavy wooden armoire.

I gasped and cringed in equal measure, instantly regretting my inexcusable behavior. My hands instinctively covered my humiliated face as he turned toward me—staring at me, standing completely still except for the hand that was tossing and catching a small black velvet box. He lobbed it into the air then clasped it into his palm half a dozen times without breaking eye contact allowing me ample time to experience the full effects of total mortification.

Chapter 50

"WOMEN ARE MADE TO BE LOVED, NOT UNDERSTOOD."

—OSCAR WILDE, THE SPHINX WITHOUT A SECRET

He sauntered toward me staring past my eyes and into my ashamed soul. I hid behind the slots in my fingers. Then in nothing but his whitey tighties and me in my bra and panties, he knelt beside me on the bed still pitching the velvet square into the air.

His expression clearly stated three things:

(1) *You really are something else, aren't you.*

(2) Did you really have any doubt?

(3) *I love you for who you are, crazy and all.*

"Told you I wasn't scared," he said as emotion welled up in his eyes. "I just wanted this moment to be perfect. That's why I waited."

I'd never seen him cry, not even close, not even a teeny drop of liquid on a cold winter's day. He was the kindest, most compassionate person I'd ever known, but he was all of those things because of logic and intelligence, not because of emotion. He simply never cried.

Except on this day.

"C.J., all of this is for you...for us," he said, "everything I do is for you." A hitch in speech revealed the knot in his throat. "I didn't want to get married here because I thought we would want our families to celebrate it with us." He cleared his throat and looked at me with watery eyes, "I've already loved you for an eternity. I've never wanted anyone but you, it's always been you, it always will be you..." A single tear melted from his icy eye down his cheek. "I never knew how lonely I was until I found you. I never want to be without you, and I never meant to hurt you. Since our first night together, this has always been my plan." He glanced at the little box, then back to me. He shook his head and shrugged as if to say...*I can't believe you didn't know?*

"Charmaine, will you marry me?"

Maybe tears are not a good measure of how much someone loves you, but I knew how much he loved me from the three vulnerable tears that fell onto the sheets that night.

"Yes. Yes!" I yelled as he opened the little box.

I was more certain of my answer than I was certain the sun would rise.

"Baby, you deserve everything you've ever dreamed of. Our life together will be so great—I promise." He said as the little box creaked open.

He slid a modest, two sizes too big ring on my finger, I straddled his lap and wrapped myself around him. We held each other and swayed for what felt like hours.

I'd finally made it home, I always knew he was my home but now I had the invitation I desperately needed to come inside, take off my coat and make myself comfortable—forever. He took me in, all of me—all the crazy, all the kindness, and I fell into him like a cup of water being poured back into the ocean.

I wish I could say that in that moment all I felt was thrilling elation and pure bliss, but shame and embarrassment cast a large shadow over my heart; my behavior had been deplorable, unworthy of the man before me and I needed to get it under control so I never did it to him again.

My chin bounced off his shoulder as I whispered, "I'm sorry I wrecked it."

"Honey, you didn't wreck anything, you don't have anything to be sorry about. This is perfect. You are perfect."

"You mean you planned it like this, in our underwear in a hotel room after I threw a tantrum?"

"Yes," he said as he wrestled me down onto the bed. "I was waiting for the perfect time and I guess this was it. Hey, we should go see if we can catch the sun set."

A dozen hues of blue smudged the sky like a water color painting. We burrowed into the cool sand and sat side by side arms and legs intertwined. I closed my eyes to feel without distraction the depth and breadth of what he had just given me. The man I respect and admire most in the universe had finally given me the closure I needed to be truly content.

After you get engaged or married, people always ask *do you feel any different?* In that very moment, my answer was yes, without a doubt, yes. The energy between us had changed instantaneously, or I had changed. Whatever it was, I was different; we were different. We were weaved emotionally and spiritually together as a unified us; a we, an our, an, if-he-goes-I-go, an, if-she-leaves-I-leave.

We both spotted a well-dressed couple walking toward us from down the beach.

"Good evening," the silver-haired man said. Then he swept his arm across the sky holding a bottle in his hand. "Now isn't this beautiful?"

"It's spectacular. We love it here," Grant replied.

The woman on his arm flashed me a familiar smile as her husband spoke with a thick Southern accent, "We saw the two of you from our balcony," he said.

"We're not weird or anything, we just thought you might enjoy some champagne."

Huh?

"We bought a bottle of champagne tonight," he went on, "and we can't drink it all. We didn't want it to go to waste. Thought the two of you might enjoy it." He held the bottle out toward Grant.

"Sure!" We said in unison as he handed us a half full bottle of bubbly and two plastic cups.

Grant and I looked at each other dumbfounded, trying to make sense of the serendipitous moment. Then it occurred to me that it was too coincidental, too much like romantic movie to be real.

Grant must have set this up.

Sand fell from our clothes as we stood up to exchange pleasantries with the dreamlike couple who'd appeared out of the dusk.

They were a quintessential charming southern duo, humble and hospitable. I instantly liked them. Somehow I felt like we'd known them for a hundred years.

They were celebrating their tenth anniversary and seemed blissfully happy. By the look of their age, I imagined their love was born from a second marriage and I couldn't help but feel like they were a vision of Grant and I, twenty years in the future.

I examined them closely to make sure they were human. I looked at their wise wrinkles and shiny flecks of gray hair, the way they held hands, and stood pressing into one another. They were truly, unequivocally happy like a married couple should be.

The men shook hands and said good-bye and I exchanged an intuitive smile with my future self.

We never saw them again.

"This is so weird," Grant said as soon as they were out of earshot.

"Did you plan this?" I accused.

"Of course not, how could I have planned this."

"Honey, why does weird stuff happen to us?"

"You know why, baby," he stuffed the cork into his pocket and poured the ginger colored fizz into our plastic cups, "because it was meant to be. We were meant to be."

I hung my head. "I'm so sorry. About earlier. I don't know why I'm so crazy sometimes." My gut flipped over in agony at the thought of the tantrum I'd thrown.

"Quit it, we never have to talk about it again. If it had happened any differently we wouldn't be drinking this champagne right now."

"You mean the champagne from our future selves?"

"Yes, you're right! That'll be us in twenty years."

I held up my cup to toast, "here's to marrying the man of my dreams."

"Here's to getting to call you my wife."

G+C

10,000

More days

Chapter 51

"TO BE ABLE TO SAY HOW MUCH LOVE IS TO LOVE BUT LITTLE."

—PETRARCH, *TO LAURA IN LIFE*

Four Months Later

The truth, our truth had made its way out of the darkness and leapt into real life—like a fairy tale jumping out of a story book. Nothing would ever be the same. *He* filled my longing, *he* erased the emptiness. A lifetime of incompleteness over. All of the things I had tried to fill myself with: religion, food, work, men, it was none of those—it was him. I had been waiting for him.

In a tiny chapel with ten rows of old church chairs, I married the man who was as much a part of me as my own soul. I won his heart by being my crazy real self, and because he knows exactly who I am, how berserk, how cruel, and how kind I can be, I have to hide nothing. With him I have no secrets, no lies, I am naked.

Our wedding was blissful. Not spectacular or stunning, glamorous or glitzy, it was romantic and blissful. The way a wedding should be when all of the ceremonious fluff is stripped away and instead of diamonds, love is allowed to shine.

Dani walked down the aisle holding a bouquet of mini purple roses I'd tied together with twine. She was excited to be a part of the celebration, but she wasn't thrilled that mom was getting remarried.

"He's nice to me, and he treats mom good." She would say when someone asked how she felt about Grant—her feelings toward him polite, but numb. Grant and Dani had yet to find real common ground. He wasn't interested in the latest nail polish trend and she wasn't interested in watching *How the Earth Was Made.* I never forced a relationship that wasn't there, I was fine with what-it-was, and what-it-wasn't.

I trusted with time they would find the right balance, and if that balance never became anything more than a mutual respect, I would be fine with that.

I wore a small Hawaiian flower in my hair and an ivory wedding dress with a champagne sash. Strips of sheer rumpled chiffon fell in waves from bust to floor. It was the only dress I never wanted to take off.

With the top button undone and his sleeves rolled up to his elbows, Grant's pale blue shirt matched his eyes. The way he looked at me made my chest ache. My respect and love for him was as expansive as the universe itself. He held my hand as we walked down the aisle. The moment he kissed me, the moment I became his wife, was as magical and as much like a fairy tale as I imagined it would be.

We spent the night at the lake cabin, naked and rolling in pleasure, in the back bedroom where our love affair had begun so many years earlier. We reminisced about the first night and all the indiscretions along the way. No matter how disapproving they might be, since they had gotten us to where we were, we agreed we would never take anything back. We talked about all the decades to come and how they would never be enough.

***

It was Christmas when we got back to Maui, seven months after our wedding. The air was filled with the sound of *mele kalikimaka* and every palm tree on the island was twinkling with lights.

Our goal: find the waterfall that had eluded us last year.

We parked our rental car on the side of the road next to the same bamboo forest. He stepped out and onto the highway, then walked around the car to get me. With his hand on the small of my back he made sure I didn't trip and fall into traffic on the narrow road.

We entered the towering green forest through a small unmarked opening that turned into an actual hiking trail.

"This is it!" I yelled. "A small opening in the trees leading into a grotto! How could we have missed this?"

"You're right!" From behind he wrapped his hands around my little growing belly and kissed my cheek. "Follow me."

We hopped from stone to stone across a shallow river bed that cleverly concealed its treasure deep within the forest. The trail picked up on the other side of the water then spit us out into another river basin where we immediately heard gushing water.

Gigantic boulders surrounded a small emerald pool, the mouth of a stunning secluded waterfall. It wasn't a hundred feet tall nor did it require a helicopter and landing pad to get to. It was better. It was private, and no one was there but him and me.

I sat on a flat polished boulder dangling my legs into the crystal green pool as Grant navigated his way to a ledge behind the falls.

"This is so amazing!" he yelled from behind a curtain of white gushing water. "I love it here!"

When he was done exploring, he came and sat beside me. He kissed me with a frisky smack and interlaced our fingers. I felt his wedding band around his right ring finger and laughed out loud.

"Honey, you do know that wearing your wedding band on your right hand means you're gay."

"I know," he said. "It doesn't bother me. It doesn't fit my left hand, and I don't want it to fall off."

"We can get you a new one," I said.

"I don't want a new one. I like this one."

"Actually, I like it that you wear it on your right hand. Other women will think that you're gay and leave you alone."

He turned his attention to my wedding ring, wiggled it from side to side, and slid it off past my swollen knuckle. We watched it sparkle under the sun as he twisted it around, and then he turned his body to face me.

"I'm so excited for our baby. You make me so happy. Since I didn't get to do this how I planned last time..." He smiled.

I cringed.

When I looked up, his unconditional loving eyes met mine.

"C.J.," he said, "you were so worth the wait. Will you marry me?"

***

*I am getting excited
for our little guy to arrive,
so I can get u prego again!*

HONEY!

IT'S SO GREAT THAT I GET TO CALL MYSELF YOUR HUSBAND! THERE IS SO ONLY ONE OF YOU ON THIS PLANET, IN THIS UNIVERSE, AND I'M THE ONE THAT HAS THE HONOR OF BELONGING TO YOU!

THIS IS A FIRST FOR ME—THE FIRST TIME I GET TO CALL SOMEONE MY WIFE :) ALL THE YEARS THAT HAVE GONE BY WITHOUT YOU ARE FINALLY OVER FOREVER, AND I LOOK FORWARD TO EVERY DAY SPENT BEING A FAMILY WITH YOU AND I, DANI, AND OF COURSE, ALL OF OUR FUTURE CHILDREN. WELL, OKAY, *ALL* MEANS NO MORE THAN TWO.

I LOVE YOU, WIFE!

LOVE, GRANT

Everyone gets a do-over
   —C.J. English

I hope you enjoyed my story as much as I enjoyed telling it.
If you did, please consider posting a brief review on Amazon.
The more honest the better.
Thank you so much!
-C.J.

If your book club is reading Affairytale and would like to skype with the author, please send your request to affairytalebook@gmail.com

Follow C.J. on social media for behind the scenes photos and deleted scenes from the book.

www.affairytalebook.com
www.pinterest.com/cjenglishauthor
www.facebook.com/cjenglishauthor
@cjenglishauthor on Twitter
cjenglishauthor on Instagram
AFFAIRYTALE on Goodreads

Acknowledgments

To my editor Hannah Kiges-Hutton who took on my manuscript in the eleventh hour and believed in it enough to commit to a crazy timeline. Thank you for letting me keep my voice and allowing me to make my own rules.

Ericka and Mandee, I speak as if you are conjoined twins but appreciate and love you both in unique ways. Ericka, thank you for listening to me ramble about this project as it was being conceived years ago and thank you for reading endless unpolished drafts until I got it right. Mandee, without the amazing cover, website and your brilliant business mind the book would never have gotten out there. You two bitches are the best.

Levi, you are a fine and decent, hard-working man and I intended no harm to come to you in writing this memoir. I hope you find love and happiness with a woman who will treat you like you deserve to be treated.

Thank you Lissy for supporting me through all the stages of my life and taking me back with open arms after I avoided you while sneaking around and pursuing my love interest. I only kept you away because you would have figured it out.

Dylan, without your very unique personality Grant probably would've never become your friend and we may have never met. I guess I owe my happiness in part to you. Also, thank you allowing me to divulge some embarrassing characteristics for the sake of sheer entertainment, I love you.

Mom and dad, without the both of you making me get me on stage, I would never have had the confidence to speak in public and be fearless in front of an audience when I need to be. I want you guys to live forever within the walls of pleasentville, I've never seen you happier and that makes me happy. You are loving, open-minded and understanding parents and I am truly grateful for everything you've done for me, and with me.

Dani, thank you for being the only one who gets my sense of humor and snarkiness when no one else does. You understand me in ways no one else does. Whether you like it or not, little by little, you're turning into me.

To my littlest guy: thank you, little monster, for plunking on the keys of my laptop when I was trying to write this book. I never want you to grow up.

Thank you to my sweet little girl who tossed and turned in my belly and gave me heart burn while I was trying to finish this book. I'll always remember the times you fell asleep in my arms by the light of the laptop and I just couldn't set you down. I love you guys.

Thanks to Shawn Rode for the cover photo, I don't know how you managed to conceal my very pregnant belly in the promo shots, but you did!

Thank you to Lewis Grant for believing in this book from the very beginning and coming along for this wild ride. You are amazing at what you do, the book trailer is fantastic.

Thank you to Grace, Kate, Sunny, Deb, Cindy, Nichole and Jeanette for your edits and honesty in the initial drafts; your feedback was invaluable.

Thank you to my in-laws or as Dylan would say (my non-blood's) you have treated me with nothing but immense respect and kindness. You've taken me and Dani in like we had been family all along. I am forever grateful and learning how to love deeper because of all of you.

My love, what more can I say? I just wrote an entire book about you! I think I've probably said enough, likely too much. I'm not sure why you came around to the idea of me airing our dirty laundry, but I'm glad you did, I've enjoyed telling the world our love story. If no other dreams of mine ever come true I will never be disappointed. You alone make life extraordinary. You have taught me things about life and love and string theory that I never knew existed. Although I've said it before, I want nothing more than to live for all eternity with you, or at least another 10,000 days. Please create some device that will allow us to upload our consciousness into a computer before we die then download it into a new youthful body when one is grown for us. Or maybe we really should freeze our brains?

To all the readers and reviewers, lovers and haters; thank you to the moon and back for your precious time and support or lack thereof. No matter what, I consider each of you my friend.

With Love,

C.J.

I'm sorry you had to find out this way.

Excerpt from

WTF am I supposed to eat?

a dieters manifesto

By C.J. English

WTF am I supposed to eat?

a dieter's manifesto

by C.J. English

The following content has not been rated but does contain graphic language, mature subject matter, some nudity, sexuality and irreverent, dry, sarcastic, WTF humor. If you're easily offended or have a tendency toward sending hate mail, consider reading a different book.

WTF am I supposed to eat? is the opinion of one person, not true and tested scientific facts. This is not a textbook. It's a manifesto written by someone who generally knows what she's talking about but readily admits that, in fact, she may actually know nothing. The content that follows is based on experiments she's done on herself and others. So for fuck's sake, try not to take anything too seriously.

Editor and Interior Design: Hannah Hutton Clark and Laura Bania
www.writeawaypublishing.com

Cover Design: MSPIRE
www.mspire.com

Cover Photo: Two Hearts Photography
www.twoheartsphotos.com
www.facebook.com/twoheartsphoto

Hair and Makeup: Molly Grundysen
www.facebook.com/mollygrundysen

Cover photo on location at The Aspens at Timber Creek, Fargo, ND.
Courtesy of Heritage Homes. www.heritagefargo.com

Paperback ISBN: 978-0-9863042-2-4

Digital ISBN: 978-0-9863042-3-1

To everyone who shares my dream of eating whatever you

want and not getting fat,

this one is for you.

Introduction

"FORGET WHAT YOU THINK YOU KNOW,

YOU MIGHT KNOW NOTHING."

Coconut or hemp milk? Wait... I haven't even tried soy milk or almond milk.

Paleo or are we still doing Atkins?

Raw nuts or roasted?

Splenda or Truvia? Or is it stevia or agave? And WTF is turbinado sugar?

What about those protein shake places, are they good for me?

Should I be eating chia seeds?

Is flax still a thing?

Steel-cut or old-fashioned oats?

What's with all these pastas?

I should be eating Greek yogurt, right?

Is red meat actually that bad for me? What if I only eat

grass-fed beef? Or bison? Or venison?

You confused?

You and everyone else. You deserve to know what it really takes to lose weight, what it really takes to keep weight off, and the truth about what's actually healthy and what will fucking kill you. You also deserve to have someone relentlessly encourage you along your journey as you pursue lifelong health, preferably someone with no ties to the food industry, supplement companies or any other entity trying to make money off getting you to buy their shit. That's me. I'm a nobody with no ties, who's spent a lifetime sifting through the sea of weight-loss information and misinformation all tangled up in knots.

It has been my mission to unravel the mess and search for WTF is the truth and WTF is total bullshit. The question I've sought the answer to is this: *how can I eat whatever I want and still stay skinny... forever? I also want to look younger than I am, have as much energy as I can possibly have, and live a long, disease-free life.*

This lifelong quest for skinnydom has turned me into a chronic dieter, information sponge, health food nut, wine drinker, juice maker, smoothie connoisseur, but above all, a plant eater—a *mostly* plant eater.

My triumphs and pitfalls attempting to lose weight have taught me how to get and stay skinny with as little effort as possible. On the pages that follow are the things I have learned along the way.

This is my manifesto.

A public declaration of what I think I know. But through all of my experiments on myself and others, and a little bit of reading too, all I've really discovered is that I know nothing. So this book is not a scientific proclamation of facts, although I will present some to you throughout—I will also scatter a few pieces of bullshit here and there to see if you're still paying attention.

I am not a dietitian, nutritionist or food scientist. Nor do I have a renowned degree in anything you'd likely be impressed with. But I am smart. I have been *edu-mac-ated* by many a college and might even have received a few pedigrees. But mostly, I just have a kinky fetish for solving problems by thinking outside the box. Not *math* problems—I fucking hate math problems. I mean I like to figure shit out; I like to play chess and not just on a chessboard. More importantly, I have the gumption to think critically and the courage to share my observations. Without questioning what we think to be true, we will never find the real truth at all.

So here is what I *do* know... for sure.

When I'm skinny, I'm happy; when I'm fat, I'm not.

I like being skinny; even more, I like *feeling* skinny.

I hate feeling fat; I *despise* feeling fat.

Feeling fat feels like shit; being fat feels even more like shit.

Don't assume I'm as shallow as a shot glass and expect

318

everyone to be skinny in order to be happy, quite the contrary is true. All I'm saying is that *I* prefer to feel skinny as opposed to *feeling* fat, and the only way for me to feel skinny is to actually *be* skinny. I've been both skinny and fat—my preference is clear.

So am I skinny?

Yes.

A tad muscular?

A tad.

A smidge flabby when I jump up and down naked in front of the mirror?

A smidge.

Am I fucking ripped? Jacked? Sliced?

Um... no.

If the physique you desire is the shredded look of the men and women on the cover of muscle magazines, you are reading the wrong book. No one who has the bad food behaviors that I have and is not willing to give them up could be that fit. But that is one of my secrets to how I stay skinny.

I *have* to be bad to stay skinny.

OK, the truth is that I have zero willpower—that's why I have to be bad. However, I've figured out how to work with this pesky willpower weakness. And it's not by going to the gym.

Overuse injuries and a strong aversion to going to the gym have forced me to figure out what food lifestyle works for me instead of forcing myself to exercise when it's actually quite boring. This journey has been a bitch at times; I'm not naturally skinny with a high metabolism, and I'm not blessed with bikini body genes. I have been way too fat, way too skinny, extremely unhealthy and un-sustainably overly healthy many times over. Simply put—I've been a hot mess and a not-so-hot mess. Being all over the spectrum of wellness and weight loss has been beneficial in pointing me toward balance.

Life is messy sometimes—chaotic, and crammed with too many things and never enough time. OK, it's that way all the time. But still, I have figured out that if I want to stay skinny with three kids, three friends, a full-time job, one Goldendoodle and keep an amazing marriage to an insanely hot husband (which I wrote about in the Amazon Kindle #1 Best Selling Book in Diaries and Journals, *AFFAIRYTALE, a Memoir,* get it here) weight loss has become more of an art than a science. Although science is the foundation on which sound knowledge is built, sometimes art is necessary to be able to see how things fit together. I am going to show you how I've pieced it all together, and I'll share how others have done it too. My hope is that you are able to figure out for yourself what will work and gain the clarity to know what won't.

You will not be reading about how much protein you should eat or getting recommendations on grams of carbs or calories, nor will I be citing a thousand peer reviewed studies that plants are a better food choice than animals—even though they are and I want to—I won't. Because there are a thousand other studies that say the opposite is true.

Both sides will be convincing; both sides will have facts and supporting evidence that seems overwhelmingly in their favor; and both sides will have flaws, mistakes, oversights and quite possibly will be contaminated with corruption and greed. None of that matters anyway. We aren't creatures who wholeheartedly believe in evidence. We live our lives by faith, hunches, gut feelings, opinions, and personal convictions regardless of the truth.

I won't be cramming chicken, tuna, or brown rice down your throat or telling you to exercise more. I'm not saying exercise is bad—that would be fucking stupid. However, the current approach to working out for weight loss is not working; two thirds of Americans are still overweight, one third of them obese. More on not exercising for weight loss in chapter three. Until then, if you are currently using exercise to lose weight and it's not working, cut it the fuck out. Go spend your time at the farmer's market and then in the kitchen where it'll actually pay off. You have my permission to not exercise until you are done reading this book and have reconsidered your plan.

Forget what you think you know; you might know nothing. All I know is that I actually know nothing, and when I can admit that to myself, only then do I begin to learn. So open your mind, ask yourself if what you've done or have been doing is really working or if you might have to re-think your plan.

Now...

If I skip right to telling you *what* to eat, you won't be successful at losing weight. Even when you know *what* to eat (which I'm certain most of you do) perhaps you haven't been able to stick with it.

To lose weight, I believe we have to have a meaningful understanding of *why* we should be doing something or why we should not. Meaningful is different for everybody, but eventually, something will click, hit home, rattle you to the core, and you'll realize that if you don't do what it is you need to, you and the people you love will suffer. If you don't change the way you think, it won't matter if you know *what* to eat because you won't have the internal motivation or tools to eat that way anyway. So before we discuss if almond milk is better than soy milk or whether or not you should be eating coconut oil by the spoonful, let's delve into a few tricks that may blow your mind and build the foundation for lasting weight-loss results.

As we go, I expect you to be curious, look shit up, ask questions, and don't take what I or anyone else says to be true without thinking critically and investigating for yourself. Form your own opinions—just don't form your own facts. Set free your inquisitiveness and have rigor in finding out what works for you... that is the key.

Did you catch that? That was important.

The key to weight loss is figuring out what works for *you*.

Part I:
How

Chapter 1

"THE BEST WEIGHT-LOSS PLAN WILL FIT YOU LIKE A RED
CARPET DRESS—TAPED, PINNED AND HEMMED TO FIT YOUR
EVERY CURVE, BULDGE, AND IMPERFECTION."

You have to create your own program.

Weight loss happens when you stop going on other people's "programs" and create your own instead. Once you have a designed a personalized weight-loss strategy, one that is integrated into your every cell—a diet you cannot go off of because it's not really a diet at all—only then, will you be successful.

Here's how to do it.

First, stop trying and re-trying the same old diets that haven't worked for you in the past. Get over it and don't even try to tell yourself *this time it'll work if I just stick with it.* Of course it will work if you stick with it—most diets do work for weight loss if you stick with it—but that's the problem: you don't stick with it.

Why? Because you haven't been honest with yourself about what you realistically can and can't do or what you are and aren't willing to give up. Did you really think you could go 30 days without eating out and working out every day at 6 a.m.? Did you really think you'd go three weeks on less carbs than a corn cob without the kernels? No—you were on someone else's program and not one that took into account your unique, sometimes weird, preferences. Anything that does not consider the things you love most or the foods you won't give up, will fail. Since no one knows you better than you, you'll have to create a plan for yourself. Once you do, your diet will not only work for you, but it will become you: it *is* you. The healthier, thinner version of you.

I will often hear this, "What do you eat? I'll just do that."

Within this question lies a widespread damaging misconception about losing weight. It implies that if so-and-so does such-and-such and you do the same, you'll both get the same results. This is what most weight-loss programs assume and understandably so. How could a diet book or program that needs to be scaled for the masses cover thousands of specific scenarios for weight loss, one for each unique reader? It can't. The information we get about what is healthy and what will help us lose weight are often over-generalized statements that assume everyone is the same and loses weight the same. We don't.

Sure, we're the same in some ways. We also have a similar biology to rats, mice, rabbits, primates, and all the other poor creatures that are forced to be our stand-ins for testing things that might be unsafe for humans. Like mascara and... weight-loss pills. [1]

So, does a weight-loss pill that causes fat loss in a mouse

---

[1] *We could do away with the barbaric practice of testing on animals, don't cha think?*

cause fat loss in a human—is that a fair comparison? What animal do you want standing in for you? My answer is none—not even another human. I don't want to be let down by trying another thingamajig that seems to work for everyone else but just doesn't work for me.

Although there are elements in common weight-loss programs that work for many people, the most successful long term weight-loss programs are not designed as one-size-fits-all. The best weight-loss plan will fit you like a red carpet dress—taped, pinned, and hemmed to fit your every curve, bulge, and imperfection; a dress that cannot be worn by anyone else because it has been sewn on you by the designer herself. The hard part is finding such a skilled designer to craft a perfectly unique dress. So if you don't have a Vera Wang of weight loss available to help you, you're going to have to figure out how to become the best damn dressmaker on your own.

A weight-loss plan that is specific to you, designed for your unique tastes, available time, preferences, and social life situations is the one that will work permanently.

This, my friends, is what we are going to attempt to do together over the course of this book—so that you never go on, or off, a *diet* ever again.

...

You'll have to get choosy.

You can't change everything. Change only what you need to

in order for you to be successful, fuck the rest—for now. Changing more than you can handle at once will slow you down or prevent success altogether. But *do* be honest with yourself about this. Small changes will produce small results over a long period of time. Like your 401K. It's worth a few nickels right now, but if you're not shortsighted and let it sit for a couple decades, maybe you'll be able to buy a yacht. Or a fishing boat. Or maybe just a beach chair and some Coronas—whatever. Depends on how much you save, right? How hard you work? How much you commit to the long term goal you know will pay off big? But if you just put in a little more effort, it could mean the difference between a body that is a retirement rust bucket that creaks and can't even sit on your floor or a luxury liner who is supple, lean, and loving life till the end.

If you're on the brink of meeting the man in the sky, then by golly, you'll need to kick it in the ass and make some serious changes. But if you have some weight to lose and are not about to float through the tunnel of white light anytime soon, then prioritizing will suffice.

Weight loss is not only about knowing *what* to eat, it's about knowing yourself well. Pre-designed diet programs set you up for failure because they do not take into account unique you.

You have to be able to do what you like (most of the time) in order to be permanently successful. So... you'll have to build naughtiness into your plan. And if you do it wisely, in the right amounts, you'll lose weight while getting to eat whatever you want. *That's* when it won't seem like a diet at all.

Ideally we'd meet in person. You would come to my office at www.rejuvclinic.com, I would ask you questions and help you come to conclusions about the reality of your willpower or lack of it, but since we most likely can't unless you move to Fargo, my goal is to preempt some of your questions. From there you'll have to decide if "this," whatever it is, will work for *you*.

In some instances, just because I've said it will work, or has worked for someone else, doesn't mean it will work for you. You'll have to do some critical thinking and discover what works in part by trial and error.

At the end of this book, someone is going to say, "Holy shit, Mary Jane, you've lost so much weight. What did you do?" The answer is simple. "I stopped going on and off diets, created my own routine, and have learned what works and what doesn't work for me. I love what I eat, and I work out when I want to."

If someone was asking me how I stay skinny, I would preface it with, "This might not work for you because it's made for my weird tastes. But I drink green tea every morning and wine every evening. Sometimes I eat nachos with jalapeños at midnight after I'm drunk, and once or twice, I've eaten so much cheese I can't shit for three days. But not often. Occasionally I've smuggled a donut, or two, into my car and ate them in secret by the railroad tracks on the outskirts of town. I've been known to hoard the left over Chinese food, and I have absolutely no willpower whatsoever against pretty much everything. But, when I'm not doing any of that, I eat really healthy. I eat plants. My diet is made up of 95 percent plants. I juice, I walk, I plan ahead when I can, and I use affirmations such as 'I like being skinny more than I like eating cheese' to remind myself to stay on track from the temptations abound. I avoid situations where I know I'll cave in and sabotage myself. I weigh myself for a slap on the ass a few times a week, and I give myself ten pounds of wiggle room before I freak out, call in sick, and then go to the gym all day."

So how the fuck is it possible for me to still be skinny doing nothing but walking and some light girly exercises on the floor?

I don't do *all* of that bad shit *all* of the time.

I do *some* of that bad shit *some* of the time.

Except wine—I do that all of the time.

The key for me is that I eat plants—it's what keeps me skinny. Lots and lots of plants. Not *only* plants, but *mostly* plants. This works for me, and I'm pretty sure this is one of those things that can work for you too. Or maybe not, because you'll have to figure that out on your own remember? But I'd recommend you give a plant-based diet a try if you want to lose weight and be optimally healthy.

There's no debate that plant eaters generally live longer, have lower weights, and suffer less major health issues. I will sprinkle my plant-eating propaganda throughout, however, I'm not going to tell you to give up anything. Well... maybe some things. But you'll have to be smart about deciding what you can and can't give up so that you're successful forever.

Since I know myself well and freely admit that I have little willpower, part of my successful skinny lifestyle is avoiding all the sabotaging food situations that I can but knowing I can't avoid them all. I am extra good when I have control over my food environment because I know there will be times when I don't. I would rather indulge my bad habits outside of my house where I have less will and more temptations than in my house where I can control what's in the fridge and pantry.

It does help that I give myself ten pounds of jiggle room to play with. Consider doing the same. I have two weights, my *on-season* weight of 115 pounds and my *off-season* weight of 125 pounds. Both are perfectly healthy weights for me. As long as I am somewhere in that range, I'm good with that.

Depending on the time of year and if I get the opportunity to wear a bikini in Hawaii or hiking gear in Alaska, I gain or lose by becoming more or less disciplined as needed. Mostly I'm less disciplined, because I fail if I try to maintain my on-season weight for too many months out of the year. This way I can screw off for most of the year and eat sweet potato fries dipped in sweet Thai chili sauce from my favorite German beer joint; then I have intermittent months of cracking down where I avoid hefeweizen, lederhosen, and hammerschlagen.

Get out your journal. Write this down. Ask yourself *"what are my three biggest weaknesses?"* The top three things that are holding you back from losing weight. This is where you will start focusing your efforts. Stop dickin' around with everything else, hit 'em where it hurts—it's time to get efficient.

Chapter 2

"FIGURE OUT WHAT YOUR BIGGEST OBSTACLE
TO WEIGHT LOSS IS AND START THERE. DON'T
WASTE YOUR TIME ANYWHERE ELSE."

If you were an Olympic swimmer, would your workouts consist of roller skating and frolfing? Of course not. So why waste time with anything that is not going to get you to your goal the quickest? I've excused you from exercise for the time being because it might not be the smartest place to spend your energy— right now, at least. Have you considered that maybe exercise just makes you more fucking hungry? And that if you're always hungry and don't know what to eat or lack the willpower to eat healthy anyway, you'll gain more weight than if you weren't working out?

Dr. Andrew Weil, founder and director of The Arizona Center for Integrative Medicine, wrote in his October, 2012 *Huffington Post* article, "Carbohydrate Density: A Better Guide to Weight Loss," that, "Excess exercise tends to be counterbalanced by excess hunger, exemplified by the phrase 'working up an appetite.' A few people with extraordinary willpower can resist such hunger day after day, but for the vast majority, weight loss through exercise is a flawed option."

Figure out who your number one enemy is and attack there first. Don't light up the wrong neighbor's doorstep with a flaming bag of poop if you're not 100 percent sure it's their dog who's leaving shit bombs in your yard. Figure out what your biggest obstacle to weight loss is and start there. Write it down. Don't waste your time anywhere else. We'll tackle the less important problems later when you've lost your first twenty pounds.

When clients ask, "What can I put in my morning coffee so I can still lose weight?" I say, "Do you think your morning coffee is one of the top three reasons you're not losing weight?" Usually the answer is no, and they can list three much bigger weight-loss saboteurs than coffee and cream. Which puts into perspective how insignificant their morning coffee is in comparison to their addiction to let's say... candy corn, alfredo pasta, and eating out.

Let's say Tamera has a sweet tooth not only for her morning coffee but everywhere else too, and in general when she eats, her portions could feed all of Mongolia. It would be a better use of Tamera's time, energy and resources, working on how to get *those* bad habits under control rather than focusing on a few extra calories in her morning coffee that are infinitesimal in comparison.

Now, for Roxanne, no amount of going to the gym is going to help her lose weight if her number one weakness is sugar. Eating too much sugar is far too damaging on her ass and her pancreas than can be fixed on the treadmill.

If sugar is your number one vice, your time would be better

spent at the grocery store and in the kitchen planning meals ahead of time to curb your sweet tooth (more on how to do this shortly) than going to the gym.

Wake up, sit straight, snap out of it—start focusing on what will really get you results. Weight loss will happen quickly if you don't dilly dally on the minor things that are important for someone else but not important for you.

Have you identified your three biggest weaknesses and written them down? If you didn't do it a minute ago, do it now. The top three things you know are preventing you from losing weight. I'm sure you know what they are and don't have to think too hard. Here are some common areas people struggle with:

No willpower.

Don't know *what* to eat.

Hungry all the time.

No time to plan.

No time to cook.

Don't like to cook.

Eating late at night.

Eating too much in general.

Eating out too much.

Not getting enough exercise.

Eating too much sugar.

Eating when you're not hungry.

Eating too much candy.

Eating too many carbs, bread, pasta, beer, etc.

Eating out of social or familial obligation.

Drinking too much alcohol.

No time to cook healthy.

Don't like vegetables.

Don't like healthy foods in general.

Depressed and emotionally eating.

So? Which ones are your reasons? Don't see yours on there? Feel free to write it in—I left space. What is the number one thing you think is preventing you from losing weight? This is where you'll begin focusing your energy first.

Onward, we'll sift through the above concerns and other issues over the course of this book to try and help you navigate your way to your goal as quickly as possible. Only when you have a handle on your three biggest areas of weakness should you continue working your way through the wellness continuum. Remember that where you focus your efforts might be different than where so-and-so focuses their efforts, and it should be this way. Don't get sucked in to someone else's diet plan or workout routine that doesn't focus on your specific areas on concern.

Did I mention exercise sucks for weight loss?

I know, I know—you can't believe I said it.

Well, it does.

Abs are made in the kitchen not in the gym.

Buckle up. We're just getting started.

Chapter 3

"EXERCISE IS A TOUCHY LITTLE BITCH."

Do not count on exercise to lose weight. Exercise is good for you, no doubt. It's good for weight loss, too, if you commit to it every day. Or at least four days a week at an intensity and duration that will actually make a difference. But if you can't rev up your mojo to hit it like it's hot and you're counting on exercise to burn calories, you're screwed like the cork I just popped from my favorite bottle of wine.

If you think that lack of exercise is one of the pesky culprits preventing your weight loss, it's probably not. Go look over the list again. Not working out enough is not likely to be the reason you are not losing weight. Duh... *it's your diet!* What you eat or don't eat is infinitely more important for weight loss *and* overall health than exercise will ever be.

Enjoy this sample?

Want to know WTF else to eat to lose weight?

Get the full version here

https://goo.gl/0stg2X

47828615R00189

Made in the USA
Middletown, DE
03 September 2017